LIONEL ROBBINS

Also by D. P. O'Brien

INFORMATION AGREEMENTS, COMPETITION AND EFFICIENCY
(*with D. Swann*)
J. R. McCULLOCH: A Study in Classical Economics
THE CORRESPONDENCE OF LORD OVERSTONE
COMPETITION IN BRITISH INDUSTRY (*with D. Swann* et al.)
CASE STUDIES: COMPETITION IN BRITISH INDUSTRY
(*with D. Swann* et al.)
J. R. McCULLOCH: Treatise on Taxation
THE CLASSICAL ECONOMISTS
COMPETITION POLICY, PROFITABILITY AND GROWTH
(*with W. S. Howe, D. M. Wright and R. J. O'Brien*)
PIONEERS OF MODERN ECONOMICS IN BRITAIN
(*edited with John R. Presley*)
AUTHORSHIP PUZZLES IN THE HISTORY OF ECONOMICS
(*with A. C. Darnell*)
ECONOMIC ANALYSIS IN HISTORICAL PERSPECTIVE
(*with J. Creedy*)

Lionel Robbins

D. P. O'Brien

Professor of Economics
University of Durham

M
MACMILLAN
PRESS

First published 1988

Published by
THE MACMILLAN PRESS LTD
Houndmills, Basingstoke, Hampshire RG21 2XS
and London
Companies and representatives
throughout the world

Typeset by Wessex Typesetters
(Division of The Eastern Press Ltd)
Frome, Somerset

Printed in Hong Kong

British Library Cataloguing in Publication Data
O'Brien, D.P.
Lionel Robbins.
1. Robbins, Lionel Robbins, *Baron*
2. Economics—Great Britain—History
—20th century
I. Title
330.1   HB103.R6
ISBN 0–333–44641–0

To the memory of Eileen

Contents

Acknowledgements

In the writing of this book I owe a special debt to Professor John Creedy. Without his encouragement the book would certainly never have been written. Moreover he has given unstintingly of his time to read and comment on draft material. Whatever the shortcomings of this volume, to which reviewers will no doubt draw attention – and since this is a book about one of the best-loved economists in history, it is a great deal more than averagely likely to attract critical comments – the work is undoubtedly a great deal better for his helpful comments. (The usual refusal to share blame of course applies in this case.)

In my efforts to produce a rounded account of a big topic (Lionel Robbins) in a small compass, this book has been through an unusual number of drafts. I am particularly grateful to Julie Bushby for her work on these. She typed, with some help from Kathryn Cowton, to whom I am also grateful, the whole of the first draft, and all subsequent drafts, dealing with these with efficiency and, perhaps even more importantly, with cheerfulness.

I am also grateful to those who have answered my queries or assisted me in other ways. Particular mention must be made of Mr Christopher Johnson who, as Lord Robbins's literary executor, gave me permission to use the lecture which I have translated in the Appendix, and who provided other helpful information. I am also grateful to Denys Gribbin for making available to me his papers on the wartime temporary Civil Service. I am also happy to acknowledge help from a number of professional colleagues particularly Mark Blaug, David Collard, Bernard Corry, Charles Feinstein (whose invitation to write an article about Robbins provided the initial impetus for the whole project), David Greenaway, Donald Winch and Jack Wiseman. I have also been grateful for the assistance of Walter Allan, Dr E. M. Hallam-Smith of the PRO, Colin Jones of *The Banker*, Eliane Perez of the Biblioteca Nacional, Rio de Janeiro, and J. R. Pinfold of the LSE Library. I must also thank the staff of Durham University Library concerned with inter-library loans, whose work has been indispensable to the completion of this book. Finally I must thank

Professor L. Kielanowski, who translated Antoni Tom's review of Robbins's *The Great Depression* into English for me.

The research for this book was at an advanced stage when my wife died. It is to her memory that this book is dedicated.

D. P. O'BRIEN

1 Introduction

This is a book which attempts to provide an overall picture of one of the dominant figures in British economics in the twentieth century. It is deliberately limited to drawing together a picture of Robbins on the basis of his published work. It is not the full-scale and full-length study which Robbins undoubtedly deserves and which, in the long run, he will undoubtedly receive – perhaps particularly as official papers are released under the thirty years' rule. Rather, it is an attempt to begin to pull together some account of the thought of a figure who, with Keynes, dominated British economics in the inter-war period. In this way it is hoped to provide a start in the process of appraisal of this major figure while making available a summary source of his thought.

I did not know Robbins very well: but each of those who did has, to some extent, a different picture, having received their strongest impression from some slightly different facet of this outsize personality. Others will undoubtedly have their say; this is, to some extent, and quite deliberately, an outside view. It seems to me too soon for detailed work on Robbins's private papers; the sort of work on Overstone's papers by the present writer which he delighted to encourage would be highly inappropriate, at this early date, on his own correspondence. In any case he knew most of the world's great economists; and a balanced assessment of the details of his interaction with them would be premature indeed. All that is attempted here is a rounded portrait of the public economist. If it makes some small contribution to keeping alive interest in the work of this great scholar, and also perhaps to keeping alive the style of analysis in which he excelled, it will have been an exercise worth undertaking.

Chapter 2 deals with Robbins's life. Any biographical work on Robbins has to start from the fact that he provided his own *Autobiography*, a fact which is both a help and perhaps, to some extent, a handicap. But if, at a later date, some Skidelsky or Holroyd should supply the full biography, a process which will not only take a great deal of time but which will require some lapse of time before a proper perspective can be drawn, then this will be of the greatest value.

Chapter 3 deals with methodology, the area in which Robbins initially rose to fame with his *Essay on the Nature and Significance of Economic Science* and which was, fittingly, the subject of his academic swansong in his astonishing address to the American Economic Association at the age of nearly 82. Robbins's work in this area is frequently cited, but more rarely read, and detailed examination reveals that his whole approach, founded in a fusion of the English tradition with Austrian general equilibrium, was not only complex but, to some extent, destructive of much that is now standard economic theory.

Chapter 4 deals with Robbins as historian of economic thought – a role in which he, almost single-handedly, reversed the decline of the subject in this country and led (and one of the things which is most noticeable about Robbins is that he believed in leadership from the front) economists in this country to a detailed appreciation not only of the history of their subject but also of decent scholarly standards. Robbins's LSE lectures on the history of economic thought are likely to be published at a later date; these will undoubtedly add further to the picture. But there is so much to be learned already from Robbins's published work in this field, in which, together with his personal contacts and supervision, the majority of his influence was exercised, that it seems right to present a picture based upon this record.

Chapter 5 deals with welfare economics. This is intimately linked with the methodological stance in Chapter 3. What is surprising, perhaps, is both the freedom with which Robbins made value judgements – at least it is surprising to those who misunderstood the message of his methodological writings and thought the precept that value judgements should be made explicit amounted to saying that they should not be made – and the basic Utilitarianism which guided his views on policy problems. He was quite explicit about being a 'provisional' Benthamite; but it was not only a rough and ready Utilitarian evaluation of problems which informed his judgements, for he took from Bentham many of the other implied attitudes, especially a passionate egalitarianism, of a non-socialist variety, the distinction between *agenda* and *non-agenda* and (from John Stuart Mill) the distinction betweeen self-affecting acts and acts affecting the rest of society. It is from Mill, perhaps above all, that his emphasis upon liberty came; his opposition to the various brands of Hegelianism (Nazism and Marxism) was sustained, deeply felt, and highly effective.

In Chapter 6 his writings on education (which began well before the Robbins Report) are considered. It is here that his egalitarianism (with a belief that nurture was more important than nature, and an emphasis upon the existence of an untapped 'pool of ability') asserted itself. In some respects, Robbins's writings on, and involvement in, education reflect an optimistic, even romantic, attitude in which Robbins the economist is somehow submerged in Robbins the Renaissance Man. They provide a notable contrast with his writings on (and involvement in) public policy in wartime (in which the marginalist Austrian general equilibrium approach predominates).

Chapter 7, dealing with microeconomics, covers not only the famous contributions like that on the elasticity of demand for income in terms of effort, but also the analysis of costs, an analysis which, if followed by the majority of the profession, would undoubtedly have destroyed very much of what is now embedded in the literature. This chapter is thus one which can be taken together with the methodology chapter, and the pairing should help to emphasise the degree to which Robbins was, to an extent to which he himself perhaps did not appreciate, an extremely unorthodox economist, not only by the standards of the England of his time, with its inward-looking and insular approach, but also by later standards in which a quasi-engineering approach to economics had made substantial strides.

Chapters 8 and 9 together represent the very substantial analysis which Robbins presented, in both the pre-war and post-war years, of macroeconomics and the open economy. In Chapter 8 the macroeconomics are discussed and it emerges that, although Robbins abandoned the specific and identifiable Mises–Hayek version of macroeconomic fluctuation (as dependent on credit expansion leading to an alteration in the relative profitability of consumption goods and investment), the roots of that analytical apparatus, in Classical economics and in Wicksell, continued to underlie his macroeconomic writing in the post-war years. They provide a degree of continuity which has not always been recognised by those who believe Robbins to have surrendered more or less completely to Keynesianism in the post-war years. In particular his very timely warnings about the need to control the credit base, and about the incompatibility of prices and incomes policy with inflation of the money supply, derived from this basic approach.

Chapter 9 deals with the open economy. Here Robbins's writings are concerned with two broad areas; commercial policy, and international monetary economics. The writings on commercial policy are very largely concerned with tariffs and were the occasion for a bitter controversy with Keynes in the inter-war years, a controversy over which Robbins later had no regrets whatever, despite his subsequent partial acquiescence in some other aspects of Keynes's inter-war writings, in particular the role of public investment.

In the monetary field we find an analysis which is based very firmly in Classical writing from David Hume to the Currency and Banking Controversy of the 1840s and 1850s. In particular we find Robbins applying the Ricardian definition of excess, so that sustained balance of payments problems necessarily meant that the money supply was at an inappropriate level. We also find – in strong contrast to what might be expected on other grounds – a very firm opposition to the idea of free exchange rates. But this opposition becomes much less surprising when it is appreciated that Robbins had a vision of a world in which there was international federation, international economic integration, and a substantial degree of supra-national authority in certain key areas. Free exchange rates would hardly be conducive to this. Alexander Hamilton's *The Federalist* is a work hardly known to economists; but to Robbins it was a document of fundamental importance in considering the ultimate goal of a world constructed on the basis of what he called 'international Liberalism', in which freedom of trade and payments would operate across federated countries in the same way as across the regions of a single country.

This leads to an exploration of Robbins's attitude towards European economic integration; his initial opposition to the EEC no longer seems paradoxical when it emerges that he wished for a wider union, embracing the United States and Canada, and feared too that European unity might distract the free world from the ever-present menace which threatened from the East.

Robbins was a major economist whose work drew inspiration from an extraordinarily wide variety of sources – English Classical economics, Austrian writings, Max Weber and Philip Henry Wicksteed. Deeply imbued with the spirit and content of these writings, Robbins was prone to allow his argument to develop by implication, in the belief (perhaps better founded in the LSE during the inter-war years than subsequently) that his hearers and readers would understand the particular theoretical implications he had in mind. In drawing out the threads of his writings, an attempt has been made to indicate the theoretical models on which the argument is based and to indicate the sources, in the belief that only in this way can the full implications of what is often a very subtle argument be drawn out.

2 Biography

1. ORIGINS

The subject of this study is unusual among economists, not only in having written an autobiography but in having produced a highly readable document in so doing.[1] Robbins was, he tells us, born on 22 November 1898 at Sipson Farm (now submerged in the environs of Heathrow Airport) Middlesex.[2] He was notably of mixed English and French Huguenot descent, with the massive solidity of Gloucester origins, although it appears that parts of his ancestry could also be traced to Wales and East Anglia.[3] The French and English parts of his inheritance were somewhat oddly juxtaposed – a strong common sense was paired with an extreme artistic sensibility, more especially to the arts of literature and painting.[4] His origins have been described as 'relatively humble',[5] but they were not straitened. His father was a successful farmer who became President of the National Farmers' Union in 1921 (and served again in 1925) and who was High Sheriff of Middlesex in 1945 and 1946.

Though father and son undoubtedly had their differences at one stage, a matter to which Robbins devoted some space in the *Autobiography*, the father's influence on Lionel was strong. His father was, particularly in his capacity as chairman of the Parliamentary, Press, and Publicity Committee of the National Farmers Union, a forceful controversialist. Robbins's own unhesitating involvement in public controversy may have owed something to this example. The elder Robbins also possessed a rolling, forceful literary style in which the origins of his son's own style are at least partially visible.[6] Robbins's father's influence over both the style and content of his son's agricultural discussions shows in Robbins's two articles on economic planning of agriculture, one of which actually contains a quotation from 'one of the most successful farmers in the home counties',[7] and Robbins's most famous book the *Essay on the Nature and Significance of Economic Science* (hereafter *ENSES*) is dedicated to his father.

Both his father's profession and his own childhood gave Robbins a strong and continuing interest in agriculture. His

Autobiography contains a touching account of growing up in what was then rural Middlesex, though it was a childhood shadowed by the distress of the loss of his mother when he was eleven and the tragic death of a younger sister. But in other respects it was a stable, orderly, almost arcadian existence. Many years later he was to write:

> All in all, although in so many respects my own career has led me into very different spheres with very different habits, I look back with love and admiration to this wholesome society, its plain seriousness of purpose, its unostentatious manners, the orderly rhythm of its life, its decent civilised standards.[8]

It was probably this childhood which gave him the strong attachment to the family as a concept which is evident in his writings.[9]

From this time, however, dates his hostility (one which he apparently shared with Jacob Viner) to theology, especially that of the seventeenth-century variety.[10] Yet he was not bigoted: in his *Higher Education Revisited* he made clear that he had no objection to the study of theology in universities nor to the training of clergymen.[11] Nor did his agnosticism affect his moral position on things like the institution of marriage, of which he strongly approved.[12]

2. EDUCATION AND EARLY INFLUENCES

Like most intelligent children Robbins became, at a very early age, a voracious reader. He was educated however not at a public school, as might have been expected given the times and his family background, but at Southall County School, a very good school it would seem, without any of the disadvantages of many public schools on which his father was prone to dwell.[13] From Southall Robbins proceeded to University College London for a short spell after which – it was late 1915 – he entered the army, and though he was long prevented by his youth from engaging in active service, he became a combatant soldier in the First World War and was wounded sufficiently seriously to bear the signs permanently.[14] Army experience also impressed upon him that the only substitute for economic incentives was firm discipline.[15]

However this recognition of the universality of the problem of incentives did not prevent him from taking an initial interest in socialism after leaving the army. Following his military service he was, at first, reluctant to return to university, and he sought methods of social reform. But he was disillusioned by the middle- and upper-class 'fun revolutionaries' and was saved, as he relates, form further involvement partly by his own common sense[16] and also by his sense of humour.[17] But for a while he devoured socialist literature, coming slowly to the realisation that it contained fundamental – and therein unanswered – economic questions. Drawn thus to professional economic literature he found, evidently with some excitement, a quality of intellect which had been entirely lacking in his previous reading matter. An extraordinarily coincidental meeting with his father, then partially estranged by his son's socialist dabblings, enabled Robbins to go to the London School of Economics,[18] which he later described as 'an entry to a new world. Here was free discussion of the great problems of man in society. Here, without abatement of personal convictions, was integrity and a search after truth.'[19]

At LSE he read Cannan, Henderson, Marshall (not only the *Principles* but also the *Economics of Industry*), Cassel, Sidgwick, Walker, Price (*Industrial Peace*), Bowley and Stamp.[20] He was taught in his third year by Harold Laski and, even at that early stage, some tensions seem to have developed.[21] Though he was lectured by T. E. Gregory and others, and regarded Gregory with particular respect,[22] the three people at LSE who seem to have made the most impression were Edwin Cannan, Graham Wallas and Hugh Dalton. For Cannan (whose mother, coincidentally, was also of Huguenot descent) Robbins seems to have felt a special affinity.[23] In his *Autobiography* Robbins pays particular tribute to Cannan and he had, many years earlier, ended his first book with a compliment to him.[24] Indeed Hicks was later to see Robbins as having tried to restore 'Cannanism' at LSE,[25] and some basis for this view can be found in Robbins's touching recollection of Cannan in 1935.[26] Books written by Robbins before and after the War contain tributes to Cannan,[27] and Robbins was clearly influenced by Cannan in his attitude to population.[28] But there is another side to all this. For, as Coats has emphasised, Cannan was strongly opposed to pure theory while Robbins ultimately stood at the opposite end of the spectrum on this[29] – indeed Marshall can be held to have stood *between* Robbins and the founders of LSE along the scale separating pure theorists from pure Institutionalists. As one who was at LSE at the time has recalled, while Plant retained Cannan's interest in institutions, Robbins did not and indeed worked largely along lines which owe little or nothing directly to Cannan.[30] Moreover *ENSES* is to a considerable extent a critique of Cannan – though one which shows how deeply Robbins had studied him – and Cannan's review of the book was not noticeably friendly, rejecting Robbins's refusal to recognise particular economic ends, and making a dig at references to 'dozens of foreign economists whom we shall never read'.[31]

It was however no doubt through the work of Cannan and of Wallas, to whom Robbins also pays tribute, that he came to the work of Hume, Smith, Ferguson and Millar, the influence of which he was later to acknowledge. The influence of Wallas was also evident in Robbins's warm romantic attitude towards Bentham and the Utilitarians.[32]

Perhaps the most important single personal influence on Robbins in his early years at LSE was, however, Hugh Dalton.[33] It was Dalton who found him a job as a research assistant and it was Dalton who went to Oxford to invite him back to a lectureship at LSE.[34] Dalton was not to everyone's taste; a later politician has described him as a nasty man with 'a voice so powerful that the windows of a private dining room had to be shut lest his remarks about his colleagues should float along the terrace of the House of Commons to their receptive ears'.[35] But he was a complex character with a warm side to his personality and Robbins became a protégé.[36] Dalton was instrumental in securing Robbins's appointment to the LSE Chair at the astonishingly early age of 30,[37] even though the economics department soon took a distinctly unsocialist turn and Dalton came to regret Robbins's appointment.[38] But Robbins had emerged very quickly as the rising star of LSE; he must have been helped by an early, and very friendly, review by Allyn Young who praised one of his first publications as 'both penetrating and judicious'.[39]

3. ACADEMIC CAREER AND RELATIONSHIPS – LSE

The bare bones of Robbins's academic career are well known. He was a lecturer at New College, Oxford in 1924, a lecturer at LSE

1925–7, and a Fellow and Lecturer at New College, Oxford 1927–29. After his accession to the LSE Chair in 1929 he remained at LSE until, in circumstances to be related below, he ostensibly retired from the Chair in 1961. The Oxford interludes were undoubtedly valuable, not least for giving Robbins some association with G. H. Hardy (who even arranged some mathematical instruction for him). In later life he retained the warmest memories both of New College and of Hardy.[40]

Robbins was clearly an outstanding teacher. According to Meade he combined, as a teacher, 'the qualities of a rowing coach with those of the conductor of a great orchestra',[41] but this in turn reflected his enormous enthusiasm for his subject. It is clear that he aimed to cover the whole field of economics in his youth 'in the main language areas' and his erudition became, in time, legendary.[42]

But his devotion to the subject is really not very surprising. Brought up against a background of strict Calvinism, he had rebelled against this with a degree of emotional violence which is still reflected in his *Autobiography*, written more than half a century later; and, after the unhappy time spent searching for salvation through the secular theology of socialism, his delight in the intellectual qualities of economics was keen indeed.

He was, then, very much the right person to set about revitalising LSE. The testimony by major British economists to his influence, especially the greatest English twentieth-century pure theorist Sir John Hicks, are too clear to doubt[43] – it was indeed Robbins who turned Hicks into a theorist.[44] And yet in the end, although Robbins was not an enthusiast for academic committees, the focus of his emotional commitment somehow transmuted itself from economics as a subject to LSE as an institution. This was widely recognised and Robbins was rightly credited not only with the building up of LSE but also with its (successful) defence against the student militants.[45] But the personal cost was, at times, considerable; he was the victim of disgusting personal attacks on him by academics in such safe havens as the correspondence columns of *The Times*, and his *Autobiography* was in fact a therapeutic exercise undertaken to ease the strain of being the central figure in the defence of LSE.[46]

His teaching was particularly important to him and, as noted and as might be expected of so remarkable a personality, he was obviously a remarkable teacher.[47] Long after his ostensible retirement, indeed, he continued to teach, and he was manifestly anxious to emphasise in public his commitment to this continuation.[48]

As an administrator he was clearly a strong-willed and powerful figure – a factor which undoubtedly led to difficulties with Beveridge, for whom Robbins had once worked as a research assistant, when the former was Director of LSE. The difficulties were in part due also to Robbins's unhappiness (at times bordering on contempt) concerning Beveridge's intellectual standards and the latter's position on several issues especially that of full employment policy.[49] Beveridge for his part was very hostile to what he considered to be Robbins's excessive emphasis on the purity of economic theory.

Beveridge's farewell address caused offence on two counts. Firstly it contained an attack on pure theory controversies conducted without reference to the possibility of empirical falsification – outsiders could not avoid the conclusion that 'economists are persons who earn their livings by taking in one another's definitions for mangling'. Secondly, it contained a substantial section warning against university teachers adopting, and delivering to their students, partisan positions. While this may very well have been aimed principally at Laski, to whose 'political' teaching Robbins also objected, it could have caused offence to anyone who was, like Robbins, a vigorous participant in public controversy.[50] But both parties also saw good in the other and they collaborated in rescuing refugees from Germany.[51] This was a remarkable story, linked to Robbins's furious opposition to any suspicion of anti-semitism,[52] and it was a proud episode in the history of LSE which made it particularly appropriate that, many years later, Robbins should be called upon to be the first lecturer under the auspices of the fund established by the refugees.[53]

Apart from difficulties with Beveridge there were inevitably some further tensions in the relationships between Robbins and Harold Laski, who had opposed Robbins's appointment to the Chair. In an attempt to defuse this, Robbins inserted a deliberately friendly reference to Laski in his inaugural lecture.[54] But relations undoubtedly became strained later on, and Robbins's recoil from some aspects of Laski's personality was far from unique.[55] Yet a genuine scholarly rapport remained even though Robbins expressed the view in later years that 'Laski – for all his erudition and amiable qualities, which were extensive – was the least reliable man I have ever known when it was a matter of casual anecdote or attribution'.[56]

Despite these difficulties, LSE became the great love of Robbins's life. Nevertheless he retained warm memories of his time at Oxford. He told the present writer that he 'left a paradise at New College' to return to LSE, and a similar expression is to be found in his *Autobiography*.[57] Yet there was something about the whole Oxbridge ambience which he found pretentious, and he was given to little digs at this.[58] The Robbins Report itself contained some slightly hostile references to Oxford and Cambridge.[59] In the case of Cambridge there was also an extra dimension; his 1947 Marshall lectures contained a number of gentle digs at the very predominantly left of centre standpoint of his audience.[60] But more broadly he was, it seems reasonable to suppose, objecting to what he perceived to be a degree of unjustified conceit – those who had got on the inside track in Oxbridge but who, by wider standards, might not be regarded as very distinguished, felt able to disdain those who had not got on to this track. Certainly he seems to have been very irritated by Oxbridge opposition to the Robbins Report.

He was also irritated by a certain insularity – provincialism in both space and time – which he felt to be a feature of English, and especially Oxbridge, economics. Robbins was a man of extraordinarily wide reading, friendships and sympathies. In particular he had a knowledge of literature written in German which was quite remarkable, and it is evident that he not only read German fluently but that he thought others should do so also.[61] However much of this literature was in fact Austrian, and Robbins was particularly appreciative of the work of Mises who, like Robbins but in a much more dangerous situation, also opposed the Nazis.[62] Robbins's attitude towards more centrally German literature, especially the philosophies which led to totalitarianism – Hegel and Marx – was caustic.[63]

But Mises and other Austrians, notably Hayek who joined him at LSE, exercised a pervasive influence on Robbins's early work. Another important influence was exercised by Jacob Viner. Robbins greatly admired Viner both as an outstanding all-round economist and as an historian of economic thought.[64] Indeed Robbins's greatest book in this area, *Robert Torrens*, is dedicated to the Viners 'to commemorate twenty-nine years of unbroken friendship'. Another close friend was Baumol – to whom *The Evolution of Modern Economic Theory* is dedicated – who provided a moving testimony of the friendship in his address at the Memorial Meeting after Robbins's death.[65] Within LSE, particularly close associations seem to have been formed with Paish – Robbins confessed in the introduction to *The Economist in the Twentieth Century* that he had been 'discussing the subject matter of these lectures since the winter of 1916' with Paish[66] and with Sayers, although in the latter case there must, it seems at least to the outsider, have been some strain over the Radcliffe Report.[67]

4. PUBLIC POLICY DEBATES

Because Robbins was such a large personality, there were bound to be public conflicts over matters of economic policy. He entered fearlessly and emphatically into public debates, regarding such participation as necessary.[68] In this he was able to use *Lloyds Bank Review* as a platform, particularly for his views on the importance of monetary and trade policy,[69] a stance which was to make him the object of controversy and even of painful abuse.[70] Some of his public interventions were in a far from popular style. A 1929 paper on hours of work[71] is one which even today requires fairly careful study despite (or perhaps because of) the lack of overt technicality (or 'rigour'). One wonders what the British Association audience to which it was delivered could possibly have made of it. But the majority of his contributions were distinguished by two characteristics: clarity, and moral courage. At an early stage he showed great moral courage after being badly treated by Keynes when, as members of the Economic Advisory Council Committee, there were differences of view over protection and public expenditure.[72] He engaged in public controversy over macroeconomic policy and over tariffs; and the courage of his positions, whether in opposing monetary reflation (in 1932) or the imposition of tariffs, is remarkable.[73]

At a later stage his *Economic Planning and International Order* must have been very unpopular at a time in the 1930s when a naive belief in 'planning' was popular with a large section of the intellectual classes, while after the war his *Economic Problem in Peace and War* was 'a remarkable tour de force' in the face of widespread favouring of planning and pro-Soviet attitudes.[74]

Again, his critique of Radcliffe, before the experience of the Heath–Barber years, was a somewhat lonely and courageous undertaking. Robbins admired academic courage;[75] but he clearly had plenty of it himself. He had need of it, especially in the pre-war years. With unemployment running at high levels, academic manners were becoming a little strained and Hayek was also the recipient of a good deal of abuse from Cambridge writers including Keynes.[76]

There is no doubt that to some extent the attacks got through to Robbins. In particular he became acutely sensitive about the accusation that he was a 'deflationist', and he came to insist that controlling inflation of aggregate expenditure was not the same thing as deflation.[77] It is however worth making the point, even at this stage of the argument – the matter will be explored in detail in Chapter 8 – that, despite the elaborate contrition expressed in the *Autobiography*,[78] Robbins in fact remained opposed to the vast majority of what were called 'Keynesian' policies. In particular he was not happy about the discretionary use of fiscal policy for fine tuning;[79] he continued to oppose Beveridge's plans for permanent excess demand in the labour market; and he told the Radcliffe Committee that forced saving was not a good way of securing economic progress.[80] His surrender to 'Keynesianism' – like his estimation of the originality of the *General Theory* – was strictly qualified, as is clear from his review of Harrod's biography of Keynes,[81] and there is some retreat from the exaggerated contrition of the *Autobiography* in his 1976 *Political Economy Past and Present*.[82] His intellectual position did not shift so *very* far, despite his sensitivity.

It is perhaps not surprising that he maintained a strong friendship with Dennis Robertson[83] who had reviewed in a friendly and serious way Robbins's *The Great Depression*[84] and who was himself the victim of very unpleasant treatment in Cambridge.[85] But his relations with Keynes, marked initially, as we have noted, by controversy, were distinctly chequered. On the one hand, Robbins in later years paid warm tribute to Keynes as 'the most remarkable man I have ever met';[86] and this was only one of several testimonies which Robbins paid to the importance of Keynes's memory.[87] Moreover, there is recollection of their wartime collaboration by no less a person than James Meade,[88] and it is clear from Harrod's biography that Robbins and Keynes made an excellent partnership in economic negotiations[89] – indeed

Harrod quotes an extract from Robbins's diary in praise of Keynes which was later used by Robbins himself in his *Autobiography* (in an interestingly abbreviated form with a comparison with Winston Churchill removed).[90] But on the other hand, the pre-war disagreements had been very deep. The tariff controversy has already been referred to[91] – and in this, it is noteworthy, Robbins was able to enlist the support of Dalton, despite the latter's unhappiness, noted above, with Robbins's non-socialist views. Dalton intervened on his behalf with Snowden, the Chancellor of the Exchequer.[92] But Robbins's clash with Keynes had roots which go back further than that. Robbins had attacked Keynes in his very first publication, a review of a book by T. E. Gregory on American banking,[93] and inserted a further dig into a notice of Cannan's *Review*.[94]

The origins of this hostility are obscure. It is perfectly true that Keynes had been involved in controversy with Cannan over money;[95] but Robbins did not accept Cannan's 'cloakroom' theory of money.[96] At all events, Robbins was critical of Keynes in his 1927 essay on population, another early piece of work;[97] and in the tariff controversy there are signs of a personal scorn for Keynes, the quasi-conscientious objector, including a biting reference to a 'funk hole'.[98] He was outraged that the man who had criticised the Treaty of Versailles so effectively should turn into a protectionist.[99] In an article in *Economica* he accused Keynes of arguing in support of tariffs because he had failed to understand the theory of international transfers;[100] and in the volume edited by Beveridge on tariffs there is a strong attack on Keynes's particular tariff proposals, which seems to have come from the pen of Robbins.[101] This hostility over protection continued into the 1930s; his *Economic Planning and International Order* of 1937 again attacked Keynes's tariff proposals.[102] Dalton's contemporary opinion was that Robbins 'over-cultivates his feud with Keynes'.[103] But some sort of feud there does seem to have been, and it may not be a coincidence that Robbins reviewed no work in the *Economic Journal* between 1930 and 1962 (when C. F. Carter became leading editor).[104] Despite the tribute to Keynes in his *Autobiography*, Robbins in the same volume remained adamant on the question of tariffs.[105] Moreover, even in later years he clearly had little time for Keynes's idiosyncratic excursions into the history of economic thought.[106]

Nevertheless, for the wartime period, collaboration between

Robbins and Keynes was clearly close. During this period Robbins worked as a member of (and from 1941 to 1945 as Head of) the Economic Section of the Cabinet Office, an experience which he found deeply impressive.[107] He was highly effective in Whitehall, and substantially established the government economic service while managing to conduct operations in part on the lines of a seminar.[108] Thanks to the researches of Denys Gribbin we have some more detailed knowledge of his work in government, a matter he passes over in his *Autobiography*, in particular of his insistence on the need to tackle restrictive practices in industry, given the commitment to a full employment policy.[109] Indeed he had a crucial role in the development of what was later to become the United Kingdom's competition policy. He was a delegate at the Bretton Woods conference,[110] and at the end of the war was one of two principal British negotiators on the Commercial Policy Commission.[111]

The return to academic life was not particularly easy. Although Robbins seems to have had little hesitation about returning, he had to engage in what he later described as 'a painful effort at re-education'.[112] Nevertheless he seems to have resumed quickly his position as the dominant personality at LSE, and to have resumed also his contributions to public debates. During the 1950s he certainly had some influence on official policy, although the extent and nature of this is at the present time not clear. Again this naturally involved him in controversy, and when he came to be examined by the Radcliffe Committee there is no doubt that he felt he was misrepresented in the course of the questioning. Indeed it is hard to reconcile some of the questions with the explicit content of his Memorandum to the Committee,[113] and his irritation is perfectly understandable – as the perceptive Dennis Robertson noted.[114]

5. A GREAT MAN OF AFFAIRS

Robbins, by virtue of his standing as an economist and of his position at LSE, was bound to be involved in such public debates as those surrounding and following the proceedings of the Radcliffe Committee. But in the post-war years, Robbins's role in the public eye went far beyond that of a prominent and influential economist. He became a great man of affairs. He had early administrative experience after the First World War, in the organisation of demobilisation,[115] and at LSE he quickly developed administrative skills. His administrative ability and force of personality were such as to equip him naturally as one of 'the Great and the Good' to be placed on public bodies, even before his wartime experiences which were undoubtedly valuable in this respect. As a man of affairs he has had few if any equals amongst academics.[116] He proved highly effective and was capable of carrying an astonishing workload.[117] He was, as Harry Johnson said, 'honourable and not opportunistic',[118] and he had a shrewdness about people, partly because he had a far wider and deeper experience of life than most academics. He was Chairman of the *Financial Times* 1961–70, and it was clear to a visitor to his office at Bracken House that this was a role which he clearly enjoyed – as indeed he acknowledged.[119] Apart from his role as Chairman of the Robbins Committee 1961–4, and as Chairman of the LSE governors 1968–74, he was a Trustee of the National Gallery 1952–74 with a long period as Chairman, a Trustee of the Tate Gallery 1953–9 and 1962–7, a Director of the Royal Opera House, Covent Garden 1955–81, and President of the British Academy 1962–7.

As if this were not enough he led the Bentham Project at UCL, was a director of British Petroleum and was a director (and eventually Deputy Chairman) of the *Economist* 1960–75, continuing as a director of the Economist Intelligence Unit until his death. That paper recorded that 'generations of those who wrote for this paper have drawn on his experience and from his counsel'.[120] It is these aspects of Robbins's life which account for the quite extraordinary response to the appeal launched in the month after his death: three months later no less than £136 000 had been promised. It is hard to imagine such a response for any other British economist except, possibly, Keynes.

Although he had little to say about his role as an economic adviser in his *Autobiography* there is no doubt that he was consulted officially.[121] Recognition of his role here may in part have lain behind Macmillan's approach to him in 1958 with the offer of a life peerage[122] – to an outsider, at least, it looks like a conciliatory gesture of typical Macmillan ambiguity following the turmoil associated with the resignation of the Chancellor of the Exchequer. But whatever the reason, the Upper House of Parliament gained by this enoblement. He attended the House of

Lords regularly and participated in debates and, perhaps not surprisingly, showed himself on at least one occasion capable of delivering a quite splendid speech, the passionate and superb 'Expansion and the Binary System' delivered in the Lords in 1965.[123] Interestingly, the tone of his speeches,[124] as of his other publications,[125] was determinedly cross-bench and non-political, setting to academics an example of how to become involved in policy without becoming involved in politics.

From one aspect of his expanded public life – arts administration – he derived enormous pleasure.[126] Pragmatic, in a Benthamite way, rather than dogmatic, he saw no objection to State involvement in the arts,[127] and he used his administrative abilities in the services of the arts to great effect. In particular his knowledge of paintings was remarkable.[128] He also found business life extremely congenial – apart from the restrictive labour practices which were much to his distaste – and indeed he contrasted business committees favourably with those encountered in academic life.[129]

But his venture into business life was not, in the first place, without considerable difficulties when, despite the agreement of his colleagues at LSE, the University of London, apparently at the instigation of one particular individual, refused to allow him to retain his Chair on a part-time basis when going to the *Financial Times*. This was undoubtedly a sad and distressing experience, and for years afterwards the memory of it rankled.[130]

6. THE ROBBINS COMMITTEE

In contrast to this unhappy and unexpected reverse, Robbins's experience on the committee which bore his name proved to be rewarding and fulfilling in a way which he clearly had not anticipated. The episode deserves, from a biographical point of view, a separate book. After being lured by civil service wiles into becoming Chairman, at a time when he was planning to write a major work on economics,[131] he became to a quite remarkable extent the moving force of the committee[132] and deeply committed to the implementation of the principles for entrance to higher education which it espoused.[133] He objected to the body which he chaired being called the Robbins Committee. Yet he certainly wrote at least parts of the report himself[134] and, to anyone reading the voluminous minutes of evidence, it is very apparent that the Chairman took an absolutely central role in the entire proceedings.[135] His natural egalitarianism is stamped on the report, and one of the things of which he was most proud in this harmonious enterprise was the 'pool of ability' demonstration.[136] The report was a remarkable seller; by 1969 the only official reports to have sold more copies were Beveridge on social insurance and Denning on Christine Keeler.[137] Partly as a result of these endeavours, honorary degrees were showered upon him; the list of them occupies ten lines in *Who's Who* and includes honours from Italy, the United States, Argentina, the United Kingdom, France and Portugal.[138]

7. WRITINGS AND INFLUENCE

Through the Robbins Report, Robbins's name had become well-known far outside the world of economists. But it should not be forgotten that, when honours were bestowed upon him, these honours were also very much a recognition of the worth of an outstanding economist. In the 1930s Robbins had two major successes – *An Essay on the Nature and Significance of Economic Science* (a book so well-known that it is now in danger of falling into Harry Johnson's category of a classic, a book that everybody has heard of and that nobody has read) and *The Great Depression*. Although Robbins was later to say that he wished that he had never written the latter book,[139] and was to disown its analysis,[140] the work was well received[141] and reprinted several times. Indeed the fourth edition was advertised, with glowing quotations from reviews of earlier editions, in 1937.[142]

These were major works written to stand on their own, as was *Robert Torrens* in the 1950s. But an extraordinarily large part of Robbins's output, though this is not generally appreciated, was composition for an occasion. This began at an early stage; his 1929 article on population was read before the Oxford Political Economy Club.[143] Later examples are *Economic Planning and International Order* (1937) which was made up of lectures delivered in Geneva in 1935, *The Economic Causes of War* (1939), *The Theory of Economic Policy* (1952), *The Theory of Economic Development* (1968) and *Political Economy Past and Present* (1976), this particular series of lectures being delivered in Cape Town in 1974. A number of his other books such as *The Economic Basis of Class Conflict* (1939), *The Economist in the Twentieth Century* (1954) and *Politics and Economics* (1963) were compilations containing pieces written for particular occasions.

Given the extraordinary variety of Robbins's career, it is perhaps not entirely surprising that he never wrote the general work he had wanted to write.[144] What is however very surprising, perhaps, to the reader of his majestic and flowing prose, is that he experienced difficulties of literary composition,[145] and he seemed sometimes to have required the pressure of an engagement to energise him into composition.[146] If that is so, we must be grateful to those who issued invitations.

The literary product of his labours had two particular characteristics which make it unusual amongst economists – a delight (like Schumpeter's) in unusual words such as 'expatiate', 'velleities', 'divagate', 'Laodicean';[147] and the rhetorical device of appealing to an unnamed authority.[148] They possessed as well a polish and a readability which, amongst economists, is very rare indeed.

It was the style, as well as the ideas, which helped to spread his influence. As Frank Knight wrote when reviewing Robbins's *Economic Planning and International Order* (1937): 'One thinks of the classics of oratory in searching for a parallel in orderliness and clarity, persuasive power and smoothness of style.'[149] But of the magnitude of that influence there can be little doubt. As Graham Hutton said when introducing a public lecture in 1954:

> next year it will be 50 years since I came to sit at the feet of Lord Robbins at the London School of Economics. I am still metaphorically sitting there. So are an untold number of economists and responsible leaders of public life in many other countries.[150]

Robbins had a powerful personality and he was extremely large, physically, mentally and morally. He was a very open-minded individual,[151] courteous and intelligent, with the marked ability to listen and a marked ability to act. He broadened the outlook not only of LSE but of English economists as a whole,[152] and he was careful (at LSE) to avoid giving the impression to his academic colleagues that there was any 'party line'.[153] The tendency to describe Robbins as 'right wing' – even in an obituary by a former Director of LSE – merely indicates how meaningless such labels are. An outspoken supporter of liberalisation of the laws on homosexuality, suicide and other matters, he was a foe to everything which pressed on, or even threatened, the liberty of the ordinary individual.[154] This made him the natural enemy of philosophical and economic doctrines associated with totalitarian regimes, whether Nazi or Communist. But it certainly did not make him reactionary.

It is true that he had his *bêtes noires*, not only the world's dictators but also less menacing figures such as Dr Thomas Balogh. They clashed publicly before the war, and again in *The Times* in 1947;[155] and Balogh's opposition to the University Grants Committee system was referred to derisively by Robbins in a Lords' speech in 1963 and in an address at Harvard in 1964.[156]

This particular enmity undoubtedly sprang, at least in part, from wounded sensitivity. For Robbins was a sensitive, and indeed at times a highly emotional, man.[157] He was also, like Alfred Marshall, a great romantic in some ways, not only in relation to LSE[158] but also about the literature of economics,[159] its authors, and its teachers.[160] Moreover, although he detested narrow nationalism, his romanticism also found expression in a deep love of his country,[161] one which is beautifully expressed in his *Autobiography*.[162] But despite this romantic patriotism, Robbins was, by instinct and intellectual belief, an internationalist.

8. INTERNATIONALISM

His detestation of narrow nationalism was the converse of a strongly and emphatically internationalist outlook. In part this may have sprung from his experiences as a soldier in the First World War; and it was very evident in his attitude towards tariffs. In the years after the Second World War his internationalism took the form of a deep personal commitment to the success of the Anglo-American negotiations at the end of the war and the implementation of their results.[163] This led him to oppose trade restrictions which interfered with unity, to defend the United States against British critics who seemed unaware of our debt to the Americans,[164] and to stress that the UK had a common interest with the United States in defending Western civilisation.[165] A belief in the fundamental and overriding importance of the

Western alliance[166] was coupled with a deep pessimism,[167] which surfaced from time to time, concerning the possible danger of an end to Western civilisation – Robbins was deeply impressed by the threat of the twin dangers of totalitarianism from the Communist world and the population explosion in the Third World. Yet in the end his basic equilibrium would re-establish itself and he would warn against excessive pessimism[168] and emphasise the duty to maintain and fight for civilised standards under all circumstances.[169]

9. CONCLUSION

Robbins was one of the major personalities in the economics profession during half a century of development in the subject. Even in old age he remained a dominant and deeply loved figure in the profession. The extraordinary scenes when, in high old age, he delivered the Ely Lecture to the American Economic Association have been unforgettably described by its then President.

> There, in a Denver ballroom, 2,000 assembled economists, made sleepy by the dinner they were digesting, sated by a full day of talks, colloquia and debates, ready to go off to their evening parties, rose to cheer Lionel as I have never seen a group of academics do. For they knew that they had that night seen and heard to what true civilisation and scholarship aspire.[170]

In July 1982 Robbins suffered a severe stroke and 'sank into a half-awake life of memories and moments of recognition'.[171] In May 1984 he suffered another severe stroke and died on 15 May. At a Memorial Meeting held on 11 October 1984 at St John's Smith Square, great names – James Meade, Lord Drogheda, William Baumol and Sir Claus Moser – paid glowing tributes to his memory.[172] Echoing Ralph Dahrendorf's obituary, Meade referred to him as 'a Great Renaissance Figure'.[173] To give an adequate biographical account of such a figure would require not a chapter but a substantial book. This chapter, then, is merely a prelude to a discussion of the work of Lionel Robbins as an economist – only a part of the whole, but a very important part of the whole and one of which it is certainly worth keeping the memory alive.

3 Methodology

1. INTRODUCTION – THE *ESSAY*

Robbins's *Essay on the Nature and Significance of Economic Science (ENSES)* is one of the two most important methodological statements by any economist this century and the single most important until the appearance of Friedman's classic essay.[1] It is, then, instructive to examine the origins of this book which first appeared in 1932. It seems clear that the book originated in at least three different considerations. The first, as Robbins recounts in his *Autobiography*, was the need, as Robbins saw it, to reformulate economics in such a way that it could take account of *non-material* welfare and also of destructive activities which nevertheless were *chosen* and which *used resources* – principally, war. This was not a difficult step, given the marginal want-satisfaction of Wicksteed and the Austrians.[2] But it was a fundamental departure from Cannan's position, in which *material* welfare was given a central place, as Robbins was very much aware.

Secondly, Robbins was anxious to separate economics and ethics. The first clear signals of this were given in a review of Hawtrey's *The Economic Problem* (which appeared five years before *ENSES*[3]) and Robbins's position evolved, as is clear from other reviews by him, between this review and the first edition of *ENSES*. Some of this review was indeed re-used in *ENSES*.[4] A major purpose of the book was, then, to purge economics of value judgements; and failure to understand this aim led to many of the misunderstandings by contemporary critics of Robbins, although the objective was achieved to a considerable extent in the longer term. The third foundation was a certain revulsion from the work of Pigou and in particular his *Economics of Welfare*. Robbins later related how he was initially predisposed towards this book but came to realise the extra-scientific nature of the interpersonal comparisons used.[5] The erection of a demarcation criterion which excluded from the domain of scientific discourse all such exercises as Pigou's then became a major objective; and it was buttressed by criticism of other aspects of Pigou's work

23

concerning increasing and diminishing returns industries, although here Robbins's criticism was simply borrowing from the fundamental critique by Allyn Young.[6]

The methodological position advanced, it should be emphasised, did not amount to the proposition that the economist should not engage in controversy over matters of economic policy and welfare.[7] Robbins was insistent on this, despite frequent misunderstanding in the early years after the publication of the book.[8] But it did amount to the proposition that the economist must *not* claim a *scientific* basis for his value judgements.[9] Although Robbins had, initially, hesitations about journalism and popularisation[10] (which may have been connected with a distaste for Keynes's activities) he emphasised that there was no question that economics was concerned with reality and he was never slow himself to give advice. Indeed, outside economics Robbins was certainly not ethically neutral but ferociously opposed to totalitarian tyranny and oppression from both the Right and the Left. But this stepped outside what the economist could say *as an economist*. All that the economist could do, in his scientific role, was to indicate the consequences of particular actions – or, as in wartime, indicate what might constitute an equi-marginal resource allocation.[11]

2. SOURCES

The sources on which Robbins drew were threefold: English Classical economics, Jevons and Wicksteed, and the Austrians.[12] As a broad generalisation one could say that the methodological postulates came from Classical economics – though the Austrians also drew upon Classical sources, producing important similarities between their methodological preconceptions and those of Robbins – and the microeconomic rationalisations came from Mises and Wicksteed.[13] It is thus not incorrect to describe *ENSES*, as Blaug has done, as a restatement of the Senior–Mill–Cairnes position in modern language where modern, for Robbins at the date of composition, meant Jevons, Wicksteed and the Austrians.[14] But there is more to the Classical part of the inheritance than indicated in the three names just cited; and in particular the distinction in the work of Hume and other Scottish philosophers, whose influence Robbins acknowledged, between 'is' and 'ought', was ever-present.[15] Bentham is also more important than the number of citations might indicate and Robbins, as a declared Utilitarian, was able to cite evidence that Bentham was well aware of the purely conventional nature of inter-personal utility comparisons, and aware too that there was no *scientific* basis for inter-personal comparisons however necessary the conventional practice.[16]

From Senior, Mill and Cairnes, Robbins took an emphasis on *a priorism*, a belief in the validity of introspection as a source of hypothesis, and a certain ambiguity about the role of data to which we shall return below.[17] The influence of Jevons was more limited, and largely confined to a reiteration of the proposition that in Utilitarian economics there was no scientific basis for interpersonal comparisons.[18] In particular Robbins did not follow Jevons into such dubious by-ways as clear-cut psychological 'laws'.[19]

Robbins's attitude to Jevons seems to have been influenced to some extent by Wicksteed, to whom he acknowledged a particular debt.[20] Certainly it is clear that Robbins had considerable admiration for Wicksteed[21] and his approach to economics, and that he had studied Wicksteed's *Commonsense* long and hard.[22] Indeed one commentator has suggested this book now reads as an introduction to Robbins's own.[23] The main thing which Robbins took from Wicksteed was the concept of the omnipresent, choosing, maximising, individual,[24] approaching allocation problems in terms of opportunity cost rather than real cost, within the framework of general rather than partial analysis.[25] Wicksteed may also have influenced Robbins in the rejection of inter-personal comparisons[26] and in his view of the limits of what could be said scientifically,[27] although it is likely that to some extent his views coincided with ones which Robbins had arrived at from other directions.

German literature influences were two-fold: Weber and the Austrians. From Weber, Robbins took what was essentially a restatement of the English Classical distinction between the science and art of economics as the distinction between positive and normative economics.[28] Seeking to rid economics of ethics, he also found valuable in Weber the concept of *Wertfreiheit* and an emphasis on the separation of value judgements from analysis[29]. Finally Weber's distinction between economics and technology – the latter has a single end, the former has multiple ends from given means, implying the concept of opportunity cost – was one to which Robbins returned on a number of occasions.[30]

It should be emphasised, however, that the German language literature to which Robbins referred was, with the exception of Weber, very largely Austrian. There was, it is clear, much in the Germanic mind which was antithetical to the flexibility and transparency of Robbins's own theoretical approach which had Gallic elements. Indeed there are scathing references to Germanic thought elsewhere in Robbins's own work which indicate not merely a lack of sympathy but an outright hostility.[31] Not surprisingly, this increased as the 1930s passed.[32]

Most of the German language literature which influenced Robbins was thus Austrian. Much of it he read directly, and parts of his early work are peppered with citations from German language literature.[33] Some of the German language material came via Wicksell and some of it, indeed, was absorbed into a mind predisposed to the Austrian approach by Wicksteed.[34] For Robbins, Austrian economics, in the late 1920s and early 1930s, was modern economics, and he used the language of Austrian economics quite consciously on occasions.[35] Although some commentators have recognised this,[36] the secondary literature in general has not placed sufficient emphasis upon this foundation of *ENSES*.[37]

Of the Austrians, the most important immediate influence was Mises, to whom Robbins acknowledged a particular debt.[38] Robbins had personal contact with Mises[39] as well as being a keen student of his writings. Of Mises's works cited by Robbins, the most important were *Money*, and *Socialism* (which was later translated into English by Robbins's friend Kahane).[40] The influence of Mises is particularly apparent in the first edition of *ENSES*, as a number of the references disappear in the second edition. Mises's work at this time had the recommendation to Robbins that it could be seen as defending the methodology of Senior and Cairnes,[41] and the further recommendation that Mises considered war to be within the subject matter of economics.[42] But it is important to distinguish the Mises of this date from the extreme *a priorist* of the later years who went much further than Robbins both in attacking mathematical economics and in the rejection of all natural science parallels.[43]

The influence of Menger on Robbins was both more distant and more diffused, even though Menger is one of those cited when Robbins gives his famous definition of economics as 'the science which studies human behaviour as a relationship between ends and scarce means which have alternative uses'.[44] Indeed, although Menger was undoubtedly an influence on *ENSES*, it is perfectly conceivable that the book could have been written without any *direct* reference to him, even though the character of economic goods and the conditions for their existence, the approach to costs, and the omnipresent economising individual in Robbins's writings, all show signs of Menger's influence.[45]

The influence of other Austrians cited – Mayer,[46] Strigl[47] and even Schumpeter (the author of an awesomely Positivist work which has never been translated into English but to which Robbins refers[48]) – is much more diffuse and peripheral to Robbins's methodological position. But the whole Austrian approach to economic problems informs Robbins's methodology, especially throughout the 1930s. It is not merely a question of obvious concepts such as opportunity cost.[49] It is rather a whole approach grounded in a disaggregated general equilibrium – with perhaps the emphasis even more upon general than upon equilibrium – leading to the insistence that production in the aggregate has no meaning and that, for the traditional theory of production and distribution, a theory of equilibrium, with comparative statics and dynamics, should be substituted.[50] Unlike Cannan, Robbins was deeply interested in questions of equilibrium and disequilibrium,[51] and his emphasis upon using a general rather than a partial equilibrium[52] frame of reference was to show later in his wartime work, when he insisted upon discussing the overall allocation of resources rather than piecemeal planning of particular industries.[53] His whole approach to costs was in these terms[54] – even though, carried to its logical conclusion, this would wreck large parts of conventional economic theory. It is interesting to note, in this context, that in some of Robbins's early writings he made extensive and ingenious use of the Marshallian tool of elasticity[55] and that as he became more Austrian he stopped doing this.

Modern Austrian economists have stressed the importance of the generation of economic information in the pursuit of economic goals, and it has been suggested that this is one area in which *ENSES*, and Robbins's position more generally, are deficient when compared with the broader Austrian approach.[56] There is some truth in this. Entrepreneurs are needed to convey information to maximisers; and while, rather later, Robbins did recognise the benefits of competition,[57] he rather took it for granted in *ENSES* and failed to spell it out in a way which would have made this vital aspect clear.

These were probably the important influences on Robbins's methodological position. Although he admired Frank Knight,[58] and although Knight became required reading at LSE,[59] it is difficult to see very much direct evidence of Knight's influence – indeed one could argue that Robbins saw a much more technocratic role for the economist than Knight did.[60] Similarly, though the elder Fetter is cited,[61] it is really only as an American Austrian rather than as having anything individual to say. Allyn Young had already brought war within economic discussion in 1925,[62] and although his treatment of the subject at all may have emboldened Robbins when he came to question Cannan's treatment which, by equating the subject matter of economics with material welfare excluded it,[63] Robbins's approach to the problem was distinct from that of Young.

It does not seem likely that Cassel was a major influence on Robbins. Although Robbins said later that in 1925–27 he was strongly influenced by Cassel,[64] he was talking about the preparation of his LSE lectures at that time – when we come to the genesis of *ENSES* it is Wicksell and the Austrians who are cited,[65] and in *ENSES* itself there are only three references to Cassel, all of them critical.[66] Cassel's *Fundamental Thoughts* (1925) actually contains a number of elements which are antithetical to Robbins's position in *ENSES*, notably the stress on induction in investigating the trade cycle[67] and the belief that it was possible to have a theory of prices without an underlying theory of value.[68] Nor did Robbins reason explicitly, as Cassel did,[69] in terms of equality of equations and unknowns. In short there was nothing in *ENSES* which Robbins could have taken only from Cassel, and vital elements – in particular the central role of individual marginal valuations – which he would not have taken from Cassel.

One outstanding puzzle about Robbins's sources is the question of the influence of John Neville Keynes – who is in any case referred to by Wicksteed.[70] It is inconceivable that Robbins had not read J. N. Keynes's famous book on methodology; yet there is only one reference to J. N. Keynes in the first edition of *ENSES* and this was itself omitted in the second edition.[71] It is all the more surprising since some commentators have, with justice, seen similarities between Robbins's methology and that of John Maynard Keynes.[72]

3. CRITIQUES

Robbins seems to have been little influenced by his critics. Cannan's adverse reaction[73] can have come as no surprise. Objection to his identification of 'economic' with 'material'[74] had been a fundamental starting point of *ENSES*.[75] His restatement of his position missed (or deliberately ignored) the central point that Robbins was making: choice, of necessity, involved non-material as well as material ends. Beveridge took the opportunity of his farewell address to reject vehemently the charge of barrenness in empirical studies[76] – but, as noted in Chapter 2 below, the effect produced seems to have been unfortunate. Many of the reviews were, in contrast to *ENSES* itself, assemblies of prolix verbiage which did little to advance the argument. Indeed, Frank Knight described one review as characterised by 'turgid, swashbuckling style and opinionated attitude'.[77] The most outspoken critic was Souter,[78] whose style it was that Knight characterised so unkindly, and his main point was that modernisation, through casting everything in terms of Austrian general equilibrium, produced a static and uninformative view of the world. Another critical reviewer was Talcott Parsons, who found the work excessively positivistic. 'In his [Robbins's] anxiety to make economics a "positive" science free from "metaphysics" he has continually been pressed into a radically positivist position which really eliminates ends altogether.'[79] Parsons also objected to the elimination of time in this 'neo-Austrian' theory[80] and, perhaps not surprisingly given his own background, rejected the idea of an exogenous scale of valuations.[81]

The critique by Harrod[82] seems to have made more impression upon Robbins, since he went to the trouble of publishing a reply. The basic point of Harrod's critique, when one penetrates the baroque prose, is that Robbins concentrated on the analysis of choice and consumer demand as the essentials of scientific economics, whereas an equally important underlying economic insight is contained in the analysis which implies equalisation of marginal net product of resources. (In fact, this is a deduction from preferences and contains no additional, independent, analysis.) Harrod's other points included the argument that, on the basis of the repeal of the Corn Laws, interpersonal comparisons were acceptable, the importance of recognising imperfect competition when addressing welfare questions, and the need for multiplicity of method, for empirical counterparts of theoretical constructs, for empirical bases for hypothesis formation, and for 'verification'. He also emphasised that the economist should not be shy of giving advice. Robbins in his reply[83] was able to meet most of these criticisms – in particular, he had never argued that the economist should not give advice, merely that he should not claim scientific sanction for this advice on all points – and to concede some ground on the question of the role of empirical work, while leaving open the nature of postulates.

Robbins's concern to deny scientific status to policy advice, and to value-judgements about distributional effects, was also criticised by Lindley Fraser. He complained that Robbins's definition of economics did not cover what economists *did*.[84] This was essentially beside the point, since Robbins knew perfectly well what they did but was arguing that much of what they did was extra-scientific. Fraser then argued that redistribution 'probably' increased welfare therefore it should be within economics – a looseness of argument that would not have appealed to Robbins. This was coupled with the view that Robbins's definition of economics implied that methodological purity required abstention from policy problems;[85] Robbins had no difficulty in replying that he was *not* asserting that economists should keep free of policy issues, merely that extra-scientific value judgements should be clearly distinguished.[86]

4. THE FULL METHODOLOGICAL POSITION

(i) Theory

Robbins's methodological position, as stated in *ENSES* and as amplified in subsequent publications, started from the position that there had been substantial progress in economics.

> The efforts of economists during the last hundred and fifty years have resulted in the establishment of a body of generalisations whose substantial accuracy and importance are open to question only by the ignorant or the perverse.[87]

On a number of occasions, especially in the 1930s, Robbins expressed considerable satisfaction at what economics had achieved, even though economists could not be expected to reach finality. Thus of the theory of costs he wrote:

> There is, indeed, no part of his subject about which the contemporary economist may legitimately feel more gratified, either as regards the quality of the work done, or as regards the temper in which it has been undertaken.[88]

There seems little doubt that Robbins's conversion from socialism made him appreciate, much more fully than those who had never been through this stage, just how much economics had really achieved; the fervour with which he embraced the subject, which was noted in the previous chapter, and his belief in its power to shed light on real world problems,[89] combined to produce an emphasis upon the achievements of the subject which the profession as a whole found highly acceptable.[90] The impression emerges from some of his post-war writings of a retreat from this; the basic position was still intact but some of the confidence seems to have evaporated.[91]

A fundamental plank in the argument was the necessity of separating economics and ethics – something which, as already noted, Robbins had been advancing since his 1927 review of Hawtrey.[92] Indeed a passage which appeared in *ENSES* and in the Hawtrey review puts the matter vividly.

> Shut Mr. Hawtrey in a room as Secretary of a Committee composed of Bentham, Buddha, Lenin and the Head of the United States Steel Corporation, set up to decide upon the ethics of usury, and it is improbable that he could produce an 'agreed document'. Set the same committee to determine the objective results of State regulation of the rate of discount, and it ought not to be beyond human ingenuity to produce unanimity – or at any rate a majority report, with Lenin perhaps dissenting.[93]

There was no *scientific* basis for *application* of economic analysis to normative problems without the use of value judgements.[94] Welfare economics with its implicit value judgements was 'a very draughty half-way house'.[95] In particular, distributive issues involved interpersonal comparisons and these had no scientific basis.[96]

The economist had thus to distinguish between positive and normative economics.[97] The positive involved the prediction of the outcome of certain economic actions or circumstances; the normative, which – and this is crucial – could not claim scientific status, involved making a judgement about the ethical status of the resulting distribution and other consequences of an economic policy measure. Robbins put the issue of a value-free positive economics most forcefully in a 1934 paper on economics and psychology.

This proposition has been much questioned in recent years by certain English-speaking economists. But they have not yet shown that propositions involving 'ought' are on the same logical footing as propositions involving 'is'. And, indeed, on examination, all their objections seem to resolve themselves into a fear that, if the scope of economics is thus defined, they may be precluded from discussing problems of social improvement from a normative point of view. But this apprehension is groundless. Nobody wishes to limit their freedom of action. Most of us think that is is very desirable that they should discuss such matters. All that is desired is that the logical division between the two types of propositions mentioned above should be clearly recognised. No-one wishes to prevent a mathematician from discussing problems of good and evil. But he may bring the multiplication table into unnecessary discredit if he suggested that his views on ethics have the same logical sanction.[98]

The scope of economics, thus delineated, covered both material and non-material costs and benefits.[99] Thus the useful fiction 'Economic Man' took into account 'net advantages' in deciding upon a course of action.[100] Economic actors were rational in the sense of consistent[101] – but economic theory did not require perfect consistency which was merely a limiting case.[102] In appraising alternatives, the individual was envisaged by Robbins as being engaged in ordinal ranking. It is tempting to see this last view as a by-product of the work of Hicks and Allen; but, in truth, ranking is to be found throughout the work of the Austrians and Wicksteed,[103] and Robbins was fond of referring to a passage from Mises (in turn citing another author) insisting that valuation was merely a process involving ranking without cardinal elements.[104] Indeed, this was a substantial point of difference between Robbins and Dennis Robertson.[105]

Given rankings, economic actors made choices in the face of scarcity.[106] When time and the means for achieving ends were limited and capable of alternative applications, and the ends could be ranked, then we had choice. Choice was the subject of economics and the role of economics was to spell out the implications of choice.[107] With competing wants and scarcity, choice became inevitable.[108]

It was the multiplicity of ends and the necessity of choice which distinguished the technical (with one end) from the economic.[109] The theory of production then, from the economic point of view, became merely the theory of factor allocation between competing uses.[110] The factor services were the means by which the given ends could be satisfied.[111] The ends themselves were not a matter on which scientific economics had any bearing.[112] Economics was neutral between ends.[113] Thus people's innate preferences for income and leisure[114] (the indifference map) were outside the scope of scientific inquiry. The desirability of increased wealth was itself a value judgement.[115] If there was only one end, such as victory in war, then this end-choice was outside economics,[116] while the resource allocation to achieve the given end was *within* economics. The only qualification to this argument was that a full understanding of the consequences of choosing particular ends might bring about some convergence of value judgements about the desirability of these ends.[117]

Not only were ends beyond the competence of the economist; there was no such thing as an 'economic' end.[118] Economics was concerned with means. Reviewing his achievements many years later, Robbins wrote:

> It disposed of the idea that there were economic ends as such, only economic ways of achieving ends – the idea of economic causes or economic motives residing properly in the sphere of generalised command over scarce means rather than in the realm of 'ultimate' objectives.[119]

The assumptions, on the basis of which the consequences of choosing given ends were to be predicted, were a somewhat loosely-defined mixture of *a priori* ones, of assumptions based upon (largely casual) empiricism, and of assumptions based upon introspection.[120] Robbins did not go to anything like the lengths of either Mises[121] or (in a different way) Friedman, but there are substantial elements of *a priorism* in his approach.[122] Essentially, this ambiguity over the precise nature of economic assumptions carries over from Classical economics – Mill is also ambiguous[123] – but, although Robbins's position has much in common with that of Cairnes,[124] he does not go as far even as Cairnes in the direction of *a priorism*. Indeed his position was essentially English; the elements of imprecision and compromise about the extent to which the basic premises of economics are hypothetical and *a priori* is to be found in many other writers.[125]

The position is further clouded by Robbins's view that introspection, as a source of premises, provides economics with an empirical base.[126] This argument, which stemmed from Mill and (especially) Cairnes, was held to provide economics with a unique source of information which rendered it superior to natural science.[127] The implication was clearly that this more than compensated for the inability to conduct controlled experiments.[128] Its only serious limitation was that it was not available as a basis for interpersonal comparisons.[129]

(ii) Empirical work – induction, testing and verification

A minimisation of the empirical basis of economic theory was not entirely surprising, given that Robbins held that there were not stable empirical regularities.[130] (Indeed, knowledge of a temporary empirical regularity might hasten its removal[131] as economic actors altered their conduct.) His argument was essentially a reflection of Hume's argument against induction – even if things have been like this, they will not necessarily be like it in the future.[132] Such criticism of the stability of economic relations has looked increasingly important in recent years, as much of the faith in regression analysis has been eroded,[133] but in the 1960s this view, coupled with the view that prediction was impossible, was deeply unpopular.[134] Critics argued both that the premise of instability was an empirical question which could not therefore rule out empirical investigation, and that the *degree* of instability was important.[135] These criticisms reflect a particular episode in the history of economic thought, when it was seriously believed that the methods of physics would yield an economics of comparable quality and when regression analysis as a tool for testing was credited with almost mystical powers, while some of the elementary philosophical criticisms concerning the testing of *one* hypothesis had not been digested by economists who declared themselves (fortunately they did not act as such) to be naive falsificationists.[136] From the vantage point of the present it does seem, without wishing to deny *all* force to these positions, that the regularity which natural science is able to posit is different in kind, and not just in degree, from that which economics is able to assume. Moreover it has to be emphasised that, as Popper has said, the notion of a regular universe is itself a metaphysical idea and one which is not capable of direct testing.[137]

There is no doubt that Robbins viewed much quantitative work in economics with a considerable degree of scepticism. It was not just that, secure in almost 200 years of unsuccessful attempts to overturn Hume's critique, he rejected induction, adding Mill's point about plurality of causes in any real-world situation;[138] it was also that he was highly critical of the usefulness of much economic data and doubtful of its correspondence with economic concepts. Thus even in the context of his critique of the Representative Firm, having disposed of the concept to his satisfaction by arraigning it in terms of Austrian General Equilibrium, he then proceeded to dismiss the concept in terms of its statistical identifiability.[139]

But such an attitude raises the whole general question of Robbins's view of quantification. Now there seems absolutely no doubt that he was, and remained, extremely sceptical about the quantitative aspects of economics and indeed of social sciences in general.[140]

> In the natural sciences the transition from the qualitative to the quantitative is easy and inevitable. In the social sciences, for reasons which have already been set forth, it is in some connections almost impossible, and it is always associated with peril and difficulty.[141]

At the end of his life he was to say that 'many of the most important propositions of the subject fall into the category where quantification is out of the question'.[142] He was strongly opposed to what he called 'pseudo-scientific bravado'.[143] He believed (not without good grounds) that there was misuse of the assumptions of probability theory in quantitative work.[144] Moreover he was strongly critical of W. C. Mitchell's quantitative work on business cycles and wrote of the Institutionalists' quantitative efforts: 'Yet not one single "law" deserving of the name, not one quantitative generalisation of permanent validity has emerged from their efforts.'[145] Time series could test the explanations of economic history, but when used as a basis for prediction were subject to changes in tastes and knowledge.[146]

To some extent this attitude was bound up with the intellectual and personal tensions between Robbins and Beveridge. Beveridge, in his farewell address which, as noted in Chapter 2, caused some offence, had bravely ('I know that in speaking thus I make enemies')[147] restated his position that economic theory should be stated in terms which made clear under what circumstances its hypotheses could be falsified.[148] Until this became the norm, economics would remain outside the area of genuinely scientific discourse.[149] But Robbins refused to accept this. Though, he argued, quantitative work in the social sciences had initially been undertaken in an optimistic spirit, this had proved an unfounded optimism.[150] He was particularly critical of Mitchell: it was not the man of science but the village idiot who considered all facts equally important. (His criticism here reflected Allyn Young's position.)[151] But he was also critical of Schultz's work: estimates of demand functions could never be stable.[152] Moreover aggregate data had particular limitations; prices which signified relative valuations could not be used for aggregations of outputs at values.[153]

And yet there is some qualification to this picture. Robbins certainly does not seem to rule out observation on all occasions; indeed he argued, in one of his most famous articles, that it was necessary to resolve differences produced by inconclusive *a priori* reasoning.[154] He approved of the quantitative work on inflation of Bresciani-Turroni[155]; his own *Great Depression* used a *great* deal of data;[156] and there were certainly occasions on which he applauded empirical research.[157] Indeed he encouraged the work of Phillips at LSE.[158]

The paradox can probably be explained by reference to the now defunct concept of verification. This, as Blaug has pointed out, is by no means the same thing as testing.[159] It is essentially designed to check the applicability of theories to particular situations, and to see whether extra auxilliary assumptions are required, as well as to discover areas where further theoretical development is also needed.[160]

Such 'verification' can lead in turn to prediction: statistics tell us the initial conditions, and our models, adjusted for the initial conditions, then predict correctly. (The corollory of this is that if there is predictive failure, the models, which are self-contained, are not falsified; rather we go back to the statistics of the initial conditions and investigate further.)[161] There are a number of Classical discussions which seem to lead in this direction, especially in the work of Cairnes, and similar lines of argument are to be found in the work of Mises and Weber.[162] Such a use of quantitative material is not necessarily valueless; Robbins's later criticism of the danger of generalising from half-baked mathematical models without reference to the facts is perfectly sound.[163] Moreover, in practice, verification can – and in Robbins's work sometimes did – shade into falsification, partly because the assumptions themselves were frequently not testable directly.[164] (A similar ambiguity may be found in the work of Cairnes[165] even though, in principle, such verification is a necessary corollary of the *a priori* approach – any other testing would be 'otiose' since the logical status of the theories is incontestable.) In practice Robbins did engage in hypothesis testing, whether in attacking the pseudo-Marxist 'market search' theory of war[166] or in criticising Hobson's over-expansion of investment theory of the trade cycle.[167] In the last resort though, even though verification and falsification can in practice shade into one another, they should be logically distinct, and there are some passages which suggest that Robbins did not care to maintain this logical distinction.[168] In almost the same breath he could talk of 'testing' and then illustrate what he meant by reference to the work of Cairnes, Bresciani-Turroni or even Viner, where the writers concerned were not engaging in 'testing' in the sense of attempted falsification, but in 'verification'.[169]

At least he was not, there is certainly no doubt, a naive falsificationist. Indeed, there were occasions on which he used the word 'tendency' in such a way as to seal a hypothesis against refutation quite as clearly as Cairnes[170] – but these occurred early on in his work. He was however clear that, if quantification and falsification are the hallmarks of natural science, economists, faced for reasons already noted with something which was clearly not a natural science, should not feel too abashed.[171]

At the same time, although he was aware of the dangers of using mathematical economics,[172] he did not share Mises's elaborate contempt for mathematical economics.[173] Indeed, he took the trouble to obtain some instruction in mathematics at an early stage of his career[174] although, like Viner, his subsequent understanding of mathematical argument was probably due more to his strong intuition than to expertise which he himself possessed.[175]

But if his atttitude to mathematics in economics was cautious rather than hostile, his attitude to psychology was completely exclusionist – it had no place in economics at all.[176] Economics simply took needs and ranking as data and left the matter at that. This did not however amount to acceptance of behaviourism – even in the particular form of revealed preference, a concept which he rejected before it had even really entered the economic literature.[177] He preferred to work with the hypothesis of the existence of motives[178] – the implication is that positing a utility function provided the basis for fruitful theorising.

Perhaps not surprisingly he was scathing about Institutionalism.

The place of institutionalism in the history of economic thought is a matter of some perplexity. That the term itself served as a war-cry congenial to quite a number of muddled and slightly disturbed spirits is clear enough. At the time of its publication in the twenties, the volume entitled *The Trend of Economics* (edited by Rexford Guy Tugwell), which, so far as it had any unity at all, was a sort of manifesto of such dissidence, had an enormous *réclame* until it was quietly and courteously deflated by a masterly essay by Allyn Young.[179] Nowadays I doubt whether five per cent of the younger generation of economists have even heard of it – which perhaps only shows that, as forecasters, its practitioners signally failed to deliver the goods. As for any influence or progress on the lines indicated, it must be admitted that it has been negligible.[180]

He was similarly unimpressed with historicism which, associating it with Hegelian philosophy, he rejected completely.[181] It is perhaps ironic that the most important single figure in the history of LSE should have moved that institution in precisely the opposite direction to that envisaged – indeed desired – by its founders.[182]

5. VALUE JUDGEMENTS

Apart from Robbins's deep distaste for all the data-dredging which he associated with Institutionalism, and his distaste also for the extraordinary generalisations of historicism (coupled with his rejection of prediction of the future, whether historicist or otherwise), there was another reason for Robbins's emphatic opposition to Institutionalism and historicism. For the literature in these areas was permeated throughout by value judgements of precisely the kind from which Robbins was seeking to free economics, in particular value judgements involving interpersonal comparisons.

As already indicated, Robbins rejected completely interpersonal comparison as something which could be made *within* the scientific apparatus of economics.[183] Such comparisons could be made – indeed the economist had to make judgements[184] – but this did not make them scientific.[185] This had not been his original position; in the *Economic Journal* in 1938 he provided an account of how, having been predisposed to the conventional Pigovian approach, he found himself unable to offer any scientific way of resolving a dispute in which a Brahmin claimed to be capable of ten times more happiness than an untouchable.[186] This was to be a frequent point of reference. In addition, of course, Jevons, Wicksteed and Mises, all of whom influenced his approach, had rejected interpersonal comparisons.[187] Such comparisons were not capable of verification by introspection, and in this context there was every danger of committing the fallacy of composition from individual diminishing marginal utility to conclusions about society – income utility could not be aggregated and its functional dependence on income determined.[188]

There are two important things to make clear in this connection. Firstly, Robbins, as a 'provisional Utilitarian' certainly believed that equality was a morally necessary working hypothesis.[189] Secondly, he was definitely not opposed to a degree of redistribution. His position was simply that redistribution goes two stages beyond what can be regarded as scientific. Firstly, it involves making implicit or explicit interpersonal comparisons;

secondly it involves an 'ought' for which there is no scientific basis, since it takes us into the realm of normative economics, even if interpersonal comparisons are admitted.[190]

6. CONCLUSION

There is no doubt about the influence of *ENSES* and indeed of Robbins's other writings on methodology, and of the methodological positions on welfare economics which he took throughout his work. In essence, he changed the face of welfare economics by his methodological critique of the Pigovian brand. The literature on hypothetical compensation – a device which, he was later to point out, was invented by Viner and re-discovered by Kaldor and Hicks[191] – was an attempt to solve the problems which he had raised; but as he pointed out, it was no use unless the compensation was actually paid.

But his methodological message was much wider, as this chapter should have indicated. His tendency to allow the argument to develop by implication does not actually seem to have hampered acceptance of the message,[192] and even those who were critical of some aspects of his argument firmly endorsed the distinction between positive and normative economics.[193] As indicated at the beginning of this chapter, *ENSES* was one of the two most important methodological statements of this century. As Baumol wrote in his Foreword to the 1984 reprint:

> It caused an upheaval in the settled habits of thought of professional economists very soon after its appearance, and it engendered controversy which has not yet abated – controversy which continues to be creative now as it was then. Even those who disagree most strongly with positions taken in this book will readily acknowledge that they are substantial, and that they have changed the course of economics by forcing economists to separate out clearly what they can derive from analysis standing firmly on logical and empirical evidence and the conclusions dependent on the observer's personal ethical precepts.[194]

4 History of Economic Thought

1. INTRODUCTION

Robbins attached great importance to the history of economic thought as part of the education of those studying economics – a subject which was too narrow on its own. Study of past theory should help us to understand the problems of the past *and* to appreciate more fully both the strengths and limitations of modern theory. History of economic thought broadened the range of intellectual possibilities under consideration, and it helped to provide a cultural background for courses.[1] He argued for compulsory courses in the history of economic thought[2] and did much to promote the subject at LSE[3] – his *Theory of Economic Policy* originated in his LSE lectures.[4] He struggled against the insularity of English economics[5] and against the curious narrowing of vision which results from knowing only very recent literature.[6] Undoubtedly he felt at some stages that he was fighting a losing battle;[7] but he was ultimately successful to a remarkable degree. There seems little doubt that the revival of interest in the subject in Britain in the post-war years owed an enormous debt to his direct influence.[8]

In Robbins's view, history of economic thought should be 'a stimulus to further thinking' and one of the things which is most remarkably clear about his own work, to anyone well versed in English Classical economic writing in particular, is the extent to which Robbins had absorbed earlier theory, adapted it to the modern world and made it his own. It would be tedious to spell out the details of such episodes; but there is no doubt that, especially in the fields of money (where the Ricardian definition of excess, and memories of Tooke and Fullarton were particularly prominent) and of trade policy, Robbins advanced essentially the Classical analysis.[9] He appreciated, unlike so many who have subsequently re-discovered bits of the Classical analysis for themselves, the quite extraordinary magnitude of the achievements of Classical theory in these fields. Moreover he acquired in this

41

way a perspective on current controversies which others lacked. During the post-war episode of passive monetary policy he observed that the 'shades of Tooke and Fullarton have reigned triumphant in Great George Street',[10] and he realised that the position of the Radcliffe Committee had been anticipated not only by Tooke and Fullarton but even by Sir James Steuart.[11]

2. THE RANGE OF VISION

Robbins's readings and sympathies in economics covered an enormous range both of time and space. The one real blind-spot in his range of vision – associated perhaps with his outspoken anti-religious views – was his treatment of the medieval writers.[12] But we all have our blind-spots; the width of his vision was incomparably greater than that of most historians of economic thought, let alone of most economists of whom Schumpeter once correctly remarked that they do not read.

His struggle was not only against 'the extraordinary provincialism in time of much contemporary professional literature'[13] but also, from the very beginning of his career, against British insularity. Indeed this was, in a sense, initially at least, the harder struggle. Cannan had after all been a major authority on the history of economic thought at LSE. But Cannan did not read over a geographically wide area and indeed, in reviewing *ENSES* he objected to the citations of foreign economists.[14] But it was these foreign economists which Robbins persuaded his colleagues (especially Hicks) and his students to read. They included in particular Cassel, Walras, Pareto, Taussig, Wicksell, the Austrians, Frank Knight – and Edgeworth, part of the British literature already in danger of falling into neglect.[15] Robbins can be said to have opened up English economic literature and helped to maintain its own heritage as well.[16] He was, not surprisingly, instrumental (with Dalton) in the planning and production of Batson's 1930 bibliography of economic theory.[17]

His knowledge of German language literature was remarkable and very evident, especially in his earlier publications.[18] This did not however give him sympathy for Hegelianism, or its Marxist derivative.[19] But, in contrast to his dismissal of the medieval literature, Robbins had taken the trouble to read the Hegelian and Marxist literature. From an early review of a book by Dobb onwards, his references to Marxism were rarely less than corrosive;[20] the Marxists had no plan for that society, in the interests of which existing society was to be destroyed,[21] and he was repelled by 'the Messianic mysticism of Marxian determinism'.[22] But he had taken the trouble to read the Marxist literature and his discussions show a good knowledge of what it contained. Had he not found so much of it, and its fruits, so remarkably repulsive, he would still have rejected it since it involved a fundamentally different conception of economics; as he pointed out in *ENSES*, the 'economic' or 'materialist' definition of history is *in substance* material and therefore not economic in the sense in which, as indicated in the previous chapter, he viewed something as being economic.[23]

He was little more sympathetic towards Institutionalism. The reasons for this have already been indicated to some extent in the previous chapter;[24] but it is also clear that the aversion was in part due to the conflict between a mind which liked to soar in theoretical speculation and the content of so much Institutionalist literature – 'how dreary and voluminous that would be' he wrote of the idea of an exhaustive history of Institutionalism.[25] His appraisal of Veblen was guarded. While acknowledging Veblen's influence and impact, and agreeing that Veblen was 'much too clever to be really taken in by the naive pseudo-explanations of pure Behaviourism', he confessed that there were difficulties in assessing the 'logical and scientific contents of Veblen's work' and pointed to a clash between the social behaviourist and the humanistic individualistic elements in Veblen.[26] But this did not prevent him from supervising Seckler's study of Veblen.[27]

3. STYLE

Robbins's style in his history of economic thought work was rather different from what has become the predominant modern style. Though the scholarship was extraordinary, the footnote references are relatively sparse; though Robbins was very much his own man, he certainly did not conduct a running debate in the footnotes with other writers whose interpretations he did not accept. Moreover the technology of modern economics is entirely absent. What is remarkable, and perhaps a little chastening, about this last is that this hardly ever leaves analytical points in need of mechanical 'rigorous' clarification. He provided a grand overview, both in works which were explicitly about the history of economic thought and in those which merely took it as a starting point, with great scholarship worn lightly.[28]

He used quotation extensively; this was 'quite deliberate' as he wrote in his Preface to *Robert Torrens*.

> It has always seemed to me wrong to write at any length about an author's opinions unless it can be assumed that one's readers have direct acquaintance, not only with the substance of these opinions, but also with the mode in which they are set forth; it is a vice of books about books that the original author tends to get lost in the commentary.[29]

Quotation had the merit of indicating clearly the basis of the interpretations advanced, while at the same time exhibiting the excellence of the originals.[30] These aims were further advanced in his great *Robert Torrens* by the inclusion of an extensive bibliographical appendix. This is a mine of information. It has not set a fashion, but of its kind it is invaluable to researchers in the field.[31]

One of the most notable characteristics of Robbins's work in the history of economic thought was the vigour and freshness of the writing. Robbins objected to

> the not inconsiderable number of contemporary academics who equate readability with superficiality and regard no contribution as deserving of respect unless it is at once overloaded with material superfluous to the argument and a positive bore to plough through.[32]

In Robbins's writing personalities are brought to life, and his history of economic thought is enlivened by his ability – without resort to 'faction' – to imagine and sympathise with the feelings of earlier writers. Thus Mill behaved badly under stress – who has not?[33] Comte was 'as pathological an egocentric as ever strutted the stage in a Strindbergian madhouse'.[34] It was partly because Robbins was really interested in, and perceptive about, people that he was able to write in this manner. To him, the characters came alive in a way that they cannot for most of us. I remember mentioning to him Overstone's dislike of Gladstone; his face lit up and he made it perfectly clear that he understood what it was about Gladstone's personality which jarred.[35] The writings too are enlivened by humour – a passage in *Robert Torrens* poking gentle fun at Marx's misrepresentation of Wakefield is a particualrly good example.[36] Another merit of the writing was the way in which analytical issues could be condensed within a small compass without loss of clarity. The Introduction to Torrens's *Letters on Commercial Policy* is a model of this kind.[37]

4. INFLUENCES ON ROBBINS

The origins of Robbins's love affair with the history of economic thought lie in the very beginnings of his love affair with economics. Sitting at the feet of Edwin Cannan he simply could not learn one without the other;[38] and as a historian of economic thought he continued the great tradition of Cannan, while not failing to note the points of disagreement.[39] Initially he seems to have absorbed Cannan's slightly abrasive attitude towards Classical economics – provoking critical comments from Allyn Young[40] – but this passed with time. Other early and important influences were Hayek and Viner. Viner's extraordinary acuteness, his total unwillingness to seek refuge in historical relativity, and his enormous knowledge of economic (especially English Classical) literature were all very much of the kind to appeal to any Cannan pupil, but to Robbins in particular.[41]

Robbins also appreciated Schumpeter's work in the history of economic thought. Indeed his review of Schumpeter's great *History* is an important document.[42] He saw accurately both the monumental strengths and the serious weaknesses of the book. There were undoubtedly issues on which Robbins saw a great deal more clearly than Schumpeter; in particular his introduction to Wicksell shows that he saw clearly what Schumpeter (amazingly) did not – the fundamental differences in the approach of Jevons, of Marshall, and of the Austrians.[43]

Great scholars and economists were one stimulus to Robbins, in this field; a stimulus of another kind was provided by reaction against bad scholarship which abounded[44] and against the use of Classical economics as an Aunt Sally. As he wrote in his *Autobiography*, about the composition of *The Theory of Economic Policy*:

I felt more and more that the classical system in general, misrepresented almost beyond belief, was being used as a convenient Aunt Sally by any writer or speaker who wished to set his *soi-disant* enlightened views against a background of black reaction. I felt this to be quite deplorable.[45]

The *Theory of Economic Policy* turned out to be a major success. By the time it reached its second edition in 1978 it had been reprinted four times after its first publication in 1952, and it had become unthinkable to discuss the topic without reference to Robbins's book.

5. ROBBINS'S HEROES

The *Theory of Economic Policy* represented a study of one particular aspect of the thought of a good many individuals. But Robbins clearly had particular heroes amongst the writers of the past. He was particularly impressed with the work of the eighteenth-century Scottish philosophers Hume, Smith, Ferguson and Millar, with their view of the evolution and development of society.[46] This was something which he came to stress in later work. His earlier view of Smith may however have involved reading more general *equilibrium* into Smith's work than was there.[47] This was perhaps partly because of his own Austrian background but it may also have been due to the influence of Allyn Young, who had advanced such a view in 1928.[48] Robbins was later to emphasise that the *Wealth of Nations* is a book about economic development.[49]

David Hume attracted Robbins's particular admiration. The influence of Hume is evident in most of Robbins's monetary writing,[50] and also to some extent in his trade writing.[51] But perhaps Hume's most pervasive influence on Robbins was his Utilitarianism.[52] Indeed, as will be clear in the following chapter, Robbins was a declared Utilitarian.[53] Bentham, whom Robbins believed to have derived his own Utilitarianism from Hume, thus became an object of particular interest in Robbins's own studies.[54] He saw Bentham as an effective and productive critic of institutions[55] and as having developed an unassailable position on law and constitutional reform.[56] The 'painstaking' Bentham was contrasted by Robbins with the 'exhibitionist Rousseau'.[57] He denied that there was any tendency to collectivism in the Greatest Happiness Principle,[58] and his writings on Bentham show an attitude so warm that it verges on the romantic.[59] It was thus entirely appropriate that he should have assumed the leadership of the Bentham Project at UCL, a role which he fulfilled with great skill and effectiveness.[60]

He delighted in Ricardo scholarship, and he undoubtedly had a warm personal regard for Ricardo both as a man and as a theorist.[61] Yet there is a certain ambiguity about his attitude; in particular he believed Malthus to have shown much greater good sense than Ricardo 'bombinating away in a stratosphere of abstract logic' on the matter of aggregate demand failure.[62]

Malthus was undoubtedly one of his heroes – and in the light of Mrs James's book, and the content of Malthus's writings, it is not difficult to see why.[63] Indeed Robbins shared Malthus's concern about population very deeply at a time when population had passed out of mainstream economics.[64]

However Malthus's theoretical achievements, and powers of abstraction, were limited. Samuel Bailey was, in this respect, very much more to Robbins's taste. In *ENSES* he cited Bailey on the relativity of economic quantities and aggregation and on the difficulties of index numbers; he drew Marian Bowley's attention to Bailey when supervising her work on Senior; he procured a reprint of Bailey's *Critical Dissertation*; and he supervised Rauner's Ph.D. dissertation on Bailey.[65]

But on Robert Torrens, after initially supervising Dr S. A. Meenai's research, he set to work himself. His study of Torrens proved to be of great significance. As a work on monetary and trade theory it is of much greater importance than the modest Preface would indicate, and it is indeed one of the major commentaries on Classical thought. The account is marked by serious analytical and historical writing enlivened by humour, the ability to bring ancient disputes – especially that involving the Cuba Case – to life, and some gentle poking of fun especially in discussing Wakefield 'whose arrival on the scene may be compared to the descent of some gorgeous tropical bird among the sober denizens of a respectable farmyard'.[66] The work is an astonishing achievement for a man with Robbins's other commitments. He had not planned to write a book although it was 'not without a certain surreptitious enjoyment' that he realised what he had really undertaken.[67] It is perhaps not surprising that the vigour and articulateness of Torrens's style, and his easy command of very high levels of abstraction, should all have appealed to Robbins; the result was a memorable book with which, more than a decade later, Robbins was still satisfied.[68]

A feature of the book on Torrens is that it contains one of the great discussions of the Currency and Banking Debate in the entire literature. There is no doubt that Robbins, long before he wrote this book, was convinced of the basic correctness of the Currency School analysis, and in particular of the proposition that the correct way to avoid a boom getting out of hand was a counter-cyclical monetary policy with early correction of expansion.[69] This did not amount to wholesale endorsement of the Currency School positions on all matters; in particular he was clear that their analysis of bank credit was unsatisfactory.[70] But the debate remained a matter of absorbing interest to him and I remember well his excitement at the discovery of Overstone's papers.

It would probably be true to say that his own position , though nearer the Currency than the Banking School, fell between the two as had the position of the Classical economist whom, of all, he probably admired the most – J. S. Mill. It is perfectly clear that his admiration was hardly uncritical, and that it did not extend to the Saint-Simonians.[71] But he had a very deep admiration for Mill indeed. After mentioning Hume, Smith and Ricardo, Robbins goes on:

> Mill yet stands out as one of the great figures of the Classical tradition, not unworthy to be mentioned in the same breath as these giants: a man of massive powers of intellectual synthesis and of burning idealism and integrity, willing to follow thought wherever it led him, somewhat over-solemn and not a very good judge of men but courageous, generous and sensitive – a rare spirit, conspicuous even in his own great age, with a message of candour and humanity.[72]

It will be clear from this that it was Mill's liberalism as well as his economics which appealed to Robbins; it was the disinterested liberalism, as he saw it, of the Cobdenites which led Robbins to admire them also.[73]

Amongst neo-classical economists, Robbins paid particular attention to Wicksteed and Wicksell. He greatly admired Jevons as an economist, both for his delight in abstraction and for his emphasis on the importance of theory at a time when the Historical School was making great strides. But he was obviously happy to have shed both Jevons's psychologism and his implications of cardinal utility.[74] He was impressed by Sidgwick's discussion of wages,[75] and he clearly respected Edgeworth.[76] Lavington he also regarded as having made significant contributions.[77] He had great reverence for Marshall,[78] although there seems little doubt that Cannan's habitually critical tone towards Marshall influenced Robbins, particularly in his early work.[79] But even in his critique of Marshall's Representative Firm he paid explicit tribute to Marshall's greatness.[80] Indeed it could be argued that he knew more of Marshall than some of those in Cambridge who affected to despise the latter. In particular Robbins pointed out that Marshall treated the equality of price with marginal revenue as a simplification for certain purposes only in Note xiv, and wrote of 'unbelievable misapprehensions' concerning the origin of the distinction between marginal revenue and price.[81] He clearly and correctly perceived that marginal utility was of small importance to Marshall and correctly perceived also that Marshall's emphasis on Ricardian elements in his work could not be afforded much weight.[82] He was obviously not prepared to defend Marshall in all respects; domestically he regarded him as 'a bit of a Turk'.[83] But in the review of Schumpeter, from which this phrase comes, he combated Schumpeter's ungenerous treatment of Marshall very judiciously.[84]

It was however Wicksteed and Wicksell with whom he felt the greatest affinity. Of the *Common Sense of Political Economy* Robbins wrote:

It is a masterpiece of systematic exposition. It is the most complete statement of the implicit philosophy of economic analysis which has been published in our day . . . It is a work which must be read slowly, conned over diligently – in short, treated with the respect with which any work of careful and intellectual architecture must be treated if it is to yield the enlightenment and aesthetic satisfaction which it is capable of yielding . . . A failure to sit through the *Common Sense* is a pretty sure sign of intellectual smallness.[85]

Robbins also regarded Wicksell as a very important economist.[86] He was impressed by his analytical contributions, while he was not repelled by Wicksell's extravagant radicalism.[87] Having at one point endorsed Marshall's *Principles* as the vital textbook, he later suggested starting with Wicksteed's *Common Sense* and then reading Wicksell's *Lectures* as a second year textbook.[88] He was impressed with the importance of Wicksell's capital theory and believed that he had succeeded, while drawing on the Austrians, in retaining much that was valuable in the Classical treatment of capital.[89] But it was in the sphere of monetary economics, and above all in the analysis of the relationship between the money and the natural rate of interest, that Robbins believed Wicksell to have made a fundamental and lasting contribution, even though he realised that the theoretical structure had Classical antecedents.[90] Indeed, with his knowledge of the historical literature forever permeating his analysis of current problems, he explicitly acknowledged the importance of Wicksell's analysis before the Radcliffe Committee.[91]

6. CONCLUSION

As an historian of economic thought Robbins's influence was enormous and is still continuing. Virtually all of those that he listed as having helped to contribute to the subject between the two editions of his *Theory of Economic Policy*[92] were influenced by him, many of them directly. He set examples of scholarship, and of the employment of a knowledge of the broad literature of economics in the analysis of current problems, without which the economics profession – and in all that he wrote in this area, Robbins wrote as an economist not as an historian – would have been much the poorer.

5 Economic Welfare

1. INTRODUCTION

This chapter deals with Robbins's writings on economic welfare. Robbins, it emerges, was a Utilitarian in the tradition stemming from Bentham and transmitted by, in particular, Jevons. From this Utilitarian base, coupled with a fundamental appreciation of the market and a crucial stress on the importance of liberty, Robbins dealt with matters of equality, State intervention, redistribution, taxation, socialism, competition and economic growth. It should already be clear from Chapter 3 that Robbins's methodological position did not involve the proposition that economists should abstain from comment on policy matters. Examination of his discussions concerning economic welfare should help to make this even more clear.

2. THE UTILITARIAN BACKGROUND

Robbins subscribed to what he called 'a provisional utilitarianism'.[1] This was partly due to the influence of Graham Wallas, one of his teachers at LSE.[2] He was contemptuous of 'refutations' of Bentham's approach and while he recognised that there were difficulties, he asked: 'How many second-rate persons and psycopathological major prophets have established reputations for superior sensibility by dwelling on these difficulties?'[3] The difficulties referred to were the standard problems with the Greatest Happiness Principle – a failure to distinguish qualities of happiness, difficulties of aggregating the happiness of different individuals, and Sidgwick's point that greatest-happiness seeking outside oneself requires moral intuition which Bentham rejected. Robbins considered neither these problems, nor the problems of implied inter-personal comparisons (he was fond of quoting Bentham to the effect that these were merely conventional and had no ultimate basis)[4] to be insuperable objections to a working Utilitarianism.

51

Nevertheless, if we consider it, not as the ultimate solution to all problems of ethics and valuation, as Bentham in the ardour of his invention was sometimes apt to claim, but rather as a working rule by which to judge legislative and administrative projects affecting large masses of people, it still seems to me to be better, more sensible, more humane, more agreeable to the moral conscience if you like, than any other I can think of . . . I submit that there is no more salutary thing for a legislator or an administrator to do than continually to be submitting his possible actions to the test [which utilitarian rules] pose: how will this affect the happiness, positive or negative, of the different members of the present and future community; where, on balance, does it stand on this criterion?[5]

In adopting a Utilitarian position, Robbins was essentially arguing for one in which the value judgements were made quite explicit. As already noted, he was very sceptical about welfare economics, which he regarded as containing a number of implicit value judgements;[6] and, as indicated, he was particularly sceptical about hypothetical compensation. It must actually be paid for general welfare to be increased; but, if it is paid, this raises other difficulties. At what rate do we compensate, and whom? Do we pay compensation before the change – which would frustrate the incentive to move – or after the change, and incur psychological costs of movement? How much should be left to private property and initiative?[7] Rather than hide the value judgements, Robbins preferred to avoid the apparatus, and to make judgements explicit, as will be seen below.

Thus the use of the word 'conventional' with reference to interpersonal comparisons was meant to indicate that these had no 'scientific' basis but were made *ad hoc* as part of value judgements external to economics. There could be a fair degree of consensus about these judgements: but this did not place them within science. The same is true of treating individuals as being of equal importance. As will become clear below, Robbins regarded this as *morally* necessary (and since he did so at a time when many British intellectuals admired Stalin, this is perhaps worth stressing). But this was a moral judgement, not a scientific result. Interpersonal comparisons were then value judgements about how the welfare of equal people could be increased. While the economist should emphatically *not* refrain from giving policy advice, the value judgements should not be clothed in 'scientific' clothing.

Precisely how Robbins proceeded on this basis should become clear in this and the following chapter, in dealing with such matters as equality, taxation and higher education (in which his strong opposition to entrenched privilege is evident).

3. ALLOCATION

Fundamental to the allocation of economic resources was the market. It might well be necessary to redistribute purchasing power, especially in wartime, but the market was robust and could accommodate intervention while any attempt to replace it would raise fundamental difficulties.[8] Experience of wartime allocation had certainly not resolved any of the doubts raised by Mises and others, in the 1930s, about the possibilities of allocation without markets. Even in wartime, with patriotic cooperation and a single objective of victory, there were difficulties; without these conditions, administrative allocation between competing ends became impossibly complicated, it had no welfare yardstick to work by, and it offered no incentives for compliance beyond criminal sanctions.[9]

On the question of wartime allocation, Robbins was particularly interesting. It will be recalled from Chapter 3 that the question of including war in economics was a moving factor in the writing of *ENSES*;[10] and the ends/means distinction was in fact, in conjunction with Robbins's Austrian general equilibrium frame of reference, to provide the basis for his work on problems of wartime allocation and indeed of planning for the transition to peacetime.[11] After his experience of the war Robbins was to argue that wartime conditions had vindicated textbook doctrine that, with a given distribution, the market mechanism works well.[12] Rationing was for distributive purposes, not to replace the market as an allocative mechanism. The points system mimicked the price system. However the points system had the drawback that the 'points profits' did not attract resources.[13] State interference in the allocation of resources in wartime was thus unavoidable. Rationing was also inevitable because the distribution which would have followed from wartime shortages would have been unacceptable.[14] But once the State interferes this raises the problem of what is to be the basis of priorities.[15] When market signals are muted by the State, resource allocation decisions become critical.[16] Clearly the concept of opportunity cost becomes a key one which has to inform such decisions.[17] This is coupled with the idea of substitution, at the margin, of different resources in a way which the market would achieve if it were operating normally.[18] The economic problem is one of allocation so as to achieve equalisation of marginal yield.[19] Command of resources through taxation is insufficient so the State must intervene directly, as well as guaranteeing entrepreneurial risk.[20] It must in any case allocate materials because, in inflationary wartime finance, market allocation signals are futher interfered with.[21] But, to reiterate, all this State interference functions only (and imperfectly) with control of inputs, control of the excess demand which the State is itself generating, and a single objective (victory) subject to the constraint of minimum necessary civilian consumption.[22]

Robbins's wartime experience, mentioned in Chapter 2, left him extremely sceptical of planning. It is not insignificant that Robbins, the major figure involved in the production of the Robbins Report, believed that manpower planning was only possible within a few limited categories of labour, such as teachers, and that 'the more detailed the manpower plan and the more specialised the training, the more likely it is to be wrong than right'.[23]

Going beyond factor markets, and individual decisions to invest in training, Robbins was a firm believer in self-directed expenditure in a broader sense. Decisions to spend should be free, though allowance has to be made for public goods and account taken of externalities.[24] But, with private goods, people pay as much as they want and there is democratic choice about what is produced.[25] This is clearly desirable. It is true that this led to the complaint that luxuries might be produced before necessities. But the 'cigars before calories' argument 'although very popular, clearly rests on a confusion between the price system considered as a mechanism and the distribution of income to which it may be made to respond'.[26] Robbins was scathingly contemptuous of those academics who believed the mass of consumers to be too stupid to judge for themselves.[27]

> The idea that most buyers of advertised goods are incapable of judging what does and what does not fulfill the object of purchase rests upon too poor a view of the perceptive apparatus

of the average man or woman. As for the business of creating demand for products which do not eventually fit the needs or the taste of the moment, anyone who has experience of such attempts must be provoked to a certain degree of wry mirth at the alleged ease of such a process. It is a facility more prevalent in the imagination of second-rate literary men than in the world of practical business.[28]

It was not that Robbins saw no need at all for consumer protection especially in matters of health; but, though we might disapprove of other people's choices more generally, choice was an aspect of liberty – and liberty was fundamental, not only to human happiness, but to the very existence of good and bad.[29] It was thus a matter of central importance to Robbins.

4. LIBERTY

Robbins held that only free actions have moral standing. Choice is only ethical, in the sense of being judged good or bad, if it is free.[30] This was Robbins's strongly held view. As a matter of fact, without a Christian theology, which he rejected, the position is completely circular: but Robbins held this view very strongly and this has to be appreciated to understand his work. Although it was not a *scientific* proposition that freedom was desirable,[31] the over-riding necessity of liberty was the *value judgement* which he made most passionately.[32] Liberty should be fought for to the bitter end.[33] Freedom was 'one of the essential constituents of a good society'.[34] He bitterly opposed the Hegelian 'sapping of the intellectual foundations of liberty'[35] and rejected Hegelian totalitarianism as much in its biological as in its Marxist form.[36] It should be emphasised, he argued, that a free society was not a natural thing;[37] freeing of the individual was the greatest achievement of the Enlightenment until threatened by Fascist and Communist tyranny.[38]

The right to a free vote – conspicuously absent in practice from such tyrannies – was a fundamental part of human liberty.[39] Then, decency and culture were intrinsic parts of a free democracy.[40] But liberty was necessary not only for such moral virtues, but also for efficiency. Totalitarian systems simply do not work. A system of free markets and private property does work because these adapt to changes in technology and to changes in demand; they register the strength of demand and the capacity of factors of production to satisfy it; they provide decentralised initiative to apply factors to the highest marginal product, and they provide incentives for managers.[41]

Robbins was in close agreement with Hayek in dismissing the alternative concept of 'positive liberty', that is freedom from want.

Professor Hayek has little difficulty in exposing the essential confusion involved in bringing under one heading the freedom involved by the absence of coercion and the so-called freedom from want which is said to flow from a certain level of real income. The limitations imposed on us by nature and technique are not the same as the limitations imposed on us by other men, and although resounding oratorical effects may be achieved by assuming that they are, yet nothing but confusion in thought and action can be the consequence.[42]

5. EQUALITY

This raises however the question of Robbins's attitude towards equality. Firstly, he believed, all men must be regarded as of equal importance. While he held that there is no *scientific* basis for this assumption, it was *morally* an absolutely necessary one to make, and all political calculations which did not make it were morally revolting.[43] Secondly, equality in some sense should be a social aim. While he was somewhat contemptuous of the pretentions of enthusiasts for the Soviet system, and not averse to contrasting their proclamations with their personal behaviour, he regarded equality as an important matter.[44]

In seeking to clarify the nature of equality as a social aim, Robbins distinguished equality before the law, equality of opportunity, equality of reward and equality of wealth.[45] Equality before the law was absolutely fundamental – a fundamental condition of a free society.[46] Equality of opportunity was an important objective – though one which was not always of over-riding importance if pursuit of it involved a threat to the family (as would be involved in removing children from their parents so as to give them an equal start) or if the search for it involved such a degree of redistribution (since opportunity could be associated with family income) that this would seriously blunt incentive and initiative.[47]

He was rather less concerned about equality of reward, so long as there was provision against poverty and so long as there were not barriers to entry into particular occupations.[48] Extreme redistribution would have damaging effects on incentives; and some inequality of wealth necessarily followed from the need for incentives.[49] He made the explicit value judgement that he did not favour a significant trade-off in favour of greater equality in return for a significant loss of output.[50] Real income differences per head in the USSR were at least as great as in the West, so collectivism offered no greater degree of equality than the market system.[51] He thought profit sharing, as a way of reducing income inequality, an attractive idea, but he had some hesitations over it. It did not actually redistribute, it could not be made compulsory (both because of the rights of existing shareholders and because of the different gearing of different companies), and it conferred privileges without responsibility. He thought it better on balance to distribute shares to the employees, a matter obstructed by revenue laws.[52]

Some inequality of wealth was unavoidable, if only because of different propensities to save.[53] He was somewhat contemptuous of the politics of envy: 'The free society is not to be built on envy; a state founded on green-eye will not stand.'[54] Imposition of collectivism with the ostensible aim of securing equality of wealth resulted in more evil than inequality of property itself – the hardships and inequality of a régime of *diffused* private property were likely to be as nothing compared to a system in which the State was the only employer.[55] In fact even the Left, though it might 'continue to get a considerable release of the soul from the reiteration of the traditional slogans' did not believe in *total* equality, and so the argument was merely one of degree.[56] To such an argument no cut and dried answer could be given – 'there are almost an infinite variety of possible patterns of inequality'.[57] It was valuable to society that there should be blocks of independent individual wealth;[58] the spread of wealth was valuable to provide centres of independent initiative,[59] and if accumulation of wealth was made difficult this harmed the prospects for small firms growing up.[60] Much 'levelling-down' had already taken place,[61] and the present tax system was relentlessly pushing us towards collectivism and propertyless uniformity.[62] But the destruction of individual wealth turns individuals into dependents of 'the collective Leviathan'.[63]

However, this should not be understood as implying that Robbins was opposed to fiscal means of reducing inequality. One measure which he favoured very strongly as a means of increasing equality of wealth was the replacement of death duties by an inheritance tax.[64] The recipients, rather than the donor, would be taxed and so there would be an incentive to divide property in order to reduce progression. In contrast to death duties, which simply appropriated property to the State's current expenditure, an inheritance tax would actually redistribute wealth rather than destroy it. A legacy duty in this way would help to maintain individuals independent of the State.[65]

As already noted, Robbins considered equality before the law to be a fundamental requirement. Law itself, although under certain circumstances possibly oppressive (for instance laws against contraception and divorce in a theocracy),[66] was a fundamental necessity to provide the framework for all economic activity. All liberty had to be within some kind of framework[67] – which was not an end in itself but a means to freedom.[68] The classical liberalism which Robbins espoused had recognised the need for a framework;[69] the Invisible Hand only operates within such a system of constraints.[70] These constraints were necessary for economic development.[71] Liberalism was not anarchism,[72] for it required a strong State and there must be a plan of rights and duties with respect to property and its use.[73] But although government had important duties – and the State was not a club because there was an irreducible minimum of force involved[74] and Public Good choice was essentially political because of the limited scope of Cost Benefit analysis[75] – it was probably better to expand the framework of law and regulation for such economic entities as companies, rather than to involve the State directly in allocation.[76]

6. THE STATE

The State had, however, an important role in relation to welfare services. Robbins approved of 'levelling-up' in matters of education and health and, to some extent, in relation to income,[77] and he distanced himself from Hayek on the matter of social security.[78]

But it was necessary to try to foster some independence, as Mill had argued, giving relief in the form of cash rather than in kind.

> If the aim of Classical Liberalism in the wide sense be the general raising of the condition of the people, the objective governing the relief of the indigent should be, as far as possible, to foster independence and to create for them the same sense of initiative and responsibility as middle-class reformers automatically assume for themselves, as for instance in the choice of food, housing, medical attention, provision for family education, and so on.[79]

But the role of government was much wider than this. Robbins's starting point was that 'It is fallacious to suppose that all government expenditure is an evil.'[80] There is much that government cannot avoid doing at all.[81] That there were extensive State functions, going beyond Public Goods, had indeed been recognised by the Classical economists.[82] Of course government had to provide a framework. Together with public health and communications,[83] the State had other important economic functions,[84] and Robbins approved Bentham's plans for a health ministry, a communications ministry, an education ministry, a Registrar General, a Statistical Office and even a meteorological office.[85] Public goods diminish inequality,[86] even though, in the course of their supply, they have the disadvantages that the preference of minorities are over-ridden, with finance by coercion rather than through purchase price, and that there is little democratic choice because elections are fought on broad issues.[87]

The argument over the State was not about whether public goods should be supported but about private goods publicly provided.[88] For the public supply of private goods, the burden of proof rests with the advocates of public supply, Robbins held.[89] In any case, there must be some limit imposed on operations of government because the very capacity of government was necessarily limited.[90] Robbins's experience in World War Two had made clear to him the foolishness of assuming a wise, unhurried, State decision-taking process as frequently posited in economic literature.[91] Moreover collective decisions on such matters as saving and investment were much more erratic than private ones.[92] There was a danger of needless and inefficient paternalism.[93] Like Bentham, he favoured leaving to the individual, and to groups of individuals, all things in which their initiative could be left to harmonise with the public good.[94] Given an initial distribution of resources, the market provides proportional representation rather than simple majority choice. It is thus better to keep the State decisions confined to areas where they are unavoidable.[95]

7. REDISTRIBUTION

However, this did not mean that Robbins believed that the State should simply accept the distribution of income produced by the market. Although he believed that no society could be built on the politics of envy,[96] and although he was sceptical about the likely efficacy of redistribution,[97] he believed that redistribution was in principle a perfectly proper role for the State,[98] despite the danger of damage to managerial incentives in seeking income equality.[99] (He agreed with what Dalton had taught him about the desirability of not taxing company profits as distinct from individual income.)[100] But redistribution, as should be clear from Chapter 3, was not a *scientific* matter.[101] This view did not amount to a self-denying ordinance concerning distribution and inter-personal comparisons. Rather the point was that because the essence of economics is choice theory, which has an identifiable logical basis, redistribution, involving choices which had no identifiable logical basis, was *extra*-scientific. We were perfectly free to make such judgements; but we had to recognise their conventional rather than scientific nature.

This aspect of Robbins's stance has been widely noted (and widely misunderstood); yet in its essence it has proved overwhelmingly persuasive. There is however another element in his critical attitude to the welfare economics literature which has attracted much less attention. This is an insistence that all economic problems, because they involve general choice, must be seen in (Austrian) general equilibrium terms. Partial equilibrium, the other leg of Cambridge welfare economics, along with inter-personal comparisons, was rejected. This partly explains Robbins's dismissive attitude towards Joan Robinsons's *Imperfect Competition*. He correctly perceived (unlike most commentators then or since, at least outside Cambridge) that this was a book on welfare economics, and one moreover which at various points made claims about general equilibrium on the basis of partial equilibrium analysis. But stressing the general equilibrium aspects of a problem was not merely sanctimonious advice. Robbins was deeply imbued with Austrian economics and the general equilibrium key of opportunity cost, and it pervades all his work on allocation including allocation in wartime. It was no use looking at industries and individuals in isolation to assess the effects of particular measures and the implications of imperfections: the whole economy had to be examined. In particular he was very critical of calculations about redistribution which assumed fixed prices and failed to take account of elasticity of supply[102] – it was necessary to take into account the adjustments which economic actors would make in response to redistribution.

Following such an examination, with the full effects of proposed policy measures traced out, particular policies could be selected. But this would require value judgements. If value judgements were to be used, then it was important that the consequences of making different value judgements should be examined in the context of the economy as a whole – indeed this might bring about some convergence of value judgements.[103]

8. PROGRESSIVE TAXATION

Despite his approval of a degree of redistribution, Robbins's attitude towards progressive taxation could not be described as enthusiastic. At a very early stage he had shown signs of distaste for the progressive tax implications of Pigou's analysis,[104] and late in life he said that he found more sense in Mill's opposition to progressive taxation than many of his contemporaries.[105] Yet he agreed with Smith's view that common sense indicated that the richer should bear heavier burdens, and he distanced himself from Hayek on the matter of progression.[106] He did not object to progression as a means of sharing public burdens. But sharing the burdens across the community by laying a heavier load on those more able to bear it he classed as 'levelling *up*'; at the same time he opposed the use of progressive taxation for 'levelling down'.[107] He was concerned about the effects (before the introduction of provision for a wife to elect to be taxed separately) of progression on marriage – he regarded it as a tax on middle-class marriage.[108]

Robbins was also concerned about the question of incentives.

While he took the sensible view that there was no basis for generalisation about the incentive effects of progressive taxation in Britain,[109] he was prone to cite the argument that, if a 100 per cent marginal rate could not possibly fail to be a disincentive, how could it honestly be argued that an 83 per cent rate (at that time the highest marginal rate on earned income) could fail to have disincentive effects?[110] He was even more sure about the disincentive effects of progressive taxation on saving – it was hardly plausible that a return on saving of 2 per cent after tax was adequate.[111]

Robbins's decidedly qualified attitude towards progression in taxation is probably best exemplified in the following:

> But to agree that *some* degree of progressiveness is desirable does not involve agreement with *all* scales of progression. And I think that it is about time that someone . . . should say bluntly that the higher reaches of our own progression are quite indefensible save upon avowedly confiscatory theory. So far as earned income is involved, they constitute a discrimination against enterprise and ability such as has never before existed for any long time in any large-scale civilised community. Certainly they are not dictated by the needs of revenue: the upper rates of surtax could be just cancelled without creating any very severe budgetary problems.[112]

That, written in 1955, inevitably reflects to some extent the legacy of the post-war Labour government's tax régime; but it does not really misrepresent Robbins's attitude, if interpreted more broadly. Needless to say he was not particularly enthusiastic about capital gains tax. It could be used if the high marginal rates on earned income were reduced: otherwise such gains remained, during the existence of high marginal rates on income, the one remaining spur to efficiency and they should be left alone. Moreover, in an inflationary economy a capital gains tax involved taxing non-existent gains.[113]

9. SOCIALISM

If Robbins's attitude to progressive taxation was lukewarm, his attitude to socialism was one of downright hostility. Disdainful of

'The Hitler beneath the skin' in the 'intellectuals of the Left',[114] he opposed socialism and collectivism both on the grounds of incompatibility with liberty (it involved adapting the people to the plan rather than the plan to the people) and on the grounds of efficiency.[115] This was not merely an academic concern; in planning for the post-war world, account had to be taken of the enthusiasm for totalitarianism which had developed in many intellectuals in the 1930s. As Robbins was later to recall:

there was a dedicated group of economists, not in government service, who in season and out of season were pressing the totalitarian alternative; and they were very articulate.[116]

To this totalitarian alternative Robbins was completely opposed. To him of course the liberty arguments were fundamental. He did not accept that Bentham's Greatest Happiness principle, which he approved, led to collectivism and he was impressed by the warning in Mill's *Liberty* against the latter. There were serious dangers to personal liberty under collectivism, and Robbins pointedly quoted Keynes in favour of individualism to his 1947 Cambridge audience at the Marshall Lectures.[117]

'Ethical neutrality' in economics thus did not prevent Robbins giving furious opposition to totalitarian oppression of both Right and Left – the particular form of interpersonal comparison ('breaking eggs to make omelettes' in the cant phrase) which judges murdering part of the population to build a 'new society' as being morally defensible, found no favour with him.

If we did not have a better system than general collectivism, we should have to create it. For in our generation we have seen the ghastly alternative – a mob of bemused slaves and prostitute intellectuals, mouthing the phrases of the Great Dictator, an ultimate degradation of the type man.[118]

Robbins's opposition to socialism and collectivism was thus grounded on explicit, and powerfully expressed, judgements. But Robbins was an economist; and he also presented a powerful economic case against socialism on the grounds of efficiency. The interests of consumers should be paramount in his judgement;[119] yet, as he informed his 1947 Cambridge audience, collectivism had all the worst features of private monopoly and little consumer sovereignty, and it thus did not meet consumer interests efficiently.[120] 'Mass production to a fixed plan may increase the volume of physical production. But if it is only made possible by the frustration of consumers' demand, it is producing mere stuff.'[121] Collectivism is inefficient because decentralised knowledge and initiative are required for efficiency;[122] and the very process of decentralisation diffuses and alleviates conflicts of sectional interest while, in contrast, such conflicts become central under socialism.[123] Socialism is characterised by bureaucracy which cannot, in its very nature, be as efficient and as adaptive as private trading.[124]

Much of Robbins's critique is based upon the classic critique by Mises.[125] This source was drawn upon extensively in *The Great Depression*; reviewing the issues more than 40 years later, Robbins was still satisfied that Mises had been correct. He argued that it was a myth that Mises had been shown to have been wrong in saying that rational allocation under collectivism was impossible – although *some* allocation is possible, in a society which *is*, rather than *having*, a military-industrial complex, allocation in accordance with the wishes of consumers was out of the question. Preferences could not be observed. The Lerner experiments with 'decentralised units all playing at competition' could not be operated without giving managers as much scope for decision-taking as in a free market society (what products to produce, how much to produce, how much working capital to reinvest in new products, what superfluous fixed capital to reinvest in new products, what superfluous fixed capital to sell) and where attempted, as in Czechoslovakia, this had been suppressed.[126]

It is important to appreciate that many of these criticisms were applied by Robbins not just to total collectivism but also to economic planning. It was not just that public ownership was inefficient and that State decision-taking involved considerable difficulties, as his wartime experience was to show him[127]. For planning would inevitably lead to socialism: 'Nothing but intellectual confusion can result from a failure to realise that Planning and Socialism are fundamentally the same.'[128] Such socialism was actually less likely to be stable 'than the so-called chaos of competitive enterprise' because restrictions of the output of individual enterprises, in the name of planning, caused conflicts of interest.[129]

The basic critique of planning, deriving from Mises, was as follows.[130] Resources have to be allocated so as to equalise marginal returns. This cannot be solved through a political voting process. We need to know not only prices which consumers would be prepared to pay, but also the opportunity costs of factors in different occupations in order to equalise the marginal return of different factor employments. This naturally poses insoluble computational problems. In competition the problem is solved by comparing costs and prices. But market costs embody competitive factor market information about opportunity costs. The solution of 'playing at competition' won't work because resources – including entire firms – have to be free to move in and out of industries. The planning approach loses sight (in assuming the prior existence of factor prices) of the fundamental distinction between the technical and the economic. A socialist government could not even use international prices as a guide to opportunity cost through trade, because it could not permit free imports to undercut the products of its own factories. But without a market system, no engineering data could tell us about opportunity costs.[131] The approach of playing at competition makes different branches of industry quasi-independent units and the prosperity of different industries, rather than the distribution of resources between industries, becomes the criterion of successful planning. Moreover, if managers play at capitalism, the community is still bearing the 'business' risk and the manager is really a bureaucrat responsible to political control and thus deprived of the scope for competitive action and initiative.[132] All this was true of *general* planning. *Partial* attempts at industrial planning had led to high prices and over-investment in particular industries, followed by their collapse, playing a part in creating the 1930s depression.[133] When attempted in a basically free society, industrial planning involved corruption, inter-governmental friction, and a political structure which threatened democracy. Such plans multiplied because their very failure seemed to lead to a need for more planning.[134]

Given all this, it is perhaps hardly surprising that Robbins was also highly critical of the syndicalism and guild socialism in which he had once been involved.[135] Not only did this give rise to problems of recruitment into (and exclusion from) the syndics, but it also implied serious problems of allocation – the outcome of establishing such a system would be 'a nightmare of uncontrolled monopolies, each seeking to maximise its gains at the expense of others'.[136] Guild socialism combined the worst features of collectivism and syndicalism and offered no criterion to the State for allocating resources between the different bodies.[137]

It was not that Robbins, in his opposition to socialism, sought to justify property through some Lockean doctrine of right; his justification for property was, not surprisingly, Hume's utilitarian justification of property which was a spontaneous social phenomenon necessary both for population control and for the capital accumulation leading to economic advance.[138] A society based upon private property would certainly be far from perfect; but it was not sufficient to point to the imperfections without specifying how any alternative system would be superior.[139]

10. MIXED ECONOMY INTERVENTION

With socialism and comprehensive economic planning resoundingly rejected by Robbins, the question arises of the degree to which he believed State intervention in a mixed, but basically free enterprise, economy could be beneficial. With regard to prices, Robbins was opposed not merely to rent restriction ('one of the meanest of all demagogic expedients')[140] but in general to the fixing of prices and incomes. Such fixing did not allow markets for goods or factors to clear, created shortages and damaged supply, perpetuating disequilibrium and excluding the less fortunate members of society from employment.[141] Any redistributive objectives of price and income control could be better met by direct redistribution.[142]

Public ownership of nationalised industries had, amongst its disadvantages, that it led to 'politicisation and bureaucratisation' of price (and investment) policy and encouraged disequilibrium wage settlements.[143] However, these were only part of the disadvantages of nationalisation which, freed from normal market pressures, had neither the incentive nor the means to conduct itself in an economically efficient manner.[144] But although Robbins wanted less nationalisation, he dissociated himself from the position taken in Hayek's *Road to Serfdom* that nationalisation necessarily led to the corporate State.[145]

Robbins was also opposed to the State inducing those industries which were in private ownership to restrict their output. In Robbins's view 'The creation of state-aided restriction is the creation of privilege.'[146] As he wrote in a Cabinet paper in 1943:

The grand question of policy of the future will not be the question of State action or *laisser-faire*. It will be the question of State action which promotes the interests of the community as a whole or State action which promotes the interests of particular groups.[147]

Output restrictions were a tax on the rest of the community.[148] As he stressed in the Cabinet paper, piecemeal planning of industries to place them 'on a sound footing' may be harmful to the community at large – as in wartime so in peacetime, it is the *overall* allocation of resources that matters.[149] As he had emphasised before the war, probably under the influence of his father's view of agricultural problems, so he again stressed that output restrictions create conflicts of interest between groups. They lead to countervailing restrictions, and at each stage both output and welfare are reduced. They lead also to price control, and to the development of competitive substitutes if output in one particular sphere is limited. The conflicts of interest themselves are magnified and made of greater permanence. As he wrote in 1939:

> The struggle for wealth becomes a struggle for privilege – a struggle not for technical efficiency and adaptation to the wants of the community of consumers, but a struggle for status and the power of monopolistic exploitation . . . Such a process in the end destroys, even for those who are most successful, the wealth and security it was originally designed to safeguard. If one line of industry practises restrictionism it may make gains which compensate the producers in question for the obvious danger they run. But if others follow suit, then these gains are likely to be wiped out in a process of general impoverishment and national and international conflict.[150]

It is better, he argued, to let a market contract and permit factors to find alternative employment, than to create immediate unemployment through restricting output.[151] Fixed capital costs need not be covered in a contracting industry – bygones are forever bygones.[152]

In his *The Great Depression* Robbins was particularly scornful of those economists who defended output restrictions.[153] It was all very well for

the dilettante economists of wealthy universities, their tables
groaning beneath a sufficiency of the good things of this world,
their garages furnished with private means of transport, to say,
'Food is cheap enough. Charabancs are vulgar. The railways are
admirable. We have enough of plenty. Let us safeguard
security.' It is for the millions to whom a slice of bacon more or
less, or a bus ride to the sea, still matter, to make the decision.[154]

Quotas did not permit market selection of the efficient,[155] while
marketing schemes achieved no economies which would not be
available without compulsion – they were merely price-fixing,
output-limiting, cartels under another name.[156] (There seems no
doubt that this is the way in which Robbins senior also saw
them.)

11. COMPETITION AND MONOPOLY

The converse of Robbins's opposition to restriction was a
recognition of the benefits of competition. Competition offered
clear benefits.[157] Any static 'wastes' of competition were merely
the price to be paid for the dynamic benefits.[158] Competition was
a spur to efficiency,[159] and there was no real substitute for
competition with free entry.[160]

But this raises the problem that monopoly might arise within
the competitive system, and destroy it. There might be no
substitute for competition with free entry; but could this be relied
upon to exist?

It was Robbins's position that competition was natural in many
industries including agriculture, manufacturing and parts of
extraction. Distribution was naturally highly competitive. Technical
efficiencies, leading to larger scale operations, were offset by
managerial diseconomies. Long run monopoly was certainly not
inevitable. *Temporary* monopoly, on the other hand, was not only
necessary but desirable; but as long as there was free entry this
monopoly could not be maintained.[161]

It was perfectly true that competition might need safeguarding
in certain areas.[162] But in fact much monopoly did not arise from
weaknesses in competition but was the direct creation of the
State.[163] Monopoly could be brought about by a friendly legal
climate, tariffs and patents, as well as by government controls;[164]

but cartels only lasted a long time with State support.[165] Moreover State-backed monopolies were less shy than the ordinary variety,[166] and thus more inclined to act harmfully: 'The predatory nature of men organised as groups of producers and backed by governmental authority, has to be seen close up at international conferences to be believed.'[167]

The emphasis upon entry indicates, as was indeed the case, that Robbins's view of competition was essentially dynamic – he had little time for the static argument, allegedly deriving from Joan Robinsons's work, that the supposed inevitability of excess capacity was an argument for limiting the number of productive units.[168] He thought the idea both stale and misconceived.

> This argument, which of course has been the small-change of discussion of the monopoly problem for the last forty years, has recently [1939] been rediscovered by the specialists of diagrammatic analysis, with results not always altogether beneficial to their general sense of proportion.[169]

But to secure the dynamic benefits of competition required a monopoly policy. In a wartime paper Robbins suggested the 'guilty till proved innocent' or qualified *per se* approach, which indeed ultimately found its way into the 1956 Restrictive Trade Practices Act[170] rather than, as his then colleagues preferred, putting the onus on the Board of Trade to prove that restriction was producing harm. He favoured an anti-trust policy and also the removal of import protection, and both during the war and afterwards he gave such an approach his strong support.[171] Only in the area of mergers was he prepared to allow the forces of consolidation to operate – and even here he believed that the parties to a proposed merger should be required to disclose much more financial information than was normally the case.[172]

But this raises in turn Robbins's attitude towards one particular kind of monopoly – the trade union monopoly. There is no question of Robbins having been unthinkingly opposed to trade unions. Though he deplored the 'mealy-mouthedness' of economists in writing about this particular form of monopoly, he saw unions as having both costs and benefits. On the positive side, the unions had done much to protect individuals. But on the other side they had succeeded in depressing wages outside their area of activity, as with the London printers (with whom he was very familiar); and they excluded women and black people from some areas and had a damaging effect on technical progress. He was not in favour of laws against trade unions, certainly; but he did not believe that they should enjoy legal privileges placing them above the law. Indeed he believed that competition policy should cover factor as well as product markets. In his view, union restrictive practices were possibly the most serious of current UK problems in the 1970s apart from monetary mismanagement.[173]

Such an attitude, which he held in both the pre-war and the post-war period, sprang in part from the analysis in his *Economic Basis of Class Conflict* (1939). The basic thesis here is that there were not homogeneous groups in horizontal strata in society (classes), but a series of vertical interest-groups, each of which may include several strata layers. There was a certainty of conflict between groups *within* the broad classification 'labour', and the struggles between different producer groups were much more influential than class struggle. It followed then that policy which limited the freedom of particular interest-groups to engage in restrictive practices was in the interest of society as a whole.[174]

12. ECONOMIC GROWTH, WELFARE AND POPULATION

Restrictive practices, by whomever exercised, interfered with economic growth. But Robbins made the judgement – and it has been noted in Chapter 3 that it was just a judgement – that economic growth was extremely desirable, not least because it was the main way to alleviate poverty.[175] Maximisation of the growth of GDP was not necessarily the final criterion; but it was extremely important.[176] He was highly critical of the anti-growth school[177] and was (surprisingly) prepared in practice to invoke hypothetical compensation in defence of technical improvement which affected the *general* level of employment adversely but provided an increase in income out of which those adversely affected could be compensated.[178] He defended technology, which was not the enemy of social welfare – it was not possible to have an advanced culture without productive power. Technology was a means not an end; but it was a means which it was essential to have 'if the good life is to be shared by any but a few'.[179] He noted that the poseurs who denounced technology also conspicuously enjoyed its benefits – the implication is clearly that he felt they were not concerned about those benefits being enjoyed widely.[180]

The critics of economic growth, however, were of course particularly concerned about externalities. Robbins was prepared to recognise the need for control of externalities in private consumption, though he warned of the danger to personal liberty,[181] and he believed that control of externalities was indeed a necessary part of the framework for economic activity discussed above.[182] While he was unimpressed by the exhaustible resources argument (such prophecies had been made even during his student days, but ignored technical progress), he was impressed by considerations of possible environmental damage[183] – even though he had, in the 1930s, expressed the view that the benefits of rural life could be somewhat over-valued.[184]

The dangers of environmental damage, especially pollution, were related to the size of population,[185] a matter which concerned him a great deal. Population indeed had been one of his very first interests,[186] stemming from the influence of Cannan.[187] In discussing population, Robbins's attention gradually turned from problems of the ageing of a population (adaptability and the increasing ratio of dependents)[188] and from questions of the optimum population (with respect to output per head – he judged that no greater population was required in 1929) to a concern with population growth.[189] At times his concern verged upon outright alarm at the threat of a population explosion.[190] Like his teacher Dalton, he became an enthusiastic advocate of contraception.[191]

Population was not just a national problem, which intensified pollution and other externalities. It was also an international problem and one which, one feels, Robbins feared could upset the entire international order. Although this chapter has dealt with questions of welfare from a national point of view, Robbins's work has an important international welfare aspect and indeed, in his *Economic Planning and International Order* (1937), he made a conscious decision to approach the whole matter of trade policy from the point of view of international rather than national welfare.[192] It is perfectly true that he believed that freedom of trade, even from a national point of view, would increase general welfare even if this was at the expense of some loss of employment – employment being a *means*, GNP being an *end*.[193] But he was opposed to nationalism,[194] as indicated in Chapters 2 and 9. Indeed in 1939 he referred to a 'nauseating backwash of historical mysticism and geographical particularism which is threatening to destroy our common culture'.[195] He saw no benefit in that off-shoot of nationalism, imperialism, either and, as will be made clear in Chapter 9, he believed that the problems arising from nationalism could be overcome by an international Federalism.[196]

13. CONCLUSION

Robbins's welfare writings are widely diffused over a number of different publications and cover a wide span of time – indeed the entire length of his writing career. Starting from a basic Utilitarian background, Robbins applied a Utilitarian standard to problems of economic welfare. Allocation through the market was the most efficient method, though this did not rule out a significant role for the State, which could also redistribute income and wealth. However Robbins was lukewarm about progressive taxation, and a powerful and effective critic of socialism. State interference in a mixed economy was not ruled out *prima facie*, but it frequently resulted in sub-optimal allocation. Competition generally produced a satisfactory allocation, and monopoly was far from inevitable in the long run, so long as it was deprived of State encouragement and, even more importantly, of State sustenance. But a competition policy – from which trade unions should not be immune – should, Robbins argued, be used to control monopolies wherever they arose. Competition could then be relied on to produce economic growth and technical progress which, he judged, was highly desirable as a way of increasing general welfare, even though externalities, intensified by population pressure, required control.

Taking together Robbins's writings on economic welfare, they represent a restatement of the Classical and Utilitarian tradition applied to twentieth-century problems. The application is in the light of, but very largely, and quite deliberately, not incorporating later welfare economics either of the Pigovian or New variety. Indeed, as was indicated in the chapter, Robbins very largely rejected formal *welfare economics*. But he wrote a good deal on *economic welfare*, and it has been necessary to give an account of his treatments of the welfare aspects of economic problems since in both positive and negative emphases (especially in the relegation of interpersonal comparisons to an area outside scientific discourse) his discussions have been highly influential.

6 Education

1. INTRODUCTION

Robbins is indissolubly associated in the British public's mind with the 1963 Robbins Report.[1] Although he was, throughout his professional career, engaged in and passionately committed to education, it is this report which accounts for much of Robbins's fame with the wider public, and it is probably better to take his involvement with it as a starting point for the discussion in this chapter. In his *Autobiography*, Robbins gives an account of how he was, to his surprise, summoned by R. A. Butler and asked to chair the Committee on Higher Education.[2] He relates how he was determined to refuse the job because, in particular, he was already launched upon what he was convinced was his last chance to write a major work on economics. Indeed there were 'dozens of things I wanted to do before the decline of my mental and physical powers set in, rather than spend all my time on the conduct of a government committee'.[3]

But he eventually gave way – indeed, in a sense, he was out-manoeuvred. The result was a major document in twentieth-century social policy, and there can be no doubt that Robbins's involvement was fundamental to its production. Not only did he take an absolutely central role in the operation of the committee, as is evident from the minutes of evidence,[4] but he spent much of the year following its publication writing and speaking on the subject.[5] For a decade, his influence was central. As the *Times Higher Education Supplement* said on his death: 'If anyone has a just claim to be regarded as father of our modern education in Britain it was Lord Robbins.'[6] He was initially satisfied with both the public reception and the implementation of the report. Yet, by the time of his death, as the obituary just quoted also indicated, it was clear that the expansion in universities had not really followed the path laid down in the report.

2. THE BASIS OF EDUCATIONAL DEVELOPMENT

Robbins's position on universities and their expansion rested on a number of points of departure. The first, was a belief in the value of public discussion.[7] This may seem obvious; yet in a field where policy has typically been decided by ministers and civil servants, often in the face of public ignorance of what was being done and public hostility to what it knew had been done, it is a point which is perhaps worth making. The second basic point is that Robbins was highly sceptical about the possibilities of manpower planning.[8] It could not, in his view, be successful except for a few limited categories of public employees; even with teachers, he was to note later on, it had gone very wrong. More generally it failed to take account of price in estimating the demand for skills, there was no idea of the relevant elasticities, and there was no possibility of forecasting changes in technical knowledge. There were also implications for limitation of human freedom in manpower planning – even implications of the danger of direction of labour.

These two principles – in a sense, both are aspects of welfare being self-perceived – led to the fundamental principle, which the committee endorsed, of open provision for those with sufficient talent to benefit by it, and the provision of places according to the demand for them.[9] Rather than manpower planning, individuals were to choose occupations on the basis of their own evaluations of the net benefits; and with open public discussion it would be much easier for individuals to appreciate the implications of their choice. Moreover, this approach was in accord with the emphasis upon equality of opportunity which, as noted in the previous chapter, was a welfare value judgement to which Robbins attached considerable importance.

3. ABILITY AND WILLINGNESS

However it is possible to detect some slight retreat from the optimism with which these principles were advanced, in some of Robbins's later writings. In particular he became worried about what he regarded as an increasing proportion of misfits amongst those admitted to university, an element he attributed in part to their possession of a mistaken belief that a degree was a royal road to higher earnings, and in part to pressure from members of an earlier generation who believed that they had missed higher education advantages. Accordingly he laid some stress on the committee's view that it was not only *ability* which was required for entry but also *willingness to take advantage* of higher education facilities which was required; these *combined* as qualifications for admittance.[10] If *both* these qualities were present then open provision to those possessed of both was superior, Robbins believed, to manpower planning.[11]

Returning to an idea he had expressed in public long before the Robbins Report,[12] Robbins also came to stress, in later years, the advantage of a year between school and university[13] – and if this resulted in a reduction in university applications, this was not a matter for concern.[14] If no grants or loans were available before the age of 20, this would improve self-selection through application.

It is quite clear from the later writings that Robbins had been – hardly surprisingly, since he had been in the forefront of resisting it – worried by the student militancy of the late 1960s.[15] In his view, the outrageous students were a tiny minority, with the vast majority of students not interested in student politics, though some joined in because of an excitable suspicion of authority.

4. THE POOL OF ABILITY

If, subject to the qualifications about ability and willingness to work, there was to be open provision, and if qualification for entry was to be crucial – a view which Robbins maintained, although he was prepared to countenance *some* relaxation of the existing entry standards[16] – then plans for university expansion required that there exist some significant pool of ability which had, prior to the report, been untapped by the higher education system. There is no doubt that Robbins regarded the work done by the committee in establishing the existence of such a pool as being of fundamental importance:[17]

the researches of Moser and Layard surely demonstrated for all time that the idea that the limits of the so-called pool of ability had anywhere been nearly reached, either among boys or girls, was without any foundation. In fact the projections which we made of numbers likely to come forward without any relaxation of existing requirements, which we were always careful to emphasise to be minimum estimates, have been vastly exceeded; I at least have derived a certain grim satisfaction from reading some pretentious commentators, who originally denounced our estimates as vast overestimates involving gross lowering of entrance standards, now reproaching us for not predicting enough.[18]

The 'more means worse' criticisms in *The Times* and elsewhere clearly rankled; but Robbins felt happy that the committee had ultimately succeeded in establishing the existence of a large pool of ability – *and* in getting this existence widely accepted.[19]

There was not only a sufficient pool of ability for expansion of the student body; there was also a sufficient pool of ability for the creation of a large enough body of university teachers, so long as expansion did not proceed too fast.[20]

At the bottom of all this emphasis on the potential for expansion is to be found Robbins's essential egalitarianism. Different participation rates between different social groups in higher eduction were, in his view, environmental rather than hereditary. Even though not everyone could have written Newton's *Principia* or the *Wealth of Nations*, there was no alternative to assuming that everyone started level – unless we were prepared to contemplate a caste system (or worse).[21]

5. THE SCHOOLS AND SPECIALISATION

Robbins was unworried that the schools which had been feeding the universities at the time of the report were replaced by comprehensives. Although he saw dangers in the comprehensive system, the dangers were, in his view, not primarily educational,[22] and it is fair to say that he believed in the comprehensive schools as a desirable development. But he had very strong views on school curricula. He believed emphatically that economics and politics should be excluded from the schools. There were much more urgent topics for school attention, especially languages and mathematics.[23] His strongest fire was directed against the teaching of economics in schools:

Fight against it as I may, I cannot resist the wish that the whole business of teaching economics in schools had never begun . . .

. . . .

No simple proposition in economics is likely to be true, unless it is understood as being subject to a whole complex of assumptions not likely to be read into it, save by those who have a sufficient knowledge both of the system of propositions as a whole and of the world of reality to which they have reference.[24]

He was also deeply concerned – again because of the effect on student quality – at the premature specialisation which he regarded as being the curse of the English school system. It was, he said, 'almost without parallel in the rest of the civilised world'.[25] He believed the Oxbridge scholarship system further encouraged this undesirable sixth form specialisation – and the scholarships themselves were an anomaly in the age of grants.[26] (It took more than 20 years but this message ultimately was accepted.) But this was, he held, only one example of the way in which the universities encouraged the schools on a wrong course of early specialisation; and they were joined, at least permissively, by the Department of Education and Science.[27] Robbins was himself anxious to see experimentation with broader first degree courses – *subject to* job preparation requirements[28] even though he distinguished clearly between education and training.[29] For some while he favoured four-year degree courses for all, although he ultimately conceded that this was not practical and settled for advocating three-year degrees plus the availability of postgraduate study.[30] He considered that the spread of the single subject honours degree in the last 50 years had been a bad development in university education in this country;[31] for those not intending to be specialists (and the proportion of intending specialists would fall with university expansion) a broader degree was necessary:[32] 'the cultivation of the *elite* starts in the graduate school rather than at the graduate level.'[33] First degree specialisation might be less harmful if the sixth forms were less specialised;[34] but the two forms of specialisation interacted. Thus fundamental changes in English universities must be linked to getting rid of most specialised A-Level requirements.[35]

Robbins had been concerned about this matter for some time before the 1963 report. In the mid-1950s he exhibited doubts about the English type of degree, and noted the superiority, as he saw it, of the American system.[36] He was an advocate of the B.Sc.(Econ.) which operated in the University of London during the 1950s with a very broad curriculum (13 papers in all), though he ultimately conceded that for this to work it would have required four years, rather than the three years taken.[37] He was worried about too much emphasis on technicality in economic education and too little emphasis on education.[38] He wanted compulsory history of economic thought courses but not compulsory mathematical economics courses[39] (although, in contrast to the 1950s B.Sc.(Econ.) degree as operated in London, he did believe in compulsory statistics courses).

Premature specialisation narrowed the windows of the mind and produced the 'two cultures' phenomenon identified by C. P. Snow.[40] With this in mind it is hardly surprising that Robbins expressed considerable admiration for the Scottish university tradition, with its four-year degrees and its broader base.[41] Indeed he relates that he became convinced of the superiority of the Scottish system.[42] There is no doubt that he wished to see the university expansion following the Robbins Report to take lines similar to those of the Scottish system, with a large increase in the number of students taking broader first degrees and an expansion of the graduate schools to supply whatever degree of specialisation might turn out to be necessary.[43] Apart from all the general cultural arguments against the existing English system, there was the straightforward economic argument that adaptability and mobility of labour were required and that these were inconsistent with narrow specialisation.

It was, then, highly appropriate that Robbins was to become the first Chancellor of Stirling – the Scottish university set up as a direct result of the Robbins Report,[44] and a university which moved some way in the direction of the American-style credits system which Robbins favoured.[45]

6. EXPANSION AND THE BINARY SYSTEM

Rightly or wrongly – and Robbins was not sure that the Committee had succeeded in demonstrating convincingly that this was the appropriate institutional pattern – the Report opted for expansion of higher education through the universities.[46] Aware of the danger of bureaucratic control and of the intrusion of politics, Robbins was a strong supporter of the University Grants Committee as a buffer between the universities and the civil servants, and of block grants to universities.[47] But a degree of unhappiness about the existing management of education by the civil service led to the recommendation of the Committee for a separate ministry for higher education, with a minister of Cabinet rank. The recommendation was deflected by an ingenious civil service fudge and ultimately neutralised.[48] Looking back over the matter many years later Robbins made it clear that, while he was not indissolubly wedded to the Committee's original proposal, he was also not very happy at the way in which the Department of Education and Science had managed to maintain control of education from primary schools to universities.[49]

But if his feelings about the rejection of the separate ministry were not strongly stated, his opposition to the so-called 'Binary System', involving the development of the polytechnics in parallel to the universities, was passionately expressed.[50] He felt that it undermined the whole basis of the report. The Robbins Committee would never have recommended the upgrading of the Colleges of Advanced Technology (CATs) to university status if they had wanted a binary system, he argued.[51] It would have been better, he believed, to reform the English universities, which were continuing to pursue the path of narrow specialisation, rather than to develop the Binary System.[52] Robbins's attack upon the Binary System brought forth what is undoubtedly his best House of Lords speech. Stressing that the Robbins Committee had seen the technical colleges as an important part of a unitary higher education system and had proposed the creation of the Council for National Academic Awards, he went on:

We recognised the need for diversity both of academic and of administrative forms. But we conceived of the system as unitary in the sense that it was flexible and evolutionary and that it contained no unnecessary barriers or limitations on growth and transformation. We emphasized the importance of the possible transfer of individuals and institutions from one sector to another.

The philosophy of the Binary System negates all this. Far from seeking to minimise barriers it positively creates them . . . Splendid experiments are possible, yet because the abracadabra of this precious Binary system prohibits transfer, all suggestions for union are ruled out. Surely, compared to such an attitude, the habits of the mandarinate at its most rigid seem enlightened and forward looking.[53]

7. FINANCE

The creation of the Binary System was an instance in which the power of the civil service and of the politicians, deriving from the power of the purse, produced results which Robbins abhorred. Nonetheless, though he regretted dependence on public funds, and believed that universities should seek more funds from outside the public sector, Robbins recognised that public funding of higher education was unavoidable.[54] But he advocated a greater reliance upon fees. Even if these were paid by local authorities, this gave universities greater independence than money from central government.[55] It also had the advantage of making universities' income sensitive to their power to attract students. He did not go as far as those who argued that fees should be raised to the level at which they covered the full cost of degrees; apart from anything else, this would result in different fees for different degrees and would raise questions about the willingness of the State to pay for different kinds of degree.[56] But some increase in reliance upon fee income would, in his view, be healthy.

The provision of funds to the students themselves was seen, in the report, as being best done through a system of grants rather than loans. The report on balance opposed loans on the grounds that they could dissuade people from entering higher education and that they might discriminate against women and against people taking degrees in subjects like theology.[57] In the period immediately following the publication of the report Robbins himself continued to advocate grants.[58] He argued that a loan system might even be contractionary, implicitly using the Mill-Senior argument about market failure, through parental ignorance leading to under-provision,[59] though recognising that there might be a case for loans when parents had become better educated. But later on he came to accept the argument that grants are a subsidy to the clever from the less clever despite 'the post-Second World War mythology of the bottomless purse'.[60] He was still concerned that there were difficulties in the operation of a loan scheme. There might be difficulties of collection of repayments; the choice of degree might be over-optimistic with regard to its earnings potential; the choice of degree might be such as would certainly not enhance income earning potential (for example, theology); and there was the 'negative dowry' problem.[61]

> It is highly desirable that talented girls should have access to higher education; only educational dinosaurs contend the contrary. But what if, at the end of the course, the girl decides that her vocation is to become a wife and a mother . . . It is not difficult to conceive of young men of prudence making surreptitious enquiries concerning the indebtedness of possible partners. I cannot believe that that would be a very satisfactory state of affairs.[62]

One can see the smile as Robbins wrote that. But the point was a serious one nonetheless.

Despite these misgivings Robbins decided that a loan scheme, on the lines put forward by Prest in which repayment would be conditional upon a sufficient level of future earnings, was desirable.[63] This represented an explicit change of mind. It was coupled with the consideration that only through some sort of loan scheme could an expansion of graduate studies, which he regarded as urgently necessary, be achieved.[64]

8. PROBLEMS OF EXPANSION

The main thrust of expansion, as urged in the Robbins Report, was, of course, to be at the undergraduate level. Here, although Robbins agreed that there could conceivably be 'some subtle deterioration in the quality of talk over nuts and wine', he was not prepared to concede that there was any danger of deterioration in the learned journals and the output of scholarly works.[65] He recognised some dangers to the universities themselves in coping with the much increased numbers[66] but believed – this was 1963 – that the pool of ability was sufficiently large to provide for extra university teachers as well as extra university students, as long as expansion did not proceed at too great a rate.[67] Many years later he was to regret not foreseeing some decline in the quality of junior staff, some of whom had insufficient 'knowledge of the essential disciplines and wider purposes of universities'.[68] Indeed it is possible that at that later date he favoured some deterioration of staff/student ratios rather than further staff expansion.[69]

The report itself recommended six new universities. By 1965 it was quite clear that these were not going to be set up; but Robbins indicated that he was not unhappy at this, if the existing universities could be expanded.[70] He was later to warn against excessive size in universities, having seen how expansion, driven by ambitious academics, could proceed. At this later date he came to believe too that students feel lost in large institutions, and that, in face of administrative problems, academics withdraw.[71] But despite having witnessed the near break-up of the University of London,[72] Robbins was, in the 1960s, fairly happy about large universities. He believed that universities needed to be large partly because of the explosion of knowledge and partly because of the benefits of division of labour, although they did not (given the example of LSE) need to be comprehensive of all subjects.[73] But to mitigate the adverse effects of size he valued the collegiate system;[74] and even when he had become much more concerned about problems of size, he argued that such a system could mitigate those problems to some extent.[75]

However, he had rather serious reservations about Oxford and Cambridge. His evidence to the commission on Oxford University shows signs of a fairly carefully concealed irritation with that university, and with Cambridge, particularly over the difficulties of obtaining even basic statistical information.[76] His reservations about the scholarship system have already been noted. But his basic criticism seems to have been that there was an almost total lack of leadership in Oxford and that the structure of the university was designed to achieve that situation.

If the failure to create six new universities was a matter about which Robbins was not unduly depressed, there were other aspects of the implementation of the report about which he was much more clearly unhappy. He was obviously disappointed by the reluctance of the government to create a set of special technological institutions of high standing;[77] and although the up-grading of the colleges of advanced technology to universities had been recommended in the report, and this was accepted, Robbins was not happy at the change of name involved if it implied an alteration in the centre of gravity of these institutions towards more traditional subjects.[78] Indeed he was rather concerned about the struggle of technological subjects to establish themselves. He was perfectly clear that he attached importance to them in their capacity *'to enlarge the general powers of the mind'* quite apart from any purely vocational skills.[79]

Again, if Robbins was happy that the creation of the CNAA was one of the achievements of the Committee,[80] he was a great deal less happy about the fate of the teacher training colleges. Although he was to express satisfaction in his *Autobiography* about the reform of the curricula in, and the governing structure of, these colleges,[81] it is perfectly clear that he felt unhappy at what he regarded as shabby treatment of these institutions. He had wanted them linked to universities and removed from the care of the local authorities so that they might supply the place of liberal arts colleges without any second class implications. But this had not happened.[82]

9. ACADEMIC FREEDOM

Not unnaturally, given Robbins's own passionate commitment to freedom, the Robbins Committee had been very much concerned with the question of academic freedom and had relied, as already noted, on the buffer of the UGC and the system of the block grant to provide for academic freedom for institutions in receipt of public subsidy.[83] Robbins was later to address squarely the question of academic freedom itself. Though it was difficult to define, its absence, he held, could easily be recognised. It involved exceptional privileges, and thus demanded exceptional justification.[84] It certainly did not mean freedom to neglect one's duties;[85] and it certainly did not mean that the individual should be freed from every last vestige of public control.[86] What he was above all concerned with was that academic freedom should permit freedom of innovation both for the institution and for the individual.[87] In practice, as somebody who was once a junior colleague of his has testified, Robbins's view in practice was that academics, as long as they did not abuse their positions, should be very free agents indeed.[88] As Robbins put it:

> The demand for academic freedom is thus essentially a demand for the freedom of a non-contractual status while in other respects in a contractual or a subsidised capacity; and it is this

which is the stumbling block in public discussions of the subject
. . . We must surely concede that these principles need a
justification which goes beyond the justification of the general
principles of liberty.

Such a justification in my judgment is to be found in the field
of results. An academic system in which individuals and
institutions are free in the ways I have described is more likely
to work well than one which is unfree. It is more likely to
achieve the ends we ask of such a system. It is more likely to
produce good teaching and fruitful speculation and to maintain
appropriate standards.[89]

Thus out of the Utilitarianism of Hume and Bentham, and
Robbins's own passionate commitment to liberty, we have his
justification of academic freedom.

In such a free institution, teaching and research should go
hand-in-hand. A university was concerned not only with education
but with the advancement of learning,[90]

> whereas without the performance of educational duties the
> universities would fail of their mission, yet, without the
> pursuance of research and the advancement of learning
> generally, the educational function itself must languish and
> indeed ossify.[91]

Of course it was possible to overdo the 'publish or perish' ethic,
and in later years Robbins showed some concern over this.[92] He
also argued that there was need for some improvement in teaching
and supervision, especially in the early stages of a degree.[93] But of
the fundamental importance which he attached to research, there
is no doubt.

A basic constituent of the academic freedom which was
necessary for fruitful research was tenure.[94] Even though Robbins
recognised that there had been clear cases of abuse, where
individuals had used universities for political indoctrination, he
regarded security of tenure as fundamental.[95]

10. INVESTMENT IN EDUCATION

There is no doubt that Robbins's dedication to the expansion of
higher education, and to the opening of higher education to all

with ability and willingness to take advantage of it, stemmed fundamentally from his egalitarianism. But there were also a number of other factors which he brought into the discussion. Firstly, there was the matter of investment in education. Here he was rather cautious. He was aware that economists, from Smith onwards, had argued that education was an investment,[96] and he accepted that there must be some connection between education and economic growth,[97] and that it might be necessary to maintain investment in education or fall behind in international competition.[98] But he did not, consistently with his methodological position, accept what he regarded as being crude correlations between higher education statistics and GNP[99] – or even take such claims of association seriously.[100] Although education clearly involves investment in human capital, Robbins was always careful to avoid glib use of this term – education has consumption as well as investment aspects.[101]

It also has external effects. As he put it:

> provided that the educational activity is not gravely misdirected, it is reasonable to suppose that, in general, society is likely to be more efficient, more progressive, more humane, the larger the proportion of people who have had the opportunity of developing their intelligence in this way.[102]

The social sciences could indeed be important in the development of society.[103] The universities helped to maintain intellectual standards; they also helped to maintain open-mindedness and tolerance of criticism (both qualities being essential to a liberal civilisation), except where idealogues took advantage of academic freedom to misuse their positions.[104]

11. CONCLUSION – THE ROBBINS ACHIEVEMENT

In his *Autobiography*, Robbins expressed some satisfaction at the achievements of his committee. After mentioning some of his disappointments he goes on:

> But I should be sorry to suggest that in my own computation of our effectiveness they over-shadowed the findings and recommendations which were accepted.[105]

After listing the achievements – a new Scottish university, the transformation of the CATs into universities, reform of the teacher training colleges, the CNAA, he continued:

> And so I could go on. In a world in which the labours of this sort of enquiry are so frequently ignored and their recommendations quietly shelved, we certainly had little cause for dissatisfaction, either with the notice attracted by our report or with the degree to which its suggestions were accepted.[106]

But towards the end of the decade at the beginning of which this *Autobiography* appeared, it was becoming clear that a degree of retrenchment in university finances was getting underway; and there seems no doubt that Robbins was bitterly disappointed.[107] Even so, and despite the fact that this is an episode in British social history on which it is still too early to get a satisfactory perspective, it does seem clear that the achievement of Robbins and his colleagues was very substantial. It is only fair to note, however, that in Robbins's writings on higher education the educationist is much more apparent than the economist.[108] The general equilibrium marginal approach, which dominates his writing about wartime work and experience, is absent. One might almost say that the romantic in him came to predominate. This is not in any way to belittle his achievements; nor is it to down-play the research findings of the Robbins Committee to which he attached such importance. Rather it is to suggest that it was this which made him vulnerable to feelings of hurt and disappointment at some aspects of later educational policy.

7 Microeconomics

1. INTRODUCTION

Robbins's treatment of microeconomic issues was never wholly systematised. This reflects his basic approach to his work as an economist – to take, pragmatically, the tools available and to use them to deal with a particular problem. Nevertheless there was an essential unity to his treatment, for underlying it were three elements derived from Austrian economics. Firstly, there was the precept that microeconomic problems must not be treated in a concept divorced from general equilibrium – a partial equilibrium conclusion should be subjected to what might be called in later language 'general equilibrium sensitivity' considerations. Secondly, cost reflected, in such a general equilibrium context, opportunity cost. It was not therefore sensible to approach cost schedules as if given and fixed, irrespective of demand changes, or to approach them as if 'real' cost meant anything other than foregone satisfactions. Thirdly, because factors always had alternative uses, including own consumption of their services, it was not helpful to reason in terms of an equilibrium model in which factor supplies were fixed.

2. EQUILIBRIUM

A key role in Robbins's approach to microeconomics was, as will be clear from Chapter 3, an emphasis upon equilibrium[1] – usually general equilibrium, analysed in terms similar to those used by the Austrians and Wicksteed.[2] Indeed his grasp of Wicksteed's theoretical approach seems to have given him early on a good feel for economic problems in a general equilibrium context.[3] For instance, in his 1927 discussion of the theory of the optimum population, Robbins approached population from a general equilibrium point of view, indicating that labour-saving inventions did not necessarily mean that the whole economy required fewer people even though particular industries did so.[4]

This standpoint made Robbins critical of several other streams in the literature of economics in the 1930s. On the one hand he was hostile to aggregation – it was necessary to analyse problems in a disaggregated way.[5] In particular the theory of production should, he held, be approached as the theory of optimum factor allocation.[6] Secondly, he was very critical of Marshall's concept of the Representative Firm.[7] He approached this concept in terms of Austrian general equilibrium and asked whether it affected equilibrium conditions, dismissing it when it appeared that it did not.[8] He thus managed to miss not only the essential nature of a Representative Firm (one which could be recognised by an individual with a detailed knowledge of the industry in question), but also the two uses to which the concept was put by Marshall – to give some idea of elasticity of supply, and as a guide to whether entry into the industry might be profitable.[9]

Robbins was also critical of Marshall's fishing industry example (in which the elasticity of supply is shown to vary with the time period under consideration). Robbins's view was that it was necessary to look at general equilibrium considerations and to ask whether the change in demand which made elasticity of supply a matter of interest had affected other industries (which could of course *shift* the supply function in the fishing industry).[10] He also stressed that, in the approach to equilibrium, adjustment was a *continuous* process; thus Marshall's separation of time into three discrete periods was unsatisfactory and was in fact identifying as separate what were different sections of the same process. Marshall's analysis also neglected the importance of expectations, Robbins argued; in the Austrian approach to equilibrium, centred around the individual's subjective perceptions, estimates of the likely duration of the change in demand could be of importance.[11]

In discussing equilibrium, Robbins made an important distinction between two different concepts of equilibrium to be found in economic literature. On the one hand there was that to be found in the writings of those like J. B. Clark, and Schumpeter in his discussion of interest, who employed a concept of equilibrium which failed to allow for variable factor supplies. On the other hand, if allowance were made for variation in factor supplies, a second and more general analysis than that put forward by writers like Clark was necessary.[12]

This distinction was then used by Robbins to resolve the controversy over 'the ultimate nature of real costs . . . Are all costs ultimately resolvable into foregone products, or are labour-

pain and abstinence to be regarded as ultimate'.[13] His solution was to argue that 'disutility' in the sense of the hedonistic calculus had become a redundant concept: even if factor supplies were variable, 'disutilities . . . are ultimately to be regarded as being the pull of foregone leisure or foregone present income – opportunity costs rather than disutilities in the sense of the old hedonistic calculus'.[14] Robbins also, as will be noted below, used the distinction as a basis for criticism of J. B. Clark's particular emphasis on marginal productivity in wage determination,[15] and of Schumpeter's analysis of interest.[16]

3. PRODUCTION

Robbins's critical attitude to much of the inter-war literature was manifested in his treatment of production. As noted above, Robbins's Austrian critique of the Representative Firm largely missed the point of its construction, as well as employing a misguided argument that if it was not obtainable from business statistics its usefulness was greatly diminished. Yet, as Blaug has noted, Robbins's critique succeeded in largely eliminating the concept from the literature.[17] Robbins's position was that because returns to factors are equalised, in equilibrium, once adjusted for their abilities, there is no more need to talk of a representative firm than of a representative piece of land or a representative worker.[18] He was approaching the problem from a completely different angle to that of Marshall, for whom the Representative Firm was essentially an informational device for telling the outsider something about an industry which was in a state of flux and concerning which information was necessarily incomplete.

The Representative Firm was essentially a partial equilibrium concept; and Robbins was critical of partial equilibrium analysis as a whole. While he was prepared to concede that there was no fundamental inconsistency between Wieser's Law of (opportunity) cost and partial equilibrium analysis, partial equilibrium required some unseen adjustment elsewhere in the system for its results to be valid, so it was not very satisfactory.[19]

It is, perhaps, worth stressing the point that the objection here implied is not to partial equilibrium analysis as such, but to partial equilibrium analysis unrelated to the general theory of equilibrium. It may be quite true that the general theory of equilibrium by itself is often too abstract and general for useful application. But it is equally true – and it is a thing which has often been forgotten in recent discussions – that partial equilibrium analysis unaccompanied by a continual awareness of the propositions of general equilibrium theory is almost certain to be misleading. It may be asserted without fear of serious contradiction that most of the confusion in the recent [1933] cost controversy has sprung from the attempt to make the constructions of partial equilibrium analysis carry more than they can legitimately bear.[20]

An example of this can be seen in Robbins's critique of Sraffa's much-cited, but arguably rather confused, article of 1926.[21] Sraffa refers to the possibility of constant or even decreasing money costs. Robbins however held that this involved an intellectual difficulty resulting from the use of partial equilibrium analysis. In his view costs are 'essentially a reflection of the strength of excluded demands' – thus only if an increase in output follows an increase in demand can we expect constant or decreasing costs.[22] If demand for one good increases, demand for some other good will fall, the services of factors of production will be released, and price need not rise. But at equilibrium in Wieser's cost analysis, *unless there is a demand shift*, factors are more highly valued in alternative occupations and thus rising costs are the norm. This as a process of reasoning was somewhat more impressive than Sraffa's reference to 'common experience' of constant or decreasing costs.[23] It is also rather ironic, since part of Sraffa's article also employed general equilibrium considerations, that general equilibrium analysis should have been so effectively employed here by Robbins.

Similar considerations also lay, in part, behind Robbins's attack on Pigou's use of supply curves (instead of marginal product curves) in his analysis of decreasing and increasing returns[24] – although here Robbins was very largely following Allyn Young.[25] He was, not unnaturally, no more sympathetic towards Joan Robinson's work. His criticism of the 'excess capacity' argument has already been noted in Chapter 5. But he was also, without explicitly citing Joan Robinson, critical of the use of partial equilibrium analysis for general equilibrium problems, pointing to the fallacy of composition which could be involved, and to the danger of drawing conclusions for aggregate distribution from marginal partial equilibrium curves.[26] But it has to be noted that, in important articles published in 1929 and 1930 Robbins, apparently under the influence of Dalton, used partial equilibrium analysis for problems which were (certainly in the first case and partially in the second) really general equilibrium problems.[27]

As already indicated, such a theoretical approach was embedded in the work of a number of previous writers. In particular, in his article on costs, Robbins cites Wieser, Wicksteed, Davenport, Knight, Henderson, Pantaleoni and Wicksell.[28] The Austrian writer Mayer, little-known today, was another source.[29] Mayer was one of those writers emphasising the Austrian demand approach to all aspects of allocation; he, like Weber, made a clear distinction between economics and technology, of the kind which Robbins, as indicated in Chapter 3, followed.[30] The influence of these writers is particularly apparent in Robbins's encyclopaedia article on Production, whcih is very Austrian in tone.[31] The influence of Wieser was most apparent in the treatment of costs, in terms of opportunity cost.[32] However the over-riding influence, it is quite clear, was Wicksteed. Wicksteed is cited as having shown that where factor supplies vary – which Robbins considered the general case, as indicated above – these changes in factor supply can be exhibited as the result of demand operating within a given technical environment.[33] Wicksteed likened the problem of distribution to that of the optimisation of personal expenditure – with balancing and substitution at the margin – and argued that factor costs were determined by the anticipated value of the product.[34] Robbins made no bones about the importance of Wicksteed's contribution.

It is nearly twenty years since Wicksteed demonstrated to the British Association the true nature of the supply curve. To-day the majority of economists would accept his demonstration as irrefutable. Yet since the war, there has appeared a great mass of literature on the cost question which, for all the awareness it displays of the essential problem at issue, might for the most part have been the same if Wicksteed had never written. Nonetheless, few things can be more certain than that until the propositions which Wicksteed stressed in this paper are incorporated into the general body of cost analysis, the whole controversy will continue to present an appearance of paradox and unreality – an intellectual backwater, full no doubt of strange fish and queer animalculae, but lacking that relation to the mainstream of general equilibrium theory which alone can give it real significance.[35]

Wicksteed's analysis was clearly distinct from Marshall's approach, as Robbins emphasised.[36]

Thus, although Robbins also drew on the work of Allyn Young (including Young's oblique criticism of Sraffa's 1926 article)[37] the predominant influence on Robbins's cost theory was undoubtedly Wicksteed. However Robbins's distribution theory represented a fusion of Classical and Austrian elements. Influenced by Taussig's *Wages and Capital*, Robbins held that wages were paid out of capital, along the lines of a Classical wage fund, and linked this to Austrian capital theory as further developed by Wicksell.[38] This leads to some elements of unresolved conflict within Robbins's treatment of wages. On the one hand, the remnants of a Classical wage-fund approach are present in the background – according to Robbins 'Nothing could be more superficial . . . than the criticisms put forward by writers such as Walker and J. B. Clark of the incontrovertible proposition that wages are paid out of capital.'[39] Indeed the Classical inheritance goes further than this: it was the Classical economists who provided the basis for Robbins's treatment of trade unions.[40] But on the other hand, in his classic article on variation of labour hours, he treated the problem in terms of the elasticity of demand for labour, with the emphasis upon the elasticity of demand for the final product as predominantly determining this.[41] It would probably be fair to say that, if pressed, Robbins would have resolved the conflict along the lines followed by Marshall in Appendix J to the *Principles*,[42] namely, that *anticipated* demand for commodities attracts capital into different employments, that wages are necessarily paid before the product is actually marketed in most cases, that such payment must come from capital, but that we can neglect both the lags and the immediate source of wage payments in analysing demand for labour since this must *ultimately* depend on the demand for the final product. But Robbins did not really do this – he insisted that he was only expounding a received position anyway and so left the matter unresolved in his own writings.[43]

But it is the cost analysis which is the most interesting part of Robbins's approach. The fundamental nature of costs, in what he stressed was *modern* economics, was displaced alternatives.[44] The process of valuation was essentially a process of choice. In the process of exchange, we chose to give things up in order to obtain others; in production, the factors employed had alternative uses. Where factor supplies were variable, factors had an opportunity cost of time and energy available for other purposes.[45] With a given technology, variations in factor supply were the result of demand changes.[46] (The technical changes themselves changed opportunity costs.[47]) Costs of production were, as already noted, 'essentially a reflection of the strength of excluded demands';[48] 'disutilities' were *foregone* leisure or income. Opportunity cost rather than the hedonistic calculus had to be used, even though there were problems of definition where factor supplies were variable because the chain of consequences was long.[49]

Following Wieser, Robbins argued that costs had to be measured by the *values* of the goods of first order (Austrian terminology for consumption goods) displaced. He quoted Wieser to the effect that the cost of production of one thing was the marginal value of another thing.[50] This led him to disagree with Frank Knight who had suggested using, instead of marginal *values*, *quantities* of goods of first order foregone.[51] Robbins accepted that this had 'an objectivity and precision which is in itself an advantage'. He accepted too that Knight (and Haberler)[52] had shown that if the amount of a commodity produced by a combination of factors of production was not the same as that set of factors could obtain *indirectly*, by producing something else and then engaging in exchange so as to obtain the first commodity, then factors would migrate to different employments until this was achieved. The argument is that whether a commodity is obtained directly, or indirectly, the marginal productivity of the factors, measured in terms of that commodity, should be the same. Knight was thus contending that when we have market equilibrium, subjective valuation has already done its work, so to speak, and we only need to look at the physical quantities of different goods.

The Knight–Haberler argument requires that the ratio of marginal value products be equalised in different occupations. Robbins however objected that if there were fixed technical coefficients then, following a shift in demand, factors used intensively in the production of the newly-favoured commodity would rise in price, altering relative values and relative costs without any change in physical opportunity cost which remains

constant if technical coefficients remain constant.[53] It was thus
necessary to measure cost by the *value* of goods of first order
displaced. Robbins also argued that you could not apply the
Knight–Haberler argument where there were specific factors,
since these had no physical opportunity cost.

The issue was confused (as in Austrian economics) by a lurking
use of the loss-principle – with fixed factor combinations, the
problem arises that if output of one good is reduced, by
withdrawing a combined unit of capital and labour, then only
part of the combination will be re-employed in a different
fixed-factor-combination industry with a different capital/labour
coefficient, so that the lost output will be greater than what is
really due to the redeployed factors. This however raises problems
of whether factor markets clear; and since all parties were
assuming that they did clear, it would have been better to avoid
this particular problem. Robbins's argument about value rather
than physical quantity of foregone goods was, however, essentially
correct. As he himself said:

> the price which the entrepreneur pays for the factors of
> production he uses is determined not by the *number* of products
> which they can produce elsewhere, but by the value of such
> products.[54]

This Austrian–Wicksteed approach to costs, inherently linked to
choice, has remained outside the mainstream of thinking in
economics. This is not entirely surprising. For such an approach,
stressing that costs have no objective existence, carried with it the
wreckage of much of what is now conventional economic theory.[55]

It also fundamentally undermines the persistent tendency of
economists to confuse the technical and the economic.[56] This was
something which Robbins attacked emphatically, drawing on
Wicksteed, Weber and Wieser. Thus Robbins's treatment of
production stressed that the 'end of all activity with an economic
aspect is the satisfaction of wants', and that production is 'the use
of scarce resources to increase opportunities of consumption' or,
formally, 'activity directed to increasing the number of scarce
economic goods of the first order'.[57] Thus:

> The business of a theory of production is not the summation of
> the technologies. It is the study of a system of relations in
> which, in its most abstract form, the subject matter of the

technologies appears merely as one set of terms in a whole series of equations.[58]

From such a position it followed, as indicated in Chapter 3, that production in the aggregate had no particular meaning and that generalisations about aggregate production, for translation into welfare purposes, were very difficult to make.[59]

Within this general equilibrium approach to production and costs, declining marginal value product is central in order to provide a basis for equi-marginal equalisation and allocation.[60] This was a static proposition, distinct from the Classical concept of diminishing returns.[61] However Robbins also, following Allyn Young, considered the possibility of increasing returns *over time*, following on general factor market developments,[62] a concept which was, as Young had pointed out, only an extension of the Smithian analysis of division of labour.[63] Thus Robbins's general equilibrium approach was couched within a moving equilibrium framework.

It did not however really extend to the search for knowledge. Though Robbins recognised clearly enough the importance of competition, the entrepreneur, as Kirzner has argued, is missing from Robbins's picture. 'A market consisting exclusively of economising, maximising individuals does not generate the market process we seek to understand.'[64]

4. DEMAND

As already indicated in Chapter 3, the basis of Robbins's approach to the demand side of microeconomics was through the ranking of given wants. That these existed was important; he was critical of Cassel's desire simply to posit a demand curve, even though he was influenced by Cassel's emphasis upon the need to consider economic problems within a general framework.[65] Thus the end of economic activity was the satisfaction of wants,[66] and the essence of technological improvement was the satisfaction of more, given, wants – Robbins rejected the idea that tastes themselves were the product of technology.[67] He also rejected, emphatically, the idea that they were the product of advertising.

Advertisement in the narrow sense of the word is simply a leading species of the much larger genus, information combined

with persuasion: and the belief is puerile that because some
advertisement is fraudulent and some methods not to our taste,
advertisement in general can be thought out of any complex
society. So too is the exaggerated view of its role in shaping
consumer (or producer) demand.[68]

Indeed this view was preceded by the comment that:

I know few subjects on which more nonsense is talked than
this. *Soi-disant* sociological and economic experts elaborate a
picture of a world in which the whole area of consumer demand
is manipulated at will by the manufacturers of shoddy and
inimical products.[69]

The origin of Robbins's own emphasis on the subjective nature
of valuation is undoubtedly Wicksteed, and the Austrians.
Wicksteed himself had switched, between his *Alphabet* and his
Common Sense, from a marginal utility approach to one purely of
ranking;[70] and it is instructive that Robbins still retained traces of
a marginal utility approach in the first edition of *ENSES*, though it
was replaced in the second.[71] Rational behaviour was, then, acting
consistently in accordance with the ranking of different
possibilities.[72] Such activity was not in itself observable, but it
resulted in market prices which were observable and with which
each individual could compare his subjective valuation.[73]

Demand on the basis of such rankings was the ultimate force in
economics; following Wicksteed,[74] Robbins viewed the supply
curve, a concept which he invoked in criticising the Representative
Firm, as the seller's own demand curve.[75]

Although, following Knight, rankings were influenced by
expected *future* prices in Robbins's analysis,[76] the question of
information was passed by here also. As Kirzner has argued, the
consumer in Robbins's work has effectively perfect information
and it shifts attention away from the market as an information-
supplying device.[77]

5. DISTRIBUTION

Robbins's treatment of distribution was never really formulated
systematically. This was partly because, as noted in Chapter 2, he

never wrote the general work on economics which he had planned. He wrote much of his output for particular occasions, and his teaching was based upon applying the tools of economics to solve particular problems. However he did produce material on distribution. That concerning land and capital derived from his discussion of the meaning of equilibrium. The discussion of labour is rather more ambitious.

(i) Land

The treatment of rent springs from the distinction between the two forms of stationary equilibrium noted above.[78] Avoiding the then common pitfall of neglecting transfer earnings,[79] Robbins argued that if all factor supplies are fixed, then the return to land is no different from the return to other factors. If factor supplies are variable then land rent does have a special nature from a *social* point of view, even though it is still a necessary payment from an individual point of view.[80]

(ii) Capital

His treatment of capital, as already noted, essentially followed Böhm-Bawerk and Wicksell. Given time preference, interest was a necessary reward since it reflected the fact that capital was demanded because it increased output while its supply was limited. He was thus critical of Schumpeter, who had argued that in a stationary state there would be no separate reward to capital.[81] Robbins argued that even if there were no new accumulation, it would still be necessary to pay interest to avoid consumption of the existing capital stock – *depreciation* payments required the existence of interest. 'Why should labour and the use of material factors be devoted to the maintenance of the produced means of production if no net remuneration is forthcoming?'[82]

Schumpeter had been misled by Clark's particular concept of static equilibrium into forgetting that factor supplies could change. 'Abstinence' should be regarded

> not only as a refusal to consume in the present in order that the sources of future income may be *enlarged*, but also as a refusal to enhance one's consumption now in order that the income of the future may not be depleted.[83]

In arguing thus, Robbins was restating J. S. Mill's position.[84] He recognised the argument that, on the grounds of equalising the marginal utility of consumption expenditure, there was no reason, in a stationary economy, for transferring expenditure from the future to the present through capital consumption. But he argued that if capital did not yield an income there would be no reason for not consuming it – even if, presumably, its consumption were evenly spaced out over time in deference to the marginal utility argument. It was in fact '*an* interest rate, which . . . keeps the stationary state stationary – the rate at which it does not pay to turn income into capital or capital into income'.[85]

Robbins's treatments of rent and capital are limited. But he paid a good deal of attention to the analysis – involving more pressing problems from a policy point of view – of wages.

(iii) Labour

Labour income was indeed the subject of Robbins's first substantial publication.[86] Although at that date he was influenced by Classical writings and notably by Sidgwick,[87] he was later to draw on Dalton and Robertson (on questions of labour supply),[88] on Chapman (on variations in hours of labour)[89] and on Marshall (for the factors affecting the elasticity of demand for labour and for the implications for labour income of the relationship between this elasticity and output).[90]

Although, as already indicated, there were residual wage-fund elements in Robbins's approach, they did not influence his analysis of wages so much as his approach to capital. In discussing wages, he insisted that there was no necessary conflict between employer and employee, because the former was interested in labour cost per unit of output, not low wages per head.[91] Following his criticism of J. B. Clark, he was perfectly clear that marginal productivity theory could only be a theory of factor demand, not a theory of distribution, once factor supplies were allowed to vary as, he argued, was the more general and correct analysis.[92] But the elasticity of demand for labour depended not only on its productivity, but also (and particularly) on the elasticity of demand for the final product as well as on the possibilities of substitution within the process.[93]

Robbins analysed the supply of labour in two famous articles, one dealing with variations in the hours of labour[94] and the other (perhaps his most famous single article) dealing with the elasticity of labour supply which, in accordance with his general demand-orientated approach, he treated in terms of the elasticity of demand for income in terms of effort.[95]

The article on variations in hours of labour is a paper which, even today, requires fairly careful study. The analysis is actually quite difficult. By avoiding the marginal revenue product curve it is illuminating. But on the other hand it attempts to employ a partial concept (elasticity) in a general equilibrium context (at least in the latter part of the article) with not entirely happy results. It is interesting that as Robbins became more Austrian, and more focused upon general equilibrium, he stopped using this kind of analysis; but both the articles under discussion employ it.

The starting point of the analysis, given that the formation of income/leisure preferences (like that of other preferences) is outside the scope of scientific enquiry,[96] is that variation of hours produces variation of output. We then assume that the elasticity of demand for labour is very largely a function of the elasticity of demand for the final product. Thus if hours are increased where elasticity of demand for goods is less than one, outlay on labour will fall and employment will fall if time wages per head remain constant.[97]

This then can give rise to a distinction between individual interests and group interests.[98] For individuals, and for society as a whole, income varies directly with output, though Robbins, perhaps mindful of Nassau Senior,[99] was careful to say that output per head was not maximised at maximum hours.[100] But when we consider groups within society (a matter he was to return to later in the *Economic Basis of Class Conflict*) the matter is more complicated. While individuals are price takers, with individual output and individual income varying directly without recourse to elasticity considerations, the elasticity of demand for the output of *groups* employed in particular industries is a significant consideration in dealing with the relationship between income and output. Where elasticity of demand for output is greater than one, income will be proportional to output, while where elasticity is less than one, income will be inversely proportional to output. In such a case, wages per man would have to fall to maintain employment as output increased. Thus the harmony between individuals and employers did not necessarily imply harmony between groups of employees and society.[101]

However Robbins then attempted to extend the analysis to all groups in economic employment moving simultaneously, while still using the partial concept of elasticity.[102] Clearly this raised difficulties which could not be solved simply through this kind of analysis, and Robbins took refuge in invoking Pigou's authority for 'the almost universal consensus of opinion among economists' that the elasticity of demand for labour in the aggregate was greater than one.[103] Given this, he developed the argument as follows. If the elasticity of demand for labour as a whole is greater than one then, as output increased, labour income would rise and, given mobility of labour, increased time wages would spread through the labour force. However, with increasing output in the economy as a whole, wages would still fall (with given employment) in some industries – in those industries where the elasticity of demand for labour was less than one. They would rise in those industries where the converse was true. This was held to be broadly true even though the demand curves for the output of each industry, and thus the demand curve for labour in that industry, was shifting (because it had to be conceded, that there were general equilibrium adjustments) so that we were not really moving along the demand curve for one product.[104]

Robbins also considered the effect of variations of labour hours (and output) in the context of an open economy.[105] Here international capital mobility introduced an extra complication. 'If man is of all luggage the most difficult to be transported, free capital is the most easy.'[106] For most open economies it was reasonable to assume, given the existence of competing sources of supply, an elasticity of demand for exports greater than one.

A reduction in labour time would make capital employment less profitable and bring about capital export. For if hours are reduced, output is reduced, and with elasticity of demand for exports greater than one, foreign expenditure on British exports would fall. The return on a given capital stock will fall and some will move to areas of higher return. The loss of capital will reduce output per head still further, and, with the same elasticity assumption, expenditure on British exports, and hence on British labour, will fall. Assuming that the labour market clears, this necessitates falling wages.

The starting point of Robbins's article on the elasticity of demand for income in terms of effort (or labour supply) was Dalton. From Dalton (Robertson is also cited) Robbins believed he had taken the 'generally accepted proposition of theoretical economics that the effects of a change in the terms on which incomes for work can be obtained depend upon the elasticity of demand for income in terms of effort'.[107] This was used as the basis for countering Knight's view that the individual supply of labour was necessarily related negatively to the wage rate.[108] If elasticity of demand for income in terms of effort is greater than one, a rise in the 'effort wage rate' (that is a reduction in the effort price of income) will cause more effort to be supplied.

Robbins's happiness with abstraction enabled him to use, as the explanatory variable, the '*effort* price of income'[109] rather than the reciprocal of wages per hour (that is hours per unit of income, which would be the *time* price of income), thereby extending the analysis to labour intensity. However, the diagrammatic analysis which he presented effectively used hours though the terminology used permitted the interpretation 'hours adjusted for intensity'. The outlay rectangle in the diagram (Figure 7.1) is then, to all intents and purposes, hours; we have the reciprocal of the wage rate on the vertical axis and income equals wh on the horizontal axis, yielding a time rectangle (that is, $wh (1/w) = h$). Knight had argued (like Robbins, without the benefit of modern terminology about income and substitution effects) that, as leisure is a normal good, the supply curve of labour must be negatively sloped. Robbins however argued that the responsiveness of labour quantity to the wage rate depended on the elasticity of demand for income in terms of effort – which we can now see as formally correct when viewed in terms of income and substitution effects. However his analogy with the Marshallian demand curve, and a total outlay curve (see Figure 7.2), did not permit him to explore these two separate effects, while his failure to make the dimensions clear is a drawback of the analysis.[110]

These two articles represent the high point of Robbins's excursions into the microeconomics of labour. Elsewhere the analysis is much more conventional. Labour supply to different *occupations* will be determined by equalisation of net advantage, with subjective valuation of the non-pecuniary conditions.[111] Robbins also tried to restore the Classical discussion of the relationship between wage levels and population,[112] and argued further that a small labour force with high productivity was

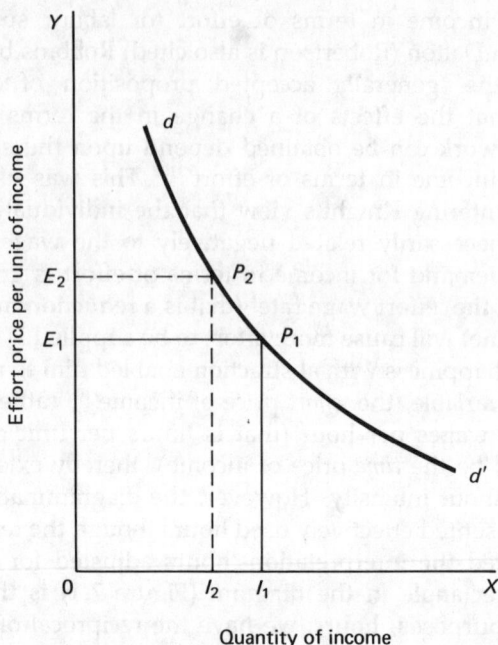

dd' is the demand curve for income.

At an 'effort price of income' $0E_1$ income, I_1 will be earned. The 'amount of work done' is $0E_1 P_1 I_1$.

An income tax would raise the effort price of income from E_1 to E_2.

The quantity of income earned becomes I_2.

If $0E_1P_1I_1 < 0E_2P_2I_2$, the supply curve of the individual's labour is negatively sloped – the elasticity of demand for income in terms of effort is less than one.

If $0E_1P_1I_1 > 0E_2P_2I_2$, the supply curve of the individual's labour is positively sloped – the elasticity of demand for income in terms of effort is greater than one.

Figure 7.1

preferable to a large labour force with low output per head because of lower fixed costs.[113]

This, like his reiteration of a view to be found in Mill, that English labour was superior to that elsewhere,[114] represents Classical influences – possibly conveyed through Cannan – rather than a fresh look at the subject. The same is very largely true of

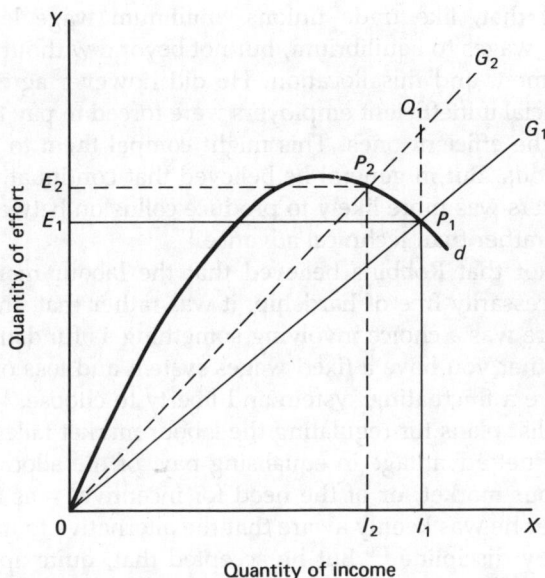

Quantity of income

'Total outlay of effort' (the rectangle $0E_iP_iI_i$ from Figure 7.1 now measured as E on the vertical axis in Figure 7.2) is related to quantity of income.

The 'effort price of income' (the wage rate reciprocal) is given by the slope of $0G$.

Equilibrium is initially at P_1.

An income tax shifts $0G$ from $0G_1$ to $0G_2$.

At the new equilibrium P_2, income has fallen to I_2 and effort increased to E_2. Thus the supply curve of individual labour supply is negatively sloped and the elasticity of demand for income in terms of effort is less than one.

Figure 7.2

his analysis of trade unions and of minimum wage legislation – despite the fact that he had at a later date substantial first-hand experience of trade unions in connection with the *Financial Times*.[115] In his very early book *Wages*, Robbins argued that trade unions could ensure that equilibrium wages were paid, and this was valuable, but they were not capable of raising wages above this level except so as to share in monopoly profits, although they could temporarily raise wages above equilibrium and harm other wage earners.[116] This remained his view 50 years later.[117] Similarly he argued that, like trade unions, minimum wage legislation could raise wages to equilibrium, but not beyond without creating unemployment and misallocation. He did however agree that it was beneficial if inefficient employers were forced to pay the same wages as the efficient ones. This might compel them to improve their methods. But in general he believed that continual pressure on employers was more likely to produce collusion between them to resist it rather than technical advance.[118]

It was not that Robbins believed that the labour market was always necessarily free of hardship; it was rather that, in the last resort, there was a choice involving something as fundamental as liberty. 'Either you have a fixed wages system and loss of liberty, or you have a fluctuating system and liberty to choose.'[119] In any case, socialist plans for regulating the labour market failed to take account of net advantage in equalising pay, of the allocative role of the labour market, or of the need for incentives – as a former army officer he was keenly aware that the alternative to incentives was military discipline.[120] But he accepted that, quite apart from the fact that labour was not homogeneous, the net advantage accruing to homogeneous labour would not be completely equalised. This was for reasons familiar to Adam Smith, such as ignorance of opportunities, excessive optimism about the rewards of particular occupations, barriers to free entry into occupations because of cost of training, and limits on occupational and geographical mobility.[121] But imperfect though the market was, it would still do better than socialist plans which failed to take any account of net advantage.[122]

Similarly, while fluctuations in the aggregate demand for labour were regrettable, many of the narrower fluctuations in the demand for labour were redistributing labour between occupations in accordance with changing preferences and technology. This was necessary in any society. In Robbins's view this process rarely caused hardship because, as people retired, new labour was directed towards new industries.[123]

6. CONCLUSION

Robbins's treatment of microeconomics reflects the diverse sources from which he drew inspiration. But it is clear that the major influences on his cost theory were the Austrians and Wicksteed while the best parts of his labour economics reflected an ingenious, if ultimately unsuccessful, attempt to make the Marshallian elasticity tool bear more weight than it could. In the last resort, neither of these elements was tremendously influential. The cost analysis would, if accepted, destroy large parts of conventional theory, and it is probably for this reason that it has not attracted very many adherents since the Second World War. The wage analysis has been rendered largely obsolete by the development of choice theory stemming from the work of Hicks and Allen (as encouraged by Robbins) although, in its own right, it is a remarkable testimony both to Robbins's theoretical ingenuity and to his powers of abstraction.

8 Macroeconomics

1. INTRODUCTION

This chapter covers Robbins's writings on macroeconomics in the pre-war and post-war periods. His pre-war contributions, most notably in *The Great Depression*, were centred on the Wicksell–Mises theory of fluctuations, though behind this there lay a profound appreciation on Robbins's part of the Classical analysis. It emerges that, in the post-war period, Robbins retained much of this analysis despite an ostensible surrender to Keynesianism. He shed the explicitly Austrian elements but retained not only the Classical but also the Wicksellian roots. From this vantage point he was able to provide commentary on, and analysis of, post-war macroeconomic policy. He was frequently a lonely figure in this context, at odds with the post-war consensus among economists; but events often vindicated his position and shifts of opinion made him less isolated as time passed.

2. PRE-WAR

(i) Sources

Robbins's pre-war macroeconomics derived from three principal sources; English Classical economics, Wicksell and a group of Austrian writers including Mises and Hayek, with these last being for long the predominant influences. Classical economics provided Robbins during this period with a background understanding of monetary economics, and with a particular appreciation of the international aspects of macroeconomic problems in an open economy. From Wicksell, Robbins took the well-known theory of the interaction of the real and the money rate of interest and the price level.[1] The theory of the real rate of interest itself, Robbins derived from Austrian capital theory, both directly and through the work of Cassel, Fetter and Wicksell,[2] though he never really spelt out the 'period of production' approach clearly. In contrast to Hayek,[3] for whom the concept was also central, Robbins simply took the real rate of interest as given by the marginal rate of return on new investment, however determined. (It is probably fair to say that, while Robbins was predisposed to the approach of Austrian capital theory by some lingering wage-fund elements in his analysis,[4] he was reluctant to commit himself to the one-dimensional and tedious numerical examples employed by the Austrians.)

Perhaps the most important single influence on Robbins's approach to the significance of changes in the quantity of money was Mises,[5] whose *Money and Credit* seems indeed to have been translated into English at Robbins's instance.[6] The vast scholarship and erudition of this book, quite apart from the analysis, would have appealed to Robbins.

Robbins was also much influenced by Hayek's *Prices and Production* which, building in part on Wicksell's work,[7] and also on that of Mises to which Hayek owed (and acknowledged) a substantial debt,[8] had developed the basic ideas further, to take account of changes in the conditions of the supply of savings. Hayek had also emphasised the need to replace the idea of a single interest rate by that of a structure of interest rates, leading in turn to such questions as the term-structure of interest rates and the relationship of interest to risk.[9] In addition, Hayek laid some stress on expectations as influencing present prices.[10]

Hayek's work had the advantages over that of Mises of being written with great clarity and of avoiding tendentious digressions, while sharing with Mises an extremely scholarly knowledge of Classical economics which would also have appealed to Robbins.

It is clear that Robbins absorbed little from Keynes's macro-economic writings in this period. This is perhaps surprising; Keynes's *Treatise*, with its two price levels, shows some remarkably Wicksellian elements, and might have provided some point of contact. But Keynes moved on from this work fairly quickly, returning in a sense to the Marshallian roots of his macroeconomics, while there seems little doubt that Robbins found some aspects of the book unattractive in any case. It seems highly likely that he shared Hayek's public irritation at a number of elements in the work – not only, on an analytical score, the strange treatment of profits, but also, on a more general scholarly plane, the 'reinvention' of well-known elements in the literature and the failure to take account of these having been worked out properly by a series of earlier authors.[11]

(ii) The model

The results of these diverse, but at that date predominantly Austrian, influences was Robbins's own trade cycle theory which, in Haberler's great 1937 survey, fitted effortlessly into the general 'Austrian' group.[12] His theory was set forth in two main publications, an article on the trade cycle and the book of which he was later so unnecessarily ashamed, *The Great Depression*. Robbins's starting point was that the correct theory of macroeconomic fluctuation must be a theory of the trade cycle. His analysis of the cycle was as follows. In the cycle, an exogenous increase in the money supply took the form of increased credit, made available to producers at a lower money rate of interest than previously. This made marginal investment profitable, producing a rise in the demand for investment goods, and labour was bid away from consumption goods industries to investment goods industries.[13] As new purchasing power worked its way through the system, spent by the labour which had experienced higher wages in being bid away to the investment goods industries, it raised the demand for consumer goods and restored the previous relative profitability of investment goods and consumer goods. This thus reversed the change produced by the initial monetary expansion because, as the relative profitability of consumer goods was restored, the consumer goods industries were able to bid for inputs. Labour costs thus rose generally. But the rise in labour costs upset the profitability calculations of the firms which had initially expanded and thus, it was argued, these firms would ask for yet more credit. But this, it was held, would require a proportionately larger credit expansion than previously, if it were met. The rate of interest then rose, because of competition for loans, coupled with the fact that the supply of loans was again becoming limited, through banking prudence. As a result, the marginal investment opportunities which seemed attractive at the start of the process became no longer profitable, and demand for investment goods fell again.

Forced saving was a part of this process. Initially it took place because the price of consumer goods rose, following a rise in the price of inputs for the consumer goods industries as the investment goods industries increased their demand for inputs. (What seems to have been envisaged is that the bidding for inputs by the expanding investment goods industries shifted the supply curves for consumer goods to the left, thus resulting in higher market clearing prices. It is also possible that, since markets were in disequilibrium, some consumer goods might have been in short supply.) The rise in the price of consumer goods reduced consumption of these goods, imposing forced saving on consumers, and thus resources were freed for the investment goods industries. But as the extra income generated by the investment boom started working through the system, and as demand for consumption goods consequently rose, the price of consumption goods rose still further, leading to an expansion of their output and a restoration of the previous level of output and consumption. Forced saving thus ceased. The investment boom, then no longer able to obtain command of extra resources, came to an end.

Monetary expansion, through a lowering of the money rate of interest, was thus the key to macroeconomic fluctuation; and because industrial costs, especially for long-lived investment, were sensitive to the rate of interest, the bulk of new borrowing would always be attracted into the investment goods sector when the rate of interest was lowered. A genuine boom could be created by an increase in *voluntary* saving; resources would be freed for the investment goods industries in this case, but the price of consumption goods would *fall*, whereas when the boom was caused by monetary expansion and depended, for resource-capture, upon *forced* saving, the prices of consumption goods would *rise*.[14]

The whole cycle would naturally give rise to unemployment. Although labour employed in the consumption goods industries could be attracted relatively easily into the investment goods industries in the initial stages of the boom, it would be difficult to reabsorb the labour back into the consumption goods industries, as initially promising investment projects were down-graded as the cycle progressed. As Haberler summarised this aspect of the matter:

In modern times especially, with inflexible wage systems and the various other obstructions represented by all kinds of State intervention, this process of shifting labour and other means of production is drawn out much longer than is necessary for purely technological reasons.[15]

The theory is not trivial. It can fit the facts of a number of episodes in twentieth-century economic history quite well, and Robbins was able to satisfy himself in *The Great Depression* that it fitted the facts of then recent history extremely well. Yet there are a number of serious difficulties with this theory.

Firstly, it is not able to explain the secondary phases of the depression,[16] nor the mechanics of recovery from depression. Secondly, the argument appears to involve a *non-sequitur* in arguing that firms will seek further credit when investment is decreasing in profitability;[17] and indeed this argument is contradicted by other parts of the analysis where it is argued that firms will only borrow with the prospect of increased profit, not because they are faced with an increased wage bill.[18] The reason why, if firms do borrow more, the increase in credit creation should be *proportionately greater* at later stages of the cycle is not spelt out. (However Tout and Hansen were able to offer the explanation that the acceleration in the rate of growth of money supply increase was due to a need to outweigh the increasing demand for consumption goods which had percolated through via wage payments.)[19] In both Hayek's and Robbins's accounts it is not really clear why the process should stop if money can go on being created.[20] (Wicksell had of course thought that it would not stop under these circumstances) although the argument seems to be that it is bank liquidity considerations which call a halt.[21]

The macroeconomic theories adopted by Robbins at this time were thus predominantly Austrian, in contrast to Keynes whose theories were, with the partial exception of the *Treatise*, Marshallian in origin. It is perhaps not surprising that bitter controversy should ensue;[22] the exchanges were acrimonious and, on the Cambridge side, patronising. Yet there were important similarities between the Austrian theory and Marshall's discussion of the monetary transmission mechanism, involving a lowering of the rate of interest, while Robbins's *The Great Depression*, like Keynes's *General Theory* of two years later, lays particular emphasis on entrepreneurial expectations.

(iii) The model applied

Robbins was able to relate the Austrian theory to the facts as he saw them.[23] In his trade cycle article he was satisfied that there was plenty of evidence that a boom in investment goods industries had been accompanied by credit expansion and that a crisis had occurred when the rate of interest had risen. He was less sure about the data on the prices of consumption goods, however. His *Great Depression* was then an exercise, with extensive research assistance (the book has 35 pages of statistical appendices), in applying the Mises–Hayek theory of the trade cycle to the years 1929–33. The problem, in his view, lay in credit expansion by the Federal Reserve in the years 1925–29, with the US credit expansion spreading throughout the whole world and affecting Germany.[24] The monetary expansion in the United States had continued even when gold had been flowing out, in a well-intentioned piece of central bank cooperation designed to take the pressure off sterling. The rate of interest changes, and the onset of the depression, had all occurred as predicted by the theory, and although wholesale prices had remained stable, this was due to exogenous productivity increase.

There were aggravating factors which made the depression worse; there was wartime dislocation and waste, the economy was losing its adaptability in both product and factor markets at a time when unprecedented readjustment was required, the World War One inflations had led to the break-up of international monetary unity and produced financial chaos, and the post-1925 industrial boom had left agriculture untouched.[25] But these were in the nature of complicating and predisposing factors rather than fundamental ones. The fundamental problems were monetary.

Robbins did not attach any importance to the idea that depression might be due to a deficiency of consumption demand, and he attacked both J. A. Hobson and Major Douglas on this matter.[26] In attacking Hobson he argued that, so long as increased investment was matched by increased voluntary saving, this was a cost-reducing activity which would actually help economic recovery. Douglas's thesis, that the sum of distributed incomes was insufficient to purchase current output, was dismissed for identifying as leakages sums which were actually part of the circular flow and necessary for the continuity of production – Robbins's residual wage-fund elements were perhaps responsible for his appreciation of circular flow.

(iv) The conditions for recovery – counter-cyclical policy

What, then, were the conditions for recovery?[27] The first essential was a return of business confidence; since the main threat to business confidence was fear of monetary disturbance, monetary stability was important here.[28] Secondly it was necessary to return to a régime of wage and price flexibility.[29] Though Robbins, even at his most austere, paid tribute to the value of trade unions in preventing exploitation, he believed that wage rigidity was a serious problem. Wage cuts were needed to restore profitability and to reduce excessive demand for consumption goods, financed by drawing on reserves as firms struggled to retain labour, so as to hasten the return to equilibrium of the relative positions of the investment and consumption goods sectors.[30] Rigid wages prevented labour markets clearing and encouraged capital consumption. They intensified depression and produced unemployment. In Robbins's view it was not 'the true humanitarian' who urged rigidity of wages.[31] With considerable moral courage, if not particularly good judgement, Robbins indicated that he was in favour of wage cuts rather than tariffs[32] as a way of increasing demand for domestic output, and that he was prepared to tolerate labour disputes rather than monetary instability.[33]

It is undoubtedly this position, at a time when wages were low, which later gave rise to Robbins's deep sense of shame noted in Chapter 2. But the analysis is neither trivial nor badly worked out, and it is unfortunate that the controversies of the time made it impossible for economists in London, Cambridge and Vienna to see what was potentially valuable in each other's position.

Even if conditions which Robbins regarded as necessary for recovery were met, there was bound to be an adjustment phase while depression worked through the system, with some unemployment of labour and capital. In the particular historical phase then operating, accidental factors were also significant. They included capital shortage in central Europe and Germany, the depressed state of agriculture because of technical improvement coinciding with poor demand for agricultural output resulting from manufacturing depression, cartels, trade unions, unemployment insurance (which produced wage rigidity), fraud, over-gearing of companies (partly because of the participation of banks and insurance companies who wanted a secondary market for the debt which they held), easy finance for crop restriction schemes, and the poor adaptability of the post-war economic structure. These all combined to make the depression worse and more prolonged than it otherwise would have been.[34] In addition, various well-intentioned activities – banks accommodating businesses which were in difficulties, government spending designed to stop the contraction of industries which should be allowed to contract, prudent investors waiting in hope of better investments[35] – all combined to prevent the system adjusting to a new equilibrium with the correct balance between the different sectors of the economy. There were also problems as countries deflated, in a struggle for international reserves, adversely affecting investment, while exchange fluctuations produced a lack of long run foreign investment – this also was deflationary.[36] But Robbins continued to maintain that the answer to depression did not lie in monetary expansion. It was monetary expansion which had brought about the main problem in the first place. Rather, he continued to maintain that the only safe monetary rule was to prevent depression in future by preventing all future booms from getting out of hand through early contraction to damp the upswing. 'It is agreed that to prevent depression the only effective method is to prevent the boom.'[37]

Given that exchange fluctuations were believed by Robbins to be deflationary, both because of the need for reserves and because of the interference with investments, it is not surprising that a second condition for recovery, apart from the removal of wage rigidity, was the reintroduction of the gold standard. Robbins argued that there was a need for unification of monetary policies in different countries through adoption of the Gold Bullion standard, with countries following the so-called 'rules of the game' in which gold losses across the exchanges necessitated monetary contraction at home.[38] Bank credit could still misbehave under such a system, but the damage would be limited compared with what could occur under a paper standard. It is perhaps rather surprising, in view of the blame he attached to the policy of the Federal Reserve under the Gold Standard, that Robbins should have shown such faith in the Gold Standard at this time, but the problem in the previous episode, he believed, lay in the fact that the Federal Reserve had not adhered to the rules of the game. Indeed he objected strongly to those who were urging the use of a managed money supply, because such management would make it difficult to operate the Gold Standard according to the rules of the game – such urging had led to admiration of the Federal Reserve's policy at the precise time when it was, in Robbins's view, sowing the seeds of the slump by ignoring those rules.[39]

It is then hardly surprising that Robbins strongly and publicly opposed proposals for monetary reflation.[40] The *Economist* had recommended that the government should pursue monetary reflation, raising the level of sterling wholesale prices by 30 per cent. While Robbins agreed that if prices did not rise there could be defaults and bankruptcies, and that a 1929 level debt burden would be much less onerous, he held that pushing the price level up could not be done without involving the Austrian trade cycle problem – it would lead to a level of investment spending which would later prove to be unprofitable. Monetary expansion would merely delay the adjustment which was necessary to achieve a return to equilibrium. Even when his attitude towards aggregate demand expansion had relaxed slightly, as it did later on, and he was prepared to concede that government expansion financed by borrowing might be a defensible course, he was still worried that there could be an adverse effect on the gilts market and on confidence,[41] and also feared that unless expansion in different countries was in step there could be international complications.[42]

There was another factor which was influencing Robbins's opposition to reflation; like the Classical economists before him, he was very concerned at the social threat which could be posed by inflation.[43] It was not just that inflation could upset exchange stability; nor was it the labour troubles, speculative booms, and the implied discriminatory capital levy on holders of fixed interest securities, which he feared most.[44] Rather, as he made clear in his criticisms of Major Douglas, he was fearful of the possibility of an inflation on the scale of that experienced by Germany in 1923; and he correctly linked the rise of the Nazis to this episode.[45] Indeed he was quite favourably disposed to the idea of holding the money suply *fixed*, so that as productivity rose the general price level *fell*, sharing the benefit of rising productivity with fixed income receivers.[46] Even after World War Two he seems to have been reluctant to discard entirely such an idea.[47]

(v) The role of government

The lessons to be drawn from the rise of the Nazis by an observer in the 1930s, especially by as acute an observer as Robbins, were indeed deeply worrying; and this no doubt helps to explain why he expressed concern about the growing size of the public sector which was in danger of taking over as the pace-maker of the entire economic system as public expenditure rose faster than national income.[48]

Moreover he was unconvinced about the merits of balancing the budget over the cycle as compared with balancing it on an annual basis, even as late as 1939. Firstly, he argued that it was not clear that the cycle itself was independent of policy. Secondly, he argued that the accumulation of a surplus in a boom, for spending in depression, might have unintended monetary effects. In particular (and this was a perfectly valid point neglected by many of those on the other side of the debate), if the surplus were invested in gilt edged, this would keep down the rate of interest in the boom while realisation of the securities in the slump would raise the rate of interest.[49]

His 1939 position did however represent some marginal retreat from the outright opposition to public investment expressed in *The Great Depression*. In this, basing himself very probably on information from Hayek, Robbins argued that public investment in Germany and Central Europe had produced a capital shortage, and that this itself had in fact worsened the economic situation. In terms of the Austrian theory of the trade cycle, this was a perfectly rational argument; if the characteristic feature of a monetary boom was insufficient *voluntary* saving, and the imposition of forced saving via price level changes, as Robbins believed, then anything which swallowed up voluntarily accumulated funds available for investment and used them in the unproductive public sector was actually harmful to macroeconomic stability.[50]

Governments, in fact, had taken on more than they were capable of performing, and they should draw back. It was not just that deficit budgeting and public works programmes had an inflationary tendency, leading to a subsequent deflationary collapse;[51] it was that governments had taken it upon themselves to protect businesses against the consequences of their own mistakes, thus preventing the economic system righting itself, and making disequilibrium worse.[52]

In particular, he was very hostile to the sort of activity associated in the United States with the National Recovery Administration, with its output restrictions and officially sponsored cartels.[53] These schemes produced higher costs, and smaller outputs, than would otherwise be the case and prevented adaptation of the economic system to shifts in demand, while turning the terms of trade against the rest of the community. They intensified depression, particularly as they were usually associated with protection.[54]

A government's correct course, Robbins held, was to pursue policies of monetary management which were counter-cyclical, choking off a boom with a rising rate of interest.[55] But this prescription raised the problem of the service charge on public debt. High interest rates on debt constituted a problem about which Robbins indeed showed some concern. While he accepted the 'Keynesian' argument that debt creation did not transfer the burden forward to future generations, because the resources were used in the present, he argued, like the Classical economists, that debt-service taxation could lead to capital export unless this was prevented by exchange control as in Nazi Germany.[56] Moreover he argued, like David Hume, that high marginal rates of taxation to pay for the debt service involved transfers to the *rentier* class and a dampening of enterprise. Nor was there any solution to the burden to be found in reducing the real value of the debt by generating inflation.[57] Robbins's very fundamental fears about the social damage which this could cause have already been noted. Such a course was a prescription for labour troubles, speculative booms and collapses; it was also, in effect, a discriminatory capital levy on those who held consols, and it would increase debt-service charges on short run debt.

Although the Austrian view of the world discussed so far remained Robbins's basic intellectual position on macroeconomic management until the war, it would be misleading to neglect the fact that there were clear signs of some shift in his position in the late 1930s, as manifested in his *Economic Basis of Class Conflict* in particular. While he was still hesitant about anti-depression public expenditure, and considered that government borrowing should be an emergency measure, he recognised that 'crowding-out' would not be a problem in a slump. Indeed he acknowledged the validity of A. L. Bowley's suggestion of concentrating public investment in depression, though warning that there were difficulties in predicting a slump and further difficulties in cutting off public investment in a boom.[58] Moreover he explicitly repudiated the 'Treasury View'[59] and (in work originally appearing in *Lloyds Bank Review* 1938) he explored the conditions for successful deficit finance.[60] These were the existence of excess capacity, the absence of implementation lags, the absence of crowding-out, and the avoidance of adverse effects on confidence.

While he held that the multiplier as a whole was, like the Fisher equation, a truism, he believed that it was advisable to distinguish the 'multiplier' effects of different forms of government expenditure and to concentrate this where excess capacity existed, so as to produce a rise in real reather than merely money income.[61] It was thus better to increase expenditure on investment goods and armaments.[62] However, the effects on business expectations would be limited because businessmen would take account of the probable duration of the expenditure as well as of the amount.[63]

It is thus possible to see Robbins moving away from the theoretically consistent but rather intransigent position of *The Great Depression* in the late 1930s, even before he entered government service and was exposed to the sustained influences of Keynes and, perhaps more importantly, of Keynes's disciples. These, building on changes which were already taking place in Robbins's position, produced some significant changes of emphasis in his post-war macroeconomic writings.[64] At the same time, as will be indicated, the importance of these changes should not be exaggerated.

3. POST-WAR

(i) A surrender to Keynesianism?

The view has been propagated – perhaps most of all by Robbins himself – that he underwent a fundamental change of thinking on macroeconomic matters during the war.

> I had become the slave of theoretical constructions which, if not intrinsically invalid as regards logical consistency, were inappropriate to the total situation which had then developed and which therefore misled my judgement. I realised that these constructions led to conclusions which were highly unpalatable as regards practical action. But I was convinced that they were valid and that therefore it was my duty to base recommendations as regards policy upon them. There was a touch of the Nonconformist conscience here.[65]

Of his conflict with Keynes on these matters, Robbins wrote:

I shall always regard this aspect of my dispute with Keynes as the greatest mistake of my professional career, and the book, *The Great Depression*, which I subsequently wrote, partly in justification of this attitude, as something which I would willingly see forgotten.[66]

During his wartime service, Robbins became convinced that governments *should* act counter-cyclically,[67] and he willingly forwarded Meade's internal paper which led to the 1944 White Paper on Employment Policy.[68] He now conceded that his

earlier diagnosis of the causes of the Great Depression had missed the mark in not recognising sufficiently the paramount role played by the catastrophic contraction of incomes brought about by the deflation due to the volatility of the then existing credit mechanism; and I had been impressed by the disappearance of mass unemployment under the impact of rearmament and war expenditure.[69]

When he came to deliver the 1947 Marshall Lectures, he paid tribute to Keynes (no doubt before an appreciative audience) and averred that he had changed his mind.[70] As he was later to write:

as a result of reflection on the events of the '30s, I had also come to realise that the forces tending to spontaneously beneficial adjustment in the sphere of relative demand and supply in a decentralised system could not be relied upon to operate so well in the sphere of aggregate income and expenditure without supplementary contrivance, both in the fiscal and the monetary spheres.[71]

The reader may feel that there was no need for such elaborate contrition, at least on the analytical score. Indeed, when so much of Robbins's pre-war analysis was persuasively argued, in the context moreover of an open economy with all the complex international ramifications, it is hard to regard the version of what 'went wrong' with economics in the 1930s, which was served up to students in the 1950s, as anything but puerile.

But examination of the content of Robbins's post-war writings on macroeconomics reveals that, after all, the shift in position was very much less than the preceding quotations might have indicated, in any case. Even in his 1947 Marshall Lectures the surrender to Keynes is strictly qualified.[72] Although it is perfectly true that Robbins supported Keynes's *How to Pay for the War* proposals, this hardly amounted to wholesale conversion to Keynesianism; deferred pay, as a way of countering an excess aggregate demand, did not go very far along the Keynesian road.[73] While Robbins continued to acknowledge his inter-war error, he also denied that the post-war situation represented any parallel with the pre-war one.[74] His review of Harrod's biography of Keynes made it quite clear that Robbins's surrender to Keynesianism was strictly qualified.[75] He was sceptical of the idea that shifts in savings and investment functions caused depressions;[76] and he was scathingly critical of those who believed that aggregate demand should be run at such a high level, in the interests of full employment, that there was perpetual excess demand in the labour market.[77] Indeed he was to state quite explicitly that he had not in fact become a Keynesian.

> It would not be true to say that then [during war service], or at any subsequent period, I had become a Keynesian in the sense of accepting *au pied de la lettre* all the analytical propositions of the *General Theory*. Although I had greatly benefitted by the intellectual shake-up involved in studying them, I found many that were confused and even wrong-headed in their formulation and much that was cogent in the arguments of some of their critics – Dennis Robertson for instance.[78]

Clearly this fell some way short of a Canossa-like obeisance. Indeed, if we compare *The Great Depression* with publications by Robbins in 1958 and 1974 on macroeconomic matters, not *much* has really changed except the jettisoning of the precise Austrian material about the relative prices and profitability of investment goods and consumption goods.[79] In the post-war material there is no explicit sign of the Mises–Hayek trade cycle theory. However the influences of Austrian general equilibrium are still perceptible in Robbins's House of Lords speeches.[80] and it would be a mistake to think that the post-war years saw any wholesale jettisoning by Robbins of his intellectual equipment.

In particular, although when we look at Robbins's citations in the post-war years we find acknowledgements of the work of Dow,[81] Sayers and Manning Dacey,[82] the influence of Wicksell is still very much in evidence (not least in Robbins's Memorandum to the Radcliffe Committee)[83] and it was indeed explicitly acknowledged in his evidence to Radcliffe.[84] Perhaps it would be true to say that while the explicitly Austrian influences are no longer evident, the sources for the Austrians – the Classical economic writings on money, and Wicksell (who, receiving Austrian influences himself, was later to be one of Hayek's sources) – are more in evidence.[85]

Unlike a number of his contemporaries in the 1950s, Robbins continued to emphasise that problems of monetary policy and aggregate expenditure must be viewed in the context of an open economy with the balance of payments acting as a necessary constraint on the inflation of aggregate demand domestically, although less constrained than under the gold standard,[86] a return to which Robbins, in contrast to his 1930s writings, did not now favour.[87]

(ii) Full employment and wage inflation

Insistence upon the problems of an open economy was part of his strongly-felt and strongly-worded critique of Beveridge's proposals for permanent excess labour-market demand.[88] This would mean, Robbins argued, permanent labour market inflation, and interference with proper labour market search, and it would cause an increase in imports, a diversion of exports to the home market, a loss of competitiveness and a deterioration in the balance of payments.

More generally, Robbins argued that the concept of full employment was itself ambiguous and that the public commitment to it had elevated expectations in the press. It was necessary to have some percentage of unemployment because of labour market turnover (as Keynes and indeed Beveridge had recognised). The commitment to maintain high levels of employment involved no reference to the rate of wages, yet if wage inflation was running ahead of the rate of productivity increase, unemployment must necessarily result unless there were monetary expansion.[89] Surely, Robbins asked, the commitment to full employment should not include accepting whatever degree of price inflation was necessary to validate wage inflation. It was not the duty of government to underwrite wage inflation with monetary expansion; trade unions could choose higher wage inflation but at the cost of unemployment.[90] We were, he believed, still so mesmerised by the 1930s that we had a permanent tendency to excess aggregate expenditure. In fact, however, the 1944 White Paper had not meant to guarantee full employment if wage inflation was running ahead of the rate of productivity increase;[91] and we now had a level of employment so 'full' that it went beyond what Keynes (and even Beveridge) thought possible and desirable.[92]

Robbins was particularly concerned about labour-market tightness – he advocated bringing in foreign labour for the mines[93] – and about wage inflation. Wage inflation, to which nationalised industries were particularly vulnerable, led to cost inflation and was one cause of price inflation.[94] It harmed exports and adversely affected those on fixed incomes, providing a disincentive to save.[95]

However, this wage inflation was critically dependent upon demand inflation.[96] Even if trade unions sought higher wages, validation through monetary expansion was required if this pressure was to lead to general inflation.[97] Neither demand nor cost inflation could operate without inflation of the credit base.[98] While he repudiated Friedman's position that *all* inflation was due to monetary influences, he stressed the permissive nature of monetary expansion.[99] 'Sociological' inflationary forces could not work without the cooperation of monetary expansion.[100]

He did not, however, completely disregard such forces. In part they were simply a response to inflation; for instance, with a wage structure upset by inflation, trade unions were bound to respond.[101] But there might also be an actual deterioration in the quality of trade union leadership[102] – Robbins clearly regarded the trade unions as a cause of wage inflation.[103] While they had limited scope for redistribution,[104] they possessed substantial market power and, he believed, their immunities should be removed, making them subject to the law like other monopolies.[105]

Government as an employer should stand firm against trade union activity. Subsidies were an expensive and disequilibrium-perpetuating anti-inflationary administrative device;[106] but the government as employer ought to have 'a permanent incomes policy'.[107]

Robbins did not however believe that prices and incomes policy in a more general sense had any significant role to play.[108] Price control was dismissed very swiftly; except in cases of obvious monopoly, and as a political device to achieve acceptance of an incomes policy, it had little to recommend it.[109] But if the money supply was under control, neither price nor income control would be necessary.[110] Public opinion was correct to resist incomes policy. It was important not to upset an historically evolved system of collective bargaining.[111] Unfortunately, despite these problems, such a policy appealed particularly to those sections of the population not affected by it: 'it smacks of no-nonsense action, strong government, a firm hand at the wheel and such-like affectively toned slogans'.[112] Robbins was a little sarcastic at the expense of the enthusiasts for such a policy.

> Our little world of *soi-disant* experts arouse in people a feeling of contempt for the policies of financial prudence and the allegedly baneful influence of the Treasury and the Bank of England which, they seem to think, are the chief obstacles to limitless prosperity. If you remonstrate with them gently, and remind them that hitherto in world history beyond a certain point high-pressure spending has always led to inflation and trouble with balances of payments, the reply is always, 'Oh, well, we need an incomes policy'.[113]

Robbins's objections to an incomes policy were substantial. Firstly, such a policy involved a fundamental interference with free allocation and raised questions about its compatibility with a free society.[114] Secondly, there was the sheer difficulty in judging appropriate levels of wage increase without market indications;[115] and there was the problem of 'relativities'.[116] Thirdly, such a policy bred 'a sense of injustice and resentment',[117] and these difficulties led to demands for limitations of dividends at a time when an increase in investment was desirable.[118] Fourthly, the policy was a stimulus to dishonesty[119] as people sought to evade it,[120] having a corrupting influence on firms[121] and leading to reclassification of jobs and the arrangement of side benefits while interfering with management. Further, if price control were coupled with this, it led to quality variation, administrative problems, queues, shortages and accumulation of unspent balances.[122]

However Robbins always stopped short of saying that an incomes policy was *impossible*. He was prepared to concede that it could be useful as a cushion to prevent an undue rise in unemployment when aggregate expenditure was checked (in order to slow inflation); wage claims, if unchecked, would be based upon expectations adapted to the previous high levels of monetary inflation, and they would generate significant increases in unemployment if 'disinflation' were not accompanied by some kind of incomes policy.[123] But such a policy was a short-term palliative at best.[124] Even here it was likely to generate divisions between the various groups affected, and end in failure.[125]

Robbins also emphasised that this use of incomes policy as a cushion could only be defended if it were not being undermined by lax monetary and fiscal policy.[126] Yet, as he pointed out, the government in the years 1970–74 both attempted to use incomes policies *and* pursued monetary inflation.[127] This was extremely foolish.[128] But even without this contradiction, a workable policy was not likely to be found.[129]

(iii) The effects of inflation

Robbins's negative attitude to incomes policies certainly did not arise because he was sanguine about inflation. He was as opposed to it as in the pre-war period. Indeed, in his 1951 Stamp Lecture, at a time when inflation was very low when compared with subsequent experiences, he argued that the need to check it was paramount.[130] Inflation was, he held, nothing less than a danger to society. There are indeed signs in Robbins's speeches in the Lords during the 1970s that he became really very alarmed.[131] In 1975, for instance, he told their Lordships:

> We are undergoing a process of inflation unprecedented in our peace-time history, and if it goes on at the present rate undoubtedly it will eventually tear our society apart.[132]

Democracy and decency were both incompatible with large inflations.[133] They had an adverse effect on 'culture', including in this the universities[134] whose planning was seriously affected by instability in the value of money.[135] Inflation was an *ethical* evil which harmed fixed income receivers,[136] involved governments in fraudulent reduction in the real rate of interest paid on its debt, and offered prospects of quick gains which fostered corruption and social divisiveness. It led to a 'lowering of public and private morale'.[137]

Its directly economic effects, apart from the impoverishment of those on fixed incomes, involved distortion of production

planning, a cumulative inadequacy of working capital, class
conflict, violent labour disputes, an adverse current account and
the danger of capital flight.[138] There was also the danger of a flight
from money into goods[139] and into equities and property.[140]

The point about working capital is an interesting one. Although
it may have derived in part from Robbins's own experience in
business, perception of the problem probably originated in
Hayek's discussion in *Prices and Production*[141] – yet another sign
that Robbins had not jettisoned entirely his pre-war apparatus.
The argument was that, with historical cost depreciation,
companies would make insufficient provision for depreciation
and run short of working capital as inflation proceeded.[142] In
addition, cost inflation harmed industry by squeezing profits and
reducing funds for investment.[143] The squeeze on company
liquidity meant that any attempt to check inflation was likely to
precipitate bankruptcies.[144]

In such a setting, tax evasion, fraudulent selling and wild
speculation in real estate became the order of the day.[145] Such a
development was not favourable to long-run economic growth,
let alone democratic stability, and it made the whole economic
structure vulnerable if there was any attempt to check inflation.[146]

Price stability had substantial advantages. Even though Robbins
seems to have decided that it was better to have a stable rather
than a falling price level with increasing productivity, in the years
after the war, it is clear that he still did not regard a falling price
level as out of the question.[147] It is then hardly surprising that he
was not in favour, unlike a number of economists in the 1950s, of
planned steady inflation.[148] Businessmen, Robbins observed, were
typically inflationists.

> But the trouble nowadays with some economists is that they
> too have become inflationists and, eschewing the traditional
> objective of stable money, think that they can determine by
> mathematics optimal rates of robbing the widows, orphans and
> other owners of fixed interest securities.[149]

Rates of inflation of between $1\frac{1}{2}$ and 3 per cent might be bearable,
at least for short periods;[150] but while it was possible to acquiesce
in past inflation, acquiescence in its continuation was quite
another matter.[151] In any case it would lose its inflationary
stimulus. Expectations adapt and thus inflation ceases to stimulate

the economy unless it is continuously running ahead of the adaptation of expectations, a prospect which gives rise to threats to social stability.[152] But factor rewards had to be adjusted for inflation, for both labour supply and saving would be affected by it.[153] It was also necessary to compensate pensioners, for electoral purposes. But the very process of compensation removed the alleged benefits of inflation – there would be no forced saving and no increase in profit margins.[154] The more people that were protected against inflation, the less its beneficial results. At the same time, indexation would actually make inflation harder to stop because it involved gearing the whole economic system into the inflationary process.[155]

It should not be thought from all this that Robbins was dismissive of the benefits of economic growth. On the contrary he was highly critical of the anti-growth economists,[156] as was indicated in Chapter 5. But he simply did not accept that inflation was the way to generate real growth.

Events were to bear him out. The economy moved from inflation with a degree of real growth to what became known as 'stagflation'. Robbins anticipated the emergence of this, which he believed was due to the attempts of firms to maintain solvency at all costs when faced with a macroeconomic check to inflation while wage costs continued to rise.[157]

(iv) Aggregate demand and inflation

The wage inflation itself was, however, only a subsidiary cause of inflation. The major factor to which Robbins ascribed inflation was excessive aggregate demand caused by monetary expansion.[158] This was coupled with a public sector borrowing requirement, an occasionally undervalued exchange rate and wage inflation. When demand inflation was checked, the danger of cost inflation then appeared.[159] However cost inflation, as already noted, required monetary validation if it were to continue.[160] Inflation was due to human action – 'it is not the product of some mysterious Zeitgeist'.[161] It was unavoidable in wartime when,[162] indeed, 'all the theoretical conditions necessary for a cumulative Wicksellian process' were present.[163]

The reference to Wicksell here is interesting. Robbins's pre-war macroeconomic theory can often be detected lurking behind his statements on inflation in the post-war period, and it is noticeable that one of the causes of inflation which he mentioned in his 1974 Wincott Memorial Lecture was credit creation unmatched by saving, with the rate of interest less than the rate of profit.[164]

He was particularly scathing about the post-war 'cheap money' policy. Despite his own connections with Dalton, he used descriptions such as 'overt folly' and 'preposterous' in connection with it.[165] This again takes us back to his Austrian pre-war theory with concern over credit extension unmatched by voluntary saving. Because of adaptive expectations, it was unlikely that forced saving could fill the gap, even had that been satisfactory.[166] But there was a shortage of voluntary savings partly brought about by taxation[167] (and the resulting reduction in investment was not offset by government investment in human capital), partly brought about by the effects of inflation in undermining saving,[168] and partly due to the effects of income redistribution.[169] Moreover what Robbins regarded as double taxation of saving (although it is not entirely clear whether he had in mind Mill's or Meade's version of this concept) discriminated against saving.[170]

The cheap money policy also encouraged spending out of capital,[171] thus adding to the excess aggregate demand which Robbins believed to be at the root of inflation.[172] Inflation could not cease if expenditure outran production.[173] Although he occasionally conceded that demand inflation at low rates might stimulate output and even investment,[174] the whole thrust of Robbins's argument is that excess aggregate demand must be controlled. Unfortunately, national monetary autonomy actually made it easier for governments to permit excess absorption.[175] Unfortunately, too, Keynes had failed to foresee the possibilities of inflationary finance: 'He was temperamentally inclined to underestimate the probability of inflation.'[176]

It was not just a monetary problem however. Robbins wanted to emphasise that there had been a failure to control aggregate expenditure altogether, rather than a failure merely to control the money supply.[177] Budget deficits produced demand inflation,[178] as well as raising the danger of monetary expansion.[179]

The problem of excess aggregate demand was connected with the very high level of public expenditure. Although Robbins recognised that there were very considerable difficulties in the way of reducing public expenditure, he believed that a fundamental reappraisal was required[180] and that it was necessary to reduce both public sector current and public sector capital expenditures.[181]

Even apart from the problem of excess aggregate demand, the very high level of taxation magnified dead-weight problems and affected incentives.[182]

Given Robbins's concerns about inflation and public sector deficits, it is hardly surprising that he should have taken an extremely hostile view both of the 1963–4 Maudling boom[183] and of the Heath–Barber deficit episodes.[184] He was scathing about the belief, apparently underlying the first of these, that monetary expansion could produce a real income growth; he believed that the second episode, involving a public sector deficit on a scale without precedent in peacetime, combined utterly contradictory policies in that government was trying to restrain inflation through an incomes policy while inflating the money supply with abandon. Inflation control was difficult enough, in all conscience, because of the political difficulties of implementing an inflation policy,[185] especially if governments failed to act at an early stage when control would be easier.[186]

(v) Monetary and fiscal policy

In this connection it should be stressed that although, as will be made clearer below, Robbins laid considerable emphasis upon monetary policy in the face of a prevailing psuedo-Keynesian orthodoxy which regarded it as derisory, he emphasised throughout the post-war period that fiscal policy was also important.[187] Aggregate expenditure should be controlled through a *combination* of fiscal and monetary policy. His pressure for a revival of monetary policy in the post-war years did not involve the advocacy of a neglect of stabilising fiscal policy.[188] Both monetary *and* fiscal policy were necessary.[189] Robbins insisted that he certainly was not advocating sole reliance on monetary policy[190] and he seems to have been enraged by his treatment by some members of the Radcliffe Committee (though he phrased his objections with characteristic courtesy),[191] who seem to have misunderstood this point despite the fact that Robbins's Memorandum was clear enough in its advocacy of *both* forms of policy. Robbins had indeed supported the idea of automatic stabilisation in his 1947 Marshall Lectures[192] and in that year, and again in 1949 and 1953, he advocated the use of a budget surplus to counter inflationary pressure – monetary policy on its own would have required too high a rate of interest.[193] He suggested using purchase tax increases, coupled with a promise of reduced rates later, as a way of restraining expenditure.[194] He was quite prepared to advocate taxation to restrict excessive consumer demand,[195] and although he saw purchase tax as having limitations, he believed the idea of a general sales tax, as well as Meade's proposal for variable National Insurance contributions, to be promising.[196]

However, fiscal policy could not be used on its own – indeed Robbins did not accept the basic Mundell assumption that monetary and fiscal policy were independent.[197] Fiscal policy could not be used *on its own* for controlling inflation if only because of inadequate and unreliable data – the full employment budget was simply a fiction.[198] In *depression*, it was true, it was perfectly possible to *increase* public investment. But it was difficult to *reduce* public investment as a means of controlling *inflation*, because there would be no parallel cut in private investment.[199] Indeed, even direct controls over private investment, which were beyond the scope of normal fiscal policy, were likely to be inadequate. Moreover, fiscal policy had no influence on wage inflation. There were in any case political obstacles to the use of budgetary policy for counter-cyclical purposes.[200] Fiscal policy was necessary; but it was unsuitable for fine-tuning. This did not mean that we should abandon fiscal policy. It simply meant that we should couple it with monetary policy.[201]

For in a world with rigidities, it was not possible to rely on fiscal policy alone.[202] In any case, because of the lags in its operation, it was unlikely to be a particularly reliable instrument of sensitive control.[203] Certainly, the use of fiscal instruments did not allow governments to ignore monetary policy altogether, particularly where there was an exchange rate to defend.[204] Monetary policy had been 'foolishly neglected' in the years after the war:[205]

> we have been attempting to drive our car through this difficult post-war country with the steering gear out of action, the wheels lashed rigidly in one direction, our only means of equilibration an occasional stop, every few months, for the wheels to be unlashed and turned at another angle – while ministers stand on the roof and deliver salutary exortations.[206]

Or as Robbins put it elsewhere:

The years since the war have witnessed a gigantic experiment, so to speak, in fiscal control applied, if not in isolation (for there have been many of the direct war-time controls in operation too) at least without recourse to the more old fashioned instruments of monetary policy. In a period in which the scarcity of capital has been such as to involve rates of return on investment not known since the First World War, we have seen important governments attempt to control inflation, with interest rates not much higher than the all-time lows of the nineties and the whole apparatus of money supply avowedly passive to the so-called needs of trade and public finance.[207]

(vi) The importance of monetary policy

Against this neglect of monetary policy, Robbins fought whole-heartedly.[208] In his view 'continuous control of the credit base' was 'absolutely indispensable'.[209] Monetary policy had, indeed, significant advantages as a policy tool. It did not depend on the accuracy of 'global statistics' required by fiscal policy, it covered the whole field of expenditure, not just special parts of it, it was flexible and easily altered with changing circumstances, and it was not subject to overt political interference.[210] It was not, it was true, capable of controlling velocity (or demand for balances) but 'both analysis and experience go to show that it [monetary policy] is quite sufficient, if properly exercised, to control the volume of expenditure – at any rate in an *upward* direction'.[211]

Thus Robbins was anxious for a revival of monetary policy during the post-war years,[212] although he emphasised that it should be in conjunction with fiscal policy. Robbins observed: 'Here I part company with extreme monetarists.'[213] As he assured Lord Boyle in the House of Lords: 'I am not a Friedmanite monetarist. I do not believe in tying one arm behind my back when coping either with inflation or deflation.'[214]

While, as Robbins attempted to make clear to the Radcliffe Committee, he would not have used monetary policy *exclusively* at any time in the period since the war,[215] he did believe that there was a need for fast and flexible use of monetary policy.[216] Its limited use had been ineffective in the preceding years, at least in the initial stages, partly because the fiscal stimulus to investment was pulling against it, and partly because monetary measures, instead of being used quickly, were adopted too late and on too

small a scale.[217] There was also the particular problem that the
authorities put a higher priority on stabilisation of the gilt-edged
market than on using monetary policy for macroeconomic
stabilisation,[218] a point which will be considered further below.
But nonetheless Robbins continued to insist, in the face of then
orthodox opinion, on the importance of monetary policy. What he
was arguing seems eminently sensible and reasonable now, but in
the 1950s, when the consensus was that money did not even
matter – and/or could not be defined, and/or could not be
controlled, and/or was endogenous – it was a lonely position and
one which Robbins was made to feel acutely.[219]

(vii) The critique of Radcliffe and the restatement of monetary control theory

It is thus hardly surprising that Robbins was completely opposed
to the report of the Radcliffe Committee, which not only endorsed
the 1950s orthodoxies but pushed them to new extremes.

Robbins attached considerable importance to his critique of
Radcliffe.[220] His Memorandum to the Committee had been part of
an attempt to reassert the importance of monetary policy;[221] and
he was naturally disappointed at the path which the committee
took. As already noted, he was also not very happy about his
examination by the committee.[222] The situation may have
been complicated by Robbins's non-deterministic methodological
position;[223] this made him sceptical about prediction and about
hard and fast economic rules, so that his answers to the questions
could have been interpreted as indicating an unwillingness to
advance a clear theoretical position.

The essence of his critique of the committee involved two main
points: firstly, he was critical of Radcliffe's attempt to substitute
'liquidity' for money; secondly, he was critical of the committee's
emphasis on control of the rate of interest rather than of the credit
base.[224]

Robbins recognised the existence of the Treasury Bill problem –
if open market operations were used to reduce the liquidity of the
banking system, banks could restore liquidity by running off
Treasury Bills so that the government was then forced to borrow
from the Bank of England, leading in turn to an increase in
bankers' deposits.[225] But he complained that the committee had
not thence concluded that control of the banking system was now

different; it had concluded instead that liquidity of the economic system as a whole was what mattered. Here, the committee were guilty of a fallacy of composition from the individual to the economy.[226] Not *everybody* could realise their assets at once, and the extent to which they could do so depended on '*the availability of liquidity in a monetary form*'. Of course Robbins recognised that the demand for money is affected by the availability of easily marketable securities; but he insisted that the distinction between money and securities was real and important.

> Needless to say, if the supply of money varies, there are likely to follow variations of interest rates which will affect in different degrees the capital values and hence the liquidity of various assets; and this in turn will affect the demand for money. But in the last analysis it is the variation in the credit base which is the causal factor. It is the credit base, moreover, which is most accessible to direct control.[227]

The committee had even committed itself to the view that there was no upper limit to velocity of circulation. While Robbins was prepared to concede that there was no fixed demand function for money 'regardless of time and place' because the demand could be affected by the rate of interest, expectations, development of the means of payment, inflation and trade credit, he pointed out that in the short run there must be some upper limit to velocity changes and that, moreover, people were likely to have desired balance levels.[228] Radcliffe's view was 'highly implausible'. In fact, velocity was substantially stable in the short run.[229] People might economise on balances, but this could not be a process without limit.[230] In Robbins's view, historical evidence supported the idea that monetary policy was effective, at least as a brake, and he thought that the committee displayed a 'curious reserve' about the effects of the 1957 credit squeeze.[231]

There is no doubt that Robbins's long-standing concern about inflation, already noted, lay behind his hostility to the 'liquidity' aspect of the committee's report. It is no coincidence that he noted that those responsible for the German inflation in 1923 took the attitude that the money supply was endogenous.[232]

On the matter of the rate of interest, Robbins accepted what the committee said about a blunting of the rate's effects through taxation and the operation of the nationalised industries.[233] But he

argued that the rate of interest could be supplemented by credit
rationing where business concerns were insensitive to the cost of
credit. He also believed that the committee had dismissed
Hawtrey's work, on the effects of the rate of interest on stocks, in
too cavalier a manner,[234] and he argued also that the rate of
interest affected the timing of investment as well as producing
wealth effects.[235]

Robbins realised that it was not possible both to support the
gilt-edged market and to have monetary control;[236] but he believed
that the committee had been far too concerned about the possible
effects of monetary policy on market institutions. Apart from
taking the view that the well-being of such institutions was not a
significant argument in the social welfare function, Robbins
thought that it was not really plausible that these institutions
were so fragile that they could not withstand the effective
operation of monetary policy.[237]

Robbins was not alone in criticising the Radcliffe Committee.
Dennis Robertson pointed to a double confusion in the report,
between planned and realised spending, and between what an
individual and what the community as a whole could do in the
realisation of liquid assets, a confusion inherent in the Committee's
strange idea of infinite velocity. Moreover it was, Robertson said, *à
propos* the committee's discussion of interest, really an empirical
matter whether, with a rise in the rate of interest, capital loss
discourages potential lenders more than the extra rate of interest
encourages other people to lend. But although there were critiques
other than Robbins's, and although many of them were extremely
well argued, the Radcliffe Report succeeded in becoming the
established orthodoxy, at least in Britain, until the monetary
inflations of the early 1970s convinced almost all economists that
money, after all, did matter.[238]

At no stage did Robbins contend that monetary policy was
without problems. The Treasury Bill problem has already been
mentioned. This was something to which he returned on a
number of occasions, after it had been pointed out by Sayers and
Manning Dacey.[239] Treasury Bills had effectively become liquid,
and control of their issue was not under the Bank of England.
This he recognised. But the answer to such a problem lay, not in
the abandonment of monetary policy, but in the replacement of
Treasury Bills by longer-dated securities to the point where the
money supply was again under the control of the Bank.[240] This

process, referred to as 'funding', could undoubtedly encounter difficulties because of the effects on the structure of interest rates. It would however be easier if the market were confident about the future purchasing power of money.[241] Robbins thought the committee 'very Laodicean' about this possibility.[242] A ceiling on advances was one possibility, but such limitations on bank deposit growth would have an unequal effect on different banks, depending on past lending, it would prevent financial competition, and it represented dealing with symptoms rather than the underlying cause.[243] Special deposits were a more attractive solution although these should not be a permanent substitute for funding.[244] Robbins recognised that, faced with a choice, the Treasury had a preference for stabilisation of the rate of interest, rather than monetary control, because this would reduce the interest charges due on government and nationalised industry debt.[245] But he did not regard this as being an overriding consideration.

What was critical was control of what Robbins referred to as the 'credit base'.[246] At times, Robbins appeared reluctant to define the constituents of this base; it was clear that it included notes[247] and some deposits,[248] but Robbins seemed almost unwilling to be tied to a particular definition. However, it emerges from his House of Lords speeches that he meant (sterling) M_3.[249]

Control of this was vital because the history of inflations did not encourage the idea that the money supply was a function of the price level.[250] On the contrary, the immediate determinant of the price level, and of the general level of activity, was the volume of expenditure, which depended on the money supply, trade credit and money substitutes. Thus the money supply was certainly a determinant of the price level. Robbins was convinced, from his knowledge of the Currency and Banking controversy, that the idea that the money supply depended on the price level could not be sustained.[251]

It was better to control the money supply than to attempt to control the structure of interest rates.[252] This structure was extremely complex, with a multiplicity of rates. In Robbins's view, the money supply was primary; the structure of interest rates was secondary, with each rate dependent on particular market situations.[253]

Given firm control of the credit base, it was unlikely that the credit structure on that base could itself really undermine monetary control for very long. If however experience proved this view to be incorrect, it would simply be necessary to devise new ways of bringing those credit developments under control.[254]

Checking the rate of growth of the money supply was not, however, something to be done suddenly. Robbins, as the discussion of incomes policy above indicated, was concerned that a sudden application of the brakes would produce high levels of unemployment. The correct policy was a gradual slowing down.[255] Such a slowing down would involve some rise in the rate of interest, as a consequence of monetary policy rather than something being used as a tool in its own right, and this could be expected to reinforce the contraction. Robbins was deeply sceptical about the evidence to the Radcliffe Committee to the effect that the rate of interest did not influence investment plans.

> Businessmen appear before government committees, beat their breasts, and swear that the rate of interest doesn't mean a thing to them, but as soon as the rate of interest is raised in some attempt to control the situation, you find them all giving interviews to financial journalists, saying what an unfortunate thing it is and how they hope that cheap money will be restored again.[256]

Although the interest rate on its own could not bear the strain without control of the monetary base and appropriate fiscal policy,[257] the use of Bank Rate was, nonetheless, a valuable element of monetary policy. It was an 'indispensable weapon' for dealing with a crisis; not only must it possess some contractionary effect, despite the Treasury Bill problem, but its use had psychological effects as signalling the onset of tight money, and effects on the exchange rate.[258] While there was no simple correlation between the level of the rate of interest and economic activity,[259] he told the Radcliffe Committee that both investment and consumer expenditure were interest elastic. His subsequent view was that the Committee failed 'conspicuously to distinguish between money rates of interest and their real equivalent' in its downplaying of the importance of the rate of interest.[260]

4. CONCLUSION

Robbins's macroeconomic thought displayed a far greater consistency throughout his career than has sometimes been thought to be the case, and indeed than the impression he himself sometimes gave. Starting from a basis of knowledge of Classical monetary theory, and of Wicksell, he espoused the Mises–Hayek theory of the trade cycle, which led him into an intransigent position, though one that was theoretically consistent, concerning fiscal policy as a means of countering depression. In the post-war years he abandoned both the opposition to fiscal policy and the close adherence to the Mises–Hayek version of monetary theory; but in doing so he retreated to the Classical and Wicksellian roots of that theory and continued to insist upon the importance of monetary control, primarily through control of the money supply and secondly through interest rates, while no longer insisting that macroeconomic disequilibrium was uniquely related to capital market disequilibrium, or that governmental fiscal policy was not only powerless but positively harmful, as he had held until the late 1930s.

9 International Economics

1. INTRODUCTION

We now come to Robbins's writings on international economics. Although a knowledge of the Classical literature background is necessary to understand fully Robbins's writings in virtually any area of economics, the problem is at its most acute in dealing with his writings on international economics. In a sense he carried forward not only the analysis but also the attitudes of the Classical writer he most admired, J. S. Mill, although of course he drew on a far wider range of sources from Hamilton to Senior and Torrens. Thus he advocated international liberalism, putting *world* before *national* welfare, attacking nationalism and protectionism, which had their origins in sectional and not class interests.

To combat these divisive tendencies, Robbins advocated international Federalism – supranational authority to bring about genuine free trade – in the pre-war years. Such an arrangement still remained an ideal, if a more distant one, in the post-war world; his hesitations over European unity after the war sprang in part from his belief that Atlantic rather than European unity should be the immediate goal, and in part from his Classical appreciation of the trade-diverting aspects of customs unions. European unity was likely to have significant protectionist aspects: Robbins opposed all forms of protectionism, drawing heavily on the Classical literature. In the search for a liberal world economic order, he also argued that fixity of exchange rates was required – the gold standard before World War Two, the Bretton Woods system (though with reform of the IMF as an objective) afterwards. Free exchange rates essentially divided the world of trade and payments. But fixed rates require macroeconomic management for their maintenance: here Robbins drew on the Ricardian definition of excess (money supply) as his principal weapon.

2. INTERNATIONAL LIBERALISM

It is important in understanding Robbins's writings on international economics to appreciate that, like J. S. Mill (but unlike the rest of the Classical economists), Robbins was concerned with world rather than with national welfare.[1] He was interested in securing an allocation of factors designed to maximise *world* welfare.[2] Robbins was in fact very committed to economic internationalism, rather than to nationalism, and he endorsed the long-term goal of international federalism as a means to this end.[3]

Nationalism was, in his view, a fragmenting influence and a basic cause of friction between countries and indeed of war.[4] National collectivism was even more objectionable than nationalism itself. Collectivism would necessarily destroy the international division of labour[5] because of its intimate connection with national planning, which trade could not be permitted to upset, leading to a reversion to seventeenth-century-style bilateralism.[6] This must necessarily involve much sacrifice of potential wealth, by limiting trade to cases of double coincidence of wants and through being forever vulnerable to technical change upsetting a balance even if one could be secured initially. With changing conditions there would be cumulative instability as bilateral agreements were reworked.[7] External competitive forces could not be allowed to affect the internal allocation of resources under collectivist planning.[8] Thus protectionism would be required; it was 'a leading species of the genus national plan'.[9] But protection intensified depression.[10] The more comprehensive the national planning, the worse all the effects. The prospect was offered by Robbins, in the 1930s, of a world market frozen into a series of geographical monopolies.[11] This would increase world fluctuations because the balance of surplus and deficit crops could not be diffused across world markets. Moreover national planning, because it obstructed change, would diminish world welfare and increase international political friction.[12] State trading introduced new frictions into international relations by substituting dealings between governments for dealings between individuals.[13] National socialism, Robbins warned from an early stage, was likely to increase the chances of war. (Unlike many intellectuals, he understood early and clearly the dangers posed by the threats from Nazi Germany and Soviet Russia even before their alliance.)[14]

What Robbins argued for, in his *Economic Planning and International Order*, was international liberalism rather than national collectivism. He wanted full international freedom of trade and payments – the market system given full *international* scope. International liberalism had not been tried because of a lack of international security.[15] But it would bring the benefits of the market – registration of demand and supply forces, decentralised initiative and incentives – to everyone, in marked contrast to planning.[16] It was superior to the pursuit of national interest, which would be cancelled out by retaliation and leave the world poorer.[17] Unlike international communism, it did not suffer from internal contradictions – the impossibility of rational factor allocations, and the impossibility of international equality.[18] Although Robbins later retreated from the idealism of his vision in *Economic Planning and International Order*,[19] there seems little doubt that international liberalism remained his ideal even if it became, in time, a more distant ideal.[20]

3. SOURCES

The sources for Robbins's idealistic international liberalism, and indeed for his writings on trade more generally, fall into two main groups. In the first group there was Alexander Hamilton, author of *The Federalist* (and also Edwin Cannan who, Robbins believed, had explored federal principles within the context of local government)[21] and Jeremy Bentham, whose opposition to aggressive wars and colonialism, and advocacy of international law and of a European fraternity, Robbins found sympathetic.[22] From these Robbins derived his view of the desirable world order in which freedom of trade and payments could develop. In the second group we have the authors of the Classical theory of international trade – perhaps the greatest single and most enduring achievement of Classical economics.

It was from this group that Robbins took his view of the mechanisms involved in international trade and payments, and his understanding of the equilibrium conditions and the equilibrating mechanisms required. Thus Robbins was able to summarise the formal content of trade theory as showing that what mattered was not national frontiers but barriers to factor mobility (citing Cairnes), and to argue that a similar case existed with regard to the monetary theory of trade in that it was not national frontiers that were critical – if there was more than one international centre of money supply, there was no automatic equilibration of the balance of payments, but different credit centres need not coincide with national boundaries. Thus the formal content of trade theory included the relations between non-competing groups and the relations between areas of independent money supply.[23] The influence of Nassau Senior was particularly evident in Robbins's writings, and he used Senior's analysis to show that wage levels and price levels resulted from the interaction of productivity with the balance of payments.[24]

We also find an application of standard Ricardian analysis in dealing with tariffs on agricultural products – farming profits would, after tariffs had raised agricultural prices, be competed to a normal level, leaving landlords as the only permanent gainers.[25] Ricardo's *Protection to Agriculture* was the source for the argument that similar burdens should be placed on home and foreign sources of supply.[26] There were later sources such as Gregory and Mises;[27] but these were usually working within the Classical mould, and the Classical origins of Robbins's trade theory are even more apparent than the Classical origins of his macroeconomic theory. Above all, the influence of David Hume's analysis of money and the balance of payments can be seen at many points.[28]

It is thus not possible to appreciate fully Robbins's writings on trade without a knowledge of the Classical literature. Almost all his writings on trade were concerned either with commercial policy or monetary matters; there is no doubt that he regarded the Classical theory as emerging 'more or less unscathed' in the context of trade policy discussions.[29] Even his analysis of the effects of tariffs on the terms of trade owed most to Robert Torrens, although it was also influenced by Mill, Marshall and Edgeworth.[30]

4. FEDERALISM

During the years before, and indeed during the early years of, the Second World War, Robbins saw Federalism as the way to a liberal international order of the kind which the Classical analysis showed to be desirable.[31] This remedy was put forward in his *Economic Basis of Class Conflict* of 1939 and in his *Economic Causes of War*, lectures delivered in Geneva in the spring of 1939.[32] It was also in his *Economic Planning and International Order* of 1937,[33] a presentation which was endorsed by Robbins as late as 1971 when he had become much more pessimistic.[34] In an essay published in 1940 and again in 1941, Robbins argued that Federal union was the only alternative to defeat and complete union under a victorious Germany.[35] His view was that construction of a Federal order was the only remedy for frictions between sovereign states over trade.[36] Its creation was the only way of avoiding international discrimination in the movement of goods and factors.[37] He believed that a structure of authority would be necessary to create such harmony;[38] and in all his discussions about the exercise of authority in Federal decisions if such a structure were realised, what Harrod was later to call the 'assumptions of Harvey Road'[39] about the operation of disinterested international civil servants are evident. This lends to the discussion a certain lack of realism, and Robbins later came to recognise this.[40] He clearly became, as will be indicated, somewhat disenchanted by the operations of the IMF;[41] and he regarded the United Nations as not 'much better than a dispiriting and expensive farce'.[42]

Nineteenth-century writers had not sufficiently recognised the need for international security to secure freedom of trade – they had failed to realise that the power of demonstration of the benefits of free trade (as enjoyed by Great Britain) was not sufficient.[43] Federalism was the only way forward, as providing the necessary international security.

The basic principle of Federalism was that the central power in the Federation should have only as much power as that which was explicitly given to it by the constituent parts. Constituent States retained all powers they did not deliberately give up. But it was essential that the Federation should take over those parts of power which had been productive of conflict.[44] These obviously included military power – and the taxation to finance it.[45] (The Federation should also have, within its public finance duties, the power to carry out public works of a particular Federal kind, such as a Channel tunnel and – and this should be noted in relation to Robbins's macroeconomic thinking in view of its date, 1941 – anti-depression public works.)[46] The Federation should also have the power to deal with any monopoly which affected inter-State trade.[47] The power of making treaties, regulation of international trade, communications, financial relations and migration must all be Federal functions.[48] Any restrictions on trade outside the Federation must in any case be reduced to a minimum to avoid clashes between the Federation and any States remaining outside it.[49]

Within the Federation trade restrictions, broadly speaking,

could not be tolerated, and the Federation should also have the power to review non-tariff barriers to trade.[50] Any economic function which could be discharged without injury to other parts of the Federation would be open to the constituent States[51] – the parallel with Mill's distinction between self-affecting acts, and acts affecting the rest of society, is clear enough.

With regard to public finance in the Federation, there would need to be, in addition to taxation for defence (and public works) mentioned already, some sort of compensation fund to cushion the effects of regional change. This would require Federal taxation. But by and large Robbins seems to have considered that public finance should remain with the constituent States in the first instance. However this would lead to differences in tax rates between States and to migration within the Federation to areas of lighter taxation.[52] This in turn would make it ultimately necessary for the Federation at least to coordinate taxation between the States.

While some regulation of migration might be necessary to avoid putting strains on the Federal system, such regulation should be a Federal function to avoid the conflicts of interest arising where productive States closed their borders to new entrants.[53] Robbins did concede from an early stage that there was a potential danger of sparsely populated regions being swamped by inward migration[54] and also, from as early as 1931, that differences in birth rates were a factor working against permitting free migration.[55] Later, as he became seriously worried about a population explosion, he recognised this as a major obstacle to allowing free migration, although he did not regard this as a serious matter within Western Europe or the Atlantic community.[56]

5. MONETARY UNION

In the heyday of his enthusiasm for, and optimism about, Federation, Robbins was a believer in complete monetary union – a strong union with a common currency. He was quite unworried about the loss of exchange-rate flexibility. The argument that exchange rate flexibility was required could be countered by the *reductio ad absurdum* that it implied the necessity of giving every industry its own currency.[57] An independent monetary policy for sovereign States would endanger the Federation – this was, of course, consistent with his point about the basic monetary theory of trade referred to above – and thus money should be under Federal control as should exchange rates within the Federation.[58] If there were national monetary freedom, the result would be inevitably, according to the basic model, balance of payments problems and these in turn would lead to trade restrictions which were unacceptable within a Federation.[59] Thus monetary union was essential.

This view is, whatever one thinks of the lack of concern about surrender of exchange rate flexibility, an important part of Robbins's writings. Indeed, 20 years before Mundell, he postulated two of the now-standard criteria for an optimum currency area – labour mobility and money illusion.[60]

However Robbins became less optimistic about the prospects of monetary union as he viewed the difficulties of monetary union within the EEC; and indeed he was certainly not prepared to support the idea of a common European monetary system if this was going to involve exchange controls. When faced with the reality there was undoubtedly some loss of the optimistic vision.[61]

6. TRADE RESTRICTIONS

(i) Protectionism, empire and war

Robbins's view, formed during the 1930s, was that protectionism and exclusion from markets was a potent source of war. Indeed he correctly foretold the effects of excluding Japan from international markets.[62] To forestall such exclusion was the only rational reason for territorial expansion.[63] There was no great advantage in extra territory; increased property might increase the income of an individual but it did not increase real income per head within a country. Extra territory was not necessary for raw material supplies, investment opportunities, migration or the supply of foreign exchange.[64] Welfare was not increased by imperialism.[65] Seeking self-sufficiency through expansion was, in itself, a futile aim – indeed while it might theoretically be possible to re-group the territories of the world so as to make each self-sufficient, this would still involve substantial welfare sacrifices.[66] The sole advantage of empire was to provide a large area within which a country had the power to prevent itself being discriminated against or excluded from trade.[67]

> It is not in the power to manipulate or to restrict trade that the advantages of wide territorial jurisdiction consist, but rather in immunity from the manipulations and restrictions which might be practised by other states if the area of jurisdiction were narrowed.[68]

In the course of developing this general thesis Robbins, in his *Economic Causes of War*, attacked to great effect the view (now obviously ludicrous, but one then held by many intellectuals of the Left) that war was brought about by the existence of private property – the pseudo-Marxist under-consumptionist theory, not held by Marx himself, and the Leninist theory of imperialism which together implied a search for new markets and/or new employments for capital as the causes of war.[69] As Robbins argued here, and in his *Economic Basis of Class Conflict*, in so far as there was conflict it was not between class interests with capitalists seeking to maintain the rate of profit, but between sectional interests.[70] The Marxist argument failed to specify *whose* economic interest was involved and failed also to show an *ex ante* connection.[71]

> To show that economic interests play a part in the causation of war, it is not enough to show that they benefit *ex-post*; it is necessary to show that it was thought that they would benefit *ex-ante*, and that this conviction was an operative factor in the actual framing of policy.[72]

Only in the case of the introduction of trade restrictions did he find the argument about sinister interests convincing; and those who sought imposition of such restrictions represented a vertical rather than a horizontal section of society. Property owners *as a whole* did not gain by trade restrictions. He did not deny a role to investment interests, in some particular conflicts, even one so major as the Boer War, but he held that in most cases the economic element, which the theory required to be universally decisive, was in fact a smoke-screen for political ambition. Typically, financial interests were *used by* governments, not the other way round.[73] Moreover some of the most aggressively expansionist countries were actually capital importers, while a number of capitalist countries – Holland, Scandinavia and Switzerland – were rigidly non-expansionist.[74] Of course, once territorial expansion had taken place, it was possible to gain some narrow national advantage by turning the terms of trade against colonial possessions; but this was certainly not an interest which was the monopoly of one single class.[75]

Neither was protectionist lobbying. If trade policy was not liberal, then particular interest groups might be able to secure gains at the expense of other (vertically constituted) groups.[76] They could use the smoke-screen of the infant industry argument to seek manufacturing protection and they could cite Wagner in support of agricultural protection.[77] Cartels were particularly anxious to try to climb on the bandwagon of international planning and it was this kind of lobbying which was the main cause of protection.[78]

> It is no accident that, speaking broadly, over the last seventy
> years [to 1939] the extent of restrictionism in various countries
> has varied with the susceptibility of governments to the pressure
> of private interests.[79]

But these were sectional and not class interests. Trade unions acted as lobbyists for sectional protection and for restrictions on migration.[80] The producer interest was 'ceaselessly active' in seeking to protect itself against competition and the effects of disagreeable change, with the struggles of different producer groups the predominant characteristic of this activity.[81] There was protectionist pressure from those industries which were not internationally competitive.[82]

The problem was basically that groups of individuals, having different economic interests within the State, sought to use the State for their common external interests. The State could be used to interfere with trade directly and also to regulate economic activity so as to interfere with trade indirectly.[83] This was a recurrent problem in human history. There had been a brief period of ascendancy of the Classical theory[84] but then the theories of List and Carey 'provided a wonderful façade for the pressure groups' with the rise of manufacturing protectionism from the 1870s. This was followed by agricultural protection with 'the ideas of Wagner [on sectoral balance which] . . . provided the necessary intellectual apologia'.[85]

The Classical economists had in fact been mistaken in thinking that freedom of trade would come about naturally. Internal freedom of trade itself had, after all, only been imposed by strong government.[86] The free trade prescriptions of the Classical economists 'were based on a gross underestimate of the strength of producer interest in shaping the economic policies of governments'.[87] They thought that the free trade example of a successful England would inspire the world. However, not only did they underestimate the strength of the producer lobby, but they failed to see the extent to which general arguments for free trade were weakened in depression or financial crisis, while they failed to appreciate 'the chronic insufficiency of the political structure of international society to safeguard peace and prosperity in general'.[88]

It was not that Robbins doubted the validity of the Classical arguments against tariffs. Indeed he probably fought harder against tariffs than any other British economist, especially in the inter-war years. He was bitterly critical of Keynes and of Keynes's endorsement of protection, and he devoted a great deal of time in both academic and more public controversy to criticising the logic of Keynes's proposals and the revenue calculations on which they were based.[89] Tariffs, he argued, were no use as a measure against unemployment. Not only were they cumulative – every depression would require yet more protection – but there was a danger of retaliation. Moreover each industry which saw other industries benefit would itself demand protection, so protection would increase while any short-run benefits would be negated by retaliation. Quotas would inevitably follow because tariffs could be adapted to, and the net result of the protective activity was simply a reduction in world trade and welfare and a worsening of world resource allocation.[90] Even though there were, Robbins recognised, sophisticated arguments concerning the optimum tariff, there was no real chance of hitting such a level in practice.[91] State involvement in the economy simply ensured that high levels of protection developed to safeguard, ostensibly at least, that involvement,[92] and depression was intensified.[93] Resource allocation was worsened[94] with precisely the wrong industries being protected[95] and, in the case of agricultural protection, the town dweller made worse off simply at the expense of the landlord[96] – Robbins's position on agricultural protection is extraordinarily Ricardian. Reducing imports through protection simply resulted in reduced exports in turn leaving us with no net gain. After the war Robbins added to these arguments the one that tariffs interfered with the Western Alliance to which, as already noted, he attached the most profound importance.[97] It is not surprising that Robbins took a central part in the creation of GATT, which accorded with a fundamental part of his philosophy.[98] He saw 'much of value' in 'the *simultaneous* negotiation of bilateral agreements with most-favoured nation arrangements to generalise the concessions thus arrived at'.[99]

Much of Robbins's discussion of tariffs is simply a restatement, with regard to particular circumstances, of the Classical case for freedom of trade as further developed by, in particular, Marshall. But the argument is so dense, since Robbins was not prepared to allow his opponents any quarter, that it is easy to miss some of the underlying theory. In particular there are a number of passing allusions to the famous 'Cuba' case posited by Torrens (in which it was shown that a country could, under highly limiting assumptions, benefit through turning the terms of trade in its favour, by the use of tariffs).[100] As so often with Robbins, only an appreciation of the Classical literature makes explicit an argument which he allows to develop by implication, and it is no coincidence that his fullest and most explicit discussion is to be found not in his writings on trade policy but in his masterly book *Robert Torrens*.[101]

(ii) Infant industries, quotas and cartels

Robbins's treatment of the particular tariff case concerned with the infant industry argument is wholly within this Classical tradition. He rejected the argument as one which could be used in support of tariffs, regarding it as largely a smoke-screen, and he suggested that subsidy would be better in any case.[102] However his treatment does have two particular aspects which take it beyond the Classical position and are of interest. Firstly, he argued that what mattered was not equalisation of costs at home and abroad, but a *discounted*, *net*, gain in prospect as a result of encouraging an industry. The industry protected must offer, in other words, the prospect of lower costs than those abroad, and this to a sufficient degree, and sufficiently early, to off-set the immediate loss from imposing some form of protection for it whether by tariff or, better, by subsidy.[103] Secondly, Robbins paid attention to the Hamilton–List statement of the infant industry argument in terms of external effects ('industrialisation'). The external effects case he rejected decisively. It involved difficulties of measuring externalities, of arriving at a balanced judgement, of resisting pressure groups, and of removing protection once in place even though it was no longer necessary.[104]

Apart from his general stance against protection, Robbins also argued against trade discrimination, in particular discrimination against the dollar in the post-war years. His preference was for an adjustment of exchange rates.[105]

Although the bulk of his attack on protection was concentrated on tariffs, he held that all the arguments against tariffs applied *a fortiori* to quotas and to licence systems. These were even worse than tariffs because producers were not faced with prices to which they could adapt. In fact quotas had unpredictable effects on prices, caused price fluctuations, and prevented the achievement of world equilibrium in trade.[106]

As already indicated, Robbins regarded the imposition of tariffs as the use of the power of the State in the interests of private individuals. However these private individuals also organised international cartels. While Robbins was certainly critical of these, for they distorted resource allocation by protecting high cost producers, and thus distorted investment flows, he believed that these cartels depended on tariffs to secure membership and that they were inherently fragile. Without the assistance of government they were unlikely to be a long term problem.[107] The main problem, and one to which he returned again and again, was tariffs.

(iii) Customs unions

But Robbins's opposition to tariffs, and his belief in some kind of international Federation, raises very clearly the question of his attitude to customs unions. Any Federation would have a common external tariff; since Robbins was fundamentally opposed to tariffs, it is necessary to ask what his attitude towards a customs union was.

It emerges that, long before the development of the modern

literature on the theory of customs unions, Robbins had appreciated the essential problem.

> From the international point of view, the tariff union is not an advantage in itself. It is an advantage only in so far as, on balance, it conduces to more extensive division of labour. It is to be justified only by arguments which would justify still more its extension to all areas capable of entering into trade relationships. The only possible vindication of the retention of old restrictions or the erection of new ones is the argument that, in their absence, the tendency to restrict would be still more rampageous. No doubt if we could coax the rest of the world into free trade by a high tariff union against the produce of the Eskimos that would be, on balance, an international gain. But it would be inferior to an arrangement whereby the Eskimos were included. The only completely innocuous tariff union would be directed against the inaccessible produce of the moon.[108]

This dates from 1937. In a later work, but one still written before he had seen the famous contribution of Jacob Viner,[109] Robbins made explicit the problem of trade diversion, as well as noting the likelihood of difficulties over division of the revenue of a common external tariff, the difficulties facing a country like Britain because of its relation to the Commonwealth, and the problems involving quotas when those imposed by different countries had somehow to be unified in the development of common external protection.[110] A customs union was essentially a limited extension of bilateral bargaining; and bilateral bargaining was likely to produce trade diversion.[111] Robbins was quite clear that the customs union case was not the free trade case, because the customs union involved trade diversion as well as trade creation. Within the union there might well be both comparative costs and scale gains, as well as a greater accumulation of capital, while national monopolies might be undermined which would produce a spur to efficiency.[112] But this was only a part of the picture.

(iv) European unity

Robbins's perception of the nature of a customs union may well have influenced his initial attitude towards European unity and the EEC, which was hostile.[113] The argument for a European customs union was not an argument based on free trade considerations, he recognised, and it might well discriminate against other members of the Atlantic Community – a grouping which, as already noted, Robbins regarded as being of over-riding importance.[114] It was better to try to move towards more liberal commercial policies through the existing organisations such as the IMF and the World Bank than to enter the EEC.[115] Initially he also took the view that there was no future in looking to European unity, because two world wars had shown that Britain was incapable of settling her differences with other European countries without the assistance of the Commonwealth and the United States.[116] It was not that Robbins had any great faith in the Commonwealth – there was little to be hoped for from an Imperial Zollverein.[117] Moreover he had indeed favoured European unity in 1939.[118] But in the years after the war he took the view that Europe on its own was not viable and that any union must involve the United States.[119] This was partly a response to the repulsive attitude of the French Left.

> Readers of Madame de Beauvoir's not very distinguished but immensely informative novel *The Mandarins* – a palpable description of the group in which she and her great friend, Jean-Paul Sartre, moved – will remember the state of mind depicted. Of all the main characters, only one – Camus in disguise, I suppose – did not feel that there was little to choose between Stalin's Russia and contemporary America, only one did not feel that to reveal the truth about Russian concentration camps and ideological murder was betraying the last best hopes of humanity. I asked myself, what had I in common with men and women capable of such attitudes.[120]

But, partly because of the response to his opposition to European unity which 'brought me much commendation, not only from some friends whose praise I valued, but also from quarters whose approbation should have given me pause for second thoughts,'[121] Robbins changed his mind and became a supporter, if a reluctant one, of European unity.[122] His new position involved a grudging acceptance of the EEC as the best – because the only – degree of Federalism attainable in the foreseeable future. There was a need for European unity in face of the ever-present Soviet threat: 'The barbarian is still at the gate. It is a folly endangering all that is most precious in the human heritage not to recognise that this is so.'[123]

(v) The Atlantic community

Robbins made no bones about the fact, however, that his preference was for Federalism within the Atlantic community, a view that he had put forward in the post-war years.

> I still think that arrangements which include the United States and Canada would be vastly superior to any which leave Europe on its own, its policies a possible prey to the odious anti-Americanism of so many *soi disant* Continental intellectuals: I am sure that such an arrangement would be much more in the interest of the United Kingdom than the more limited association. But I am afraid that history . . . has made this unlikely, at any rate as the next step; and I am therefore now a positive supporter of our proposed conjunction with Western Europe [1971].[124]

We needed a wider grouping in the Atlantic community,[125] above all for reasons of defence rather than economics – Robbins was bitingly dismissive of the advocates of a European Third Force, 'second-rate publicists and pathological American-haters who, if they were not definitely infected with the virus of the fellow-traveller, were at least so weak in understanding as to believe that, by proclaiming neutrality without being willing to fight for it, they could enjoy immunity both from obligations and misfortunes'[126] – but also particularly because the Americans, who were now part of the European tradition, would provide a balance not available in a Europe dominated by the larger countries.[127] These were political considerations; Robbins's economic understanding, especially his understanding of the essential nature of customs unions (though this should not surprise us since the roots of his understanding, like that of Jacob Viner, lay in Classical economics),[128] impelled him in the same direction. But, as already indicated, one of his recurrent fears was of an end to Western civilisation; and the only security against that would be provided by union of the Western countries around the United States.[129]

One aspect of either a broader or a narrower area of economic union is monetary unification, as already indicated in discussing

Robbins's Federalist vision. Although he had recognised, from an early stage, the existence of European resistance to monetary union with North America,[130] he continued to hope that this might eventually come about.[131] This in its turn reflected changes which had taken place in his attitude towards international monetary arrangements and in particular towards the Gold Standard.

7. EXCHANGE RATES

(i) The Gold Standard

In the years up to the Second World War, Robbins was a supporter of the Gold Standard and of the adherence of countries which were on it to the 'rules of the game' whereby the money supply was contracted when gold was lost over the exchanges. He believed that we should have returned to gold in 1932.[132] The problem was not with the Gold Standard but with hit-and-miss rate fixing, and the United States mismanagement of its money supply in the late 1920s.[133] If we had returned to a low parity after the first war then (despite a number of particular British problems such as poor export performance and wage and price rigidity, and despite Britain's vulnerability to hot money flows), the Gold Standard would still have been workable and it would have produced unification of monetary policies in different countries and global stabilisation, with only an irreducible minimum of inflationary booms. The latter would be on a small scale compared with those experienced under paper standards.[134] Once gold parities were correctly fixed, however, Robbins was anxious that they should stay fixed; exchange stability was fundamental to the operation of the Gold Standard system. If movable gold parities were permitted they would encourage local experiments in inflation, erode money illusion, and interfere with international investment while encouraging hot money flows.[135]

Looking back on pre-war experience, after the second war, Robbins believed that the Gold Standard had worked well when it was in operation, with a few large financial centres and an important international capital market. It had been cushioned by the gold discoveries and the development of credit systems so that means of payment proceeded to develop with economic growth, and under the system an adverse balance of payments did not necessitate depression, merely a slowing of the relative rate of advance.[136] The system had a good theory worked out by Hume and Ricardo. However he conceded that the Gold Standard had not always operated well, partly because there had been two (1819 and 1925) episodes of wrong parities, and partly because of recurrent failures to follow the 'rules of the game'.[137] Though there are points at which his analysis is open to question,[138] the account given, which is wholly Classical in its approach, reflects a satisfaction with both the analytical basis and the historical operation – subject to the qualification about incorrect parities – of the system.

But after the war, although Robbins undoubtedly looked back with nostalgia to the Gold Standard,[139] he did not advocate a return to it. But the nostalgia was strong. Money supplies had been internationally equilibrated under the Gold Standard, despite the growth of the credit system. The hardships of the Gold Standard were greatly exaggerated: they were no greater than the effects on particular industries of internal demand shifts.[140] He clearly still hankered after the monetary discipline involved in the Gold Standard.[141] Without a common international money, there was a lack of an automatic adjustment mechanism, and a lack of control of global aggregate demand.[142] Of course the Gold Standard necessitated a degree of inflation or deflation in accordance with the balance of payments; but such adjustment was required of regions, within one country, and moreover a *stable* world paper system would be open to the same objections.[143] It was true that the development of banking systems had undermined the automatic equilibration of payments-balance. But the metal systems had still done better than the paper systems.[144]

Nevertheless, he did not favour a return to the Gold Standard.[145] He approved Rueff's analysis, but not his proposal to return to gold.[146] Apart from the historical importance of precious metal discoveries in easing the actual operation of the Gold Standard system, which were a special factor which could not be expected to recur, the modern world *should* be able to devise a paper system which would out-perform gold even though it had failed to do so thus far.[147] Return to the Gold Standard was impracticable because central banks determined reserve ratios and thus central banks determined the world money supply;[148] and the way forward lay in turning the IMF into a central bank for the free world, in which the national banks keep a substantial part of their reserves, and which, by way of open-market policy, has the power of easing or curbing the availability of purchasing power for the entire area over which it operates.[149]

But he did not believe that gold should be demonetised;[150] and he favoured an upward change in the price of gold (in 1967) despite the benefits to Russia and South Africa.[151]

(ii) Balance of payments problems with fixed paper exchange rates

Robbins's analysis of the source of balance of payments difficulties was conducive to the idea that a world central bank was required. Balance of payments difficulties arose from two broad groups of causes. There were real causes, and there were monetary causes.[152] The real causes, especially in the case of Britain in the post-war world, were substantial enough. They included downward shifts in the demand for exports, export disorganisation, loss of overseas assets, adverse turns in the terms of trade and the necessity of making debt repayments.[153] In particular, the debts in the form of sterling balances posed a problem.[154]

But it is clear from Robbins's writings that he considered the majority of balance of payments problems to have monetary causes. Considerations of external equilibrium had usually, he told his 1951 audience at the Stamp Memorial Lecture, been subordinated to domestic policy.[155] Aggregate demand had been allowed to run at too high a level so that output of potential exports was diverted into the home market, and the rate of growth of the money supply had been excessive.[156] Money income had risen in the United States in line with productivity; but other countries had run into balance of payments difficulties with the United States because they had allowed money income to rise even faster.[157] But if the rate of growth of the money supply were not disciplined with respect to the balance of payments, and exchange rates were fixed, then balance of payments crises would necessarily result.[158]

It was relative rates of price inflation, rather than excess absorption, on which Robbins placed most of his emphasis. If price inflation were uniform internationally, there would not be balance of payments problems.[159] All that other countries had to do was to keep behind the United States price inflation, but they had wasted their opportunities.[160] The UK had inflated faster not only than the United States but also than Germany.[161]

(iii) Monetary and fiscal policy and the Ricardian definition of excess

Taking together Robbins's recognition of the effects of real factors on the balance of payments, and his emphasis upon the predominance of monetary factors, it comes as no surprise, in the light of what has already been indicated about the sources of Robbins's approach to international problems, that the Ricardian definition of excess – if the balance of payments is persistently adverse then, by definition, the money supply is excessive – lay behind his analysis of the problem. Robbins argued that

> given a fixed rate of exchange, there is always a level of internal prices and incomes at which the balance of payments would tend to equilibrium. It follows, therefore, that if there is disequilibrium, for any long period of time, this ideal level has been missed.[162]

If there were a real change, such as a fall in the level of exports, then finance must react to this.[163]

> If difficulties persist in the exchange market, there is a strong presumption that the internal financial conditions have been incompatible with the requirements of external equilibrium.[164]

But the authorities had failed to note the lessons of Ricardo. Instead: 'The shades of Tooke and Fullarton have reigned triumphant in Great George Street.'[165] The result was a quite remarkable fragility of the British balance of payments. As Robbins told his audience, in a famous passage:

> If a car fails to reach its destination, if it is continually running into the side, or if it is continually having to solicit hauls from passing lorries, we should not regard it as a sufficient explanation that the roads are not level and straight, that there are hills to ascend and corners to turn.[166]

In other words, financial policy should be able to accommodate the real shocks by adhering to the Ricardian definition of excess.

Thus monetary policy was of central importance in relation to the balance of payments.[167] While, as already noted, Robbins did not accept Mundell's basic assumption that monetary and fiscal policy are independent[168] (which is of course vital for Mundell's targets/instruments – EMC – approach), the emphasis is undoubtedly upon monetary policy. Although, as noted in Chapter 8, Robbins was insistent in the post-war period on the coupling of monetary and fiscal policy, he did not consider fiscal policy on its own as suitable for balance of payments correction:

> how clumsy and inadequate an instrument is budgetary policy, if operated by itself? I say nothing against policy of this kind in conjunction with other measures. Indeed I am sure that we cannot afford to dispense with it; in present circumstances, the rate of interest necessary to restrain outlay without a substantial budget surplus would be very inconvenient. But when it is a matter of maintaining external equilibrium in a situation in which conditions of external supply and demand are continually changing, surely the probabilities are that budgetary policy *by itself* will only succeed as a matter of lucky accident.[169]

Robbins's emphasis upon the monetary aspects of macroeconomic policy was a natural deduction from his application of the Ricardian definition of excess. Indeed one can see, lying behind some of his statements, the principle of 'metallic fluctuation' (that the money supply should fluctuate in accordance with the balance of payments exactly as if it were entirely of specie), which was the guiding principle of the framers of the Bank Charter Act of 1844.[170] At the same time he did not believe that it was necessary, in a progressive world, for actual deflation to take place; a slowing in the relative rate of advance was all that was required.[171]

As will be clear from Chapter 8, the majority of his emphasis when dealing with monetary policy is on control of the money supply, with the rate of interest occupying a subsidiary, though important, place. The same was true when considering correction of the balance of payments; a high rate of interest could be used to protect the sterling balances, to procure short run capital flows and to provide an international signal about indications concerning inflation.[172] But control of aggregate monetary demand was central.

Control of excess aggregate demand was particularly important because there was only limited scope for off-setting potentially inflationary monetary expansion by productivity rises.[173] With inflation under way, money wages would rise and depart from the level which (Robbins's keen grasp of Classical analysis made clear) was required by any given exchange rate, thus rendering that exchange rate inappropriate.[174]

A monetary policy and an exchange rate which were compatible with freedom of trade and payments must be the aim. Convertibility could be delayed (and Robbins was in no doubt that it had been attempted prematurely after the war) but in the long run it was of fundamental importance.[175] Thus, in both his pre-war and post-war writings, Robbins opposed the use of exchange controls as anything more than a temporary expedient.[176] He told his 1951 audience: 'I share the classical view that, as a rule, this is a cumbersome and superfluous policy. My Utopia does not lie in that prison-house.'[177] Exchange control was always out of touch with the market, resulting in last minute crises with 'big men flying about wildly in aeroplanes . . . grandiose conferences . . . last minute compromises'.[178]

Even if the exchange rate were an equilibrium one, and monetary policy adjusted to ensure this, there was still the problem of reserves. Robbins was concerned about the adequacy of world reserves, but more especially with the British case, when faced with leads and lags and with flights of hot money. With sometimes explicit reference to Tooke he was arguing, even up until the late 1960s, that reserve shortage was a serious problem for Britain.[179]

(iv) The Bretton Woods system and fixed rate adjustment

With an attachment to the concept of equilibrium exchange rates in conjunction with an appropriate monetary policy, and an emphasis upon the need for adequate reserves, all of which derived from the Classical literature that related to the Currency and Banking controversy of the mid-nineteenth century, it is hardly surprising that Robbins was a keen supporter of the Bretton Woods system of fixed exchange rates. He believed that it had provided a much superior exchange rate system to what he saw as the chaos operating in the 1930s.[180] Robbins was indeed a member of the Bretton Woods delegation from Britain,[181] and undoubtedly saw the system created there as a remedy for the unhappy experiences of the 1930s. However he conceded that on the British side only Hawtrey saw the danger of inflation in conjunction with the arrangements then negotiated.[182] These arrangements had not made any provision against world inflation, and a world on a dollar standard had not been foreseen. But a dollar standard which then inflated had led to the breakdown of the system.[183] The answer, after the breakdown of that system, lay, Robbins believed, in a return to a modified Bretton Woods system with declared key-currency parities, with wider margins either side of those parities, and with greater flexibility.[184]

He does not however seem to have questioned that keystone of the Bretton Woods system, the concept of 'fundamental disequilibrium'. While in his pre-war writing he had poured scorn on the idea of internationally agreed exchange rate changes – they would only be agreed to when the need was desperate and by that time there would have been speculation and aggravation of the disequilibrium[185] – he seems, in his post-war writings, to have been happy to accept the idea of such negotiated adjustments,[186] even though experience of the Bretton Woods system would seem to have borne out many of the criticisms which he made before the war (in criticism, indeed, of the ideas of Keynes which became partially embodied in the IMF system). So in the post-war years he believed that fixed exchange rates which had become unrealistic should be altered under IMF supervision – a course which would remove pressure for trade discrimination.[187]

This represented some shift in his position compared with the pre-war years. Before the Second World War, he seems to have disapproved of the 1931 devaluation as introducing an era of exchange rate uncertainty affecting trade and investment, and leading to competitive depreciation.[188] But in the post-war years he seems to have been prepared to regard devaluation as a viable option, although not as a way out for perpetually inflation-prone countries[189] – he believed in the value of the discipline of the exchanges.[190] He was doubtful about the relevance of purchasing power parity;[191] and he was prepared to contemplate a temporary float as a method of finding an equilibrium fixed rate.[192]

It is true that in a sense the change in Robbins's attitude between the pre-war and post-war years represented a shift of emphasis rather than a fundamental break; even in his *Economic Planning and International Order* of 1937, in which he had poured scorn on the general idea of rate flexibility, he had acknowledged that there was a case for adjustable paper exchange rates after periods of monetary nationalism, to avoid deflation – though he had argued that this should not become a permanent expedient, or trade and investment would be interfered with.[193] Correspondingly, in the post-war years, when he favoured greater exchange rate flexibility, he still opposed devaluation in 1958[194] and again in 1964–6.[195]

A world in which exchange rates were fixed, but could be changed if fundamental disequilibrium manifested itself, was half-way, Robbins believed, to the ideal world of full international monetary integration with a surrender of national monetary control.[196] But for this compromise world to work it was necessary that there should be firm national monetary control[197] – Robbins rejected emphatically the idea that the money supply was somehow endogenous.[198] Given such monetary control, however, devaluation could be successful – Robbins dismissed as 'worthless' estimates of elasticities in international trade which appeared to show that they were so low as to provide a basis for elasticity pessimism. Such estimates were only short run, whereas the relevant ones were long run elasticities, he argued, and he pointed out that the estimates assumed a fixed range of export goods whereas the range of export goods itself altered with changes in the exchange rate. So long as the devaluing country was not encountering tariffs and quotas, the elasticities should be high enough to make devaluation successful.[199]

(v) The IMF and world liquidity

For a world of fixed exchange rates to operate successfully, however, reform of the IMF was urgently required.[200] He favoured the proposal by J. H. Williams for a system with a few key countries in control as the desirable way forward.[201] With his aims of international Federation ever at the back of his mind, he argued that the IMF should seek to stabilise *world* demand[202] – and for such a fundamental role, reform of the IMF was highly necessary. The IMF was a valuable institution;[203] but it needed a reform both of its government and of its objectives. It was also necessary to reform the key-currency system. Rather than have the world on a dollar standard, with the gold price of dollars a matter for American discretion, each key currency should be able to adjust its own rate in relation to the Fund's unit of account, using the SDR for this purpose.[204] SDRs should be used *strictly* as an international standard; he was opposed to the proposal to use SDRs as a form of aid, because he believed that extra resources should not be made available by an institution which he wished to see operating as a world central bank, on non-banking grounds.[205]

A reformed IMF became, for Robbins, something of an ideal. In terms of practical politics, Robbins was not optimistic about it being achieved, and he was perfectly clear that even then a reformed IMF would be subject to limitations; there had been plenty of price inflation within the US, despite the Federal Reserve System which, having at the back of his mind his international Federal proposals, he took as his model for world monetary organisation.[206]

The most immediate need was not, however, for the creation of greater world liquidity. Despite his concern, until the late 1960s, about the state of British reserves, he seems to have come quite early to the view that there was no shortage of *world* liquidity – indeed there was too much rather than too little – and his support for the SDR was as a unit of account, not as a means of increasing world liquidity.[207]

This attitude is however hardly surprising, given the deterioration in the United States balance of payments during the 1960s. By 1968 Robbins was warning that, unless the US deficit was checked, the dollar exchange standard would break down (which of course it did). Either contraction of American expenditure, or the demonetisation of gold and the floating of the dollar, appeared possible outcomes.[208] There was the danger of a flight from the key currencies into gold. If this happened there would be a gold shortage, countries would find themselves with inadequate reserves and they would then have to apply deflationary pressure.[209]

The flood of dollars was a strange development in a world which had seen economists convinced in the preceding decade that a world dollar shortage was likely to persist into the foreseeable future.[210] Robbins deserves credit for having seen clearly, during the 1950s, how very misguided some of this literature on the dollar shortage was. He pointed out that the dollar shortage was only a shortage in relation to existing policies and exchange rates. The persistence of the problem was due to monetary policies which were inappropriate in relation to the balance of payments – an application of the Ricardian definition of excess again.[211] He was particularly unconvinced by MacDougall's essay on the dollar problem, emphasising that the main source of difficulty was simply a lack of control of monetarily induced inflation outside the United States.[212] The problem certainly did not arise from the practice of deflation by the United States itself.[213]

In discussing this matter Robbins showed a degree of perception, derived from a deep appreciation of the Classical model, which is instructive. Although it is undoubtedly true that much of the literature on the supposed dollar shortage was due to a fixed-exchange rate mentality,[214] Robbins, despite being strongly attached to the idea of fixed exchange rates, was not a prisoner of this mentality.

(vi) Free exchange rates

He was, however, consistently opposed to the idea of free exchange rates.[215] Free exchange rates, breaking the world up into competing national centres of monetary expansion, were in his view the complete antithesis of the truly liberal international order which he had been advocating since *Economic Planning and International Order* in 1937.[216] They would require, for reasons to be indicated below, a ban on contracts in monies other than the national one, and they moved in completely the opposite direction to the international economic integration which Robbins regarded as the ideal to be aimed for.[217] Indeed he believed that they could threaten the stability of the whole free world.[218]

He was prepared to accept that they could be used on a temporary basis, as a way of deciding on the equilibrium level of a new fixed rate[219] (particularly for countries up-valuing)[220] and he was even prepared to consider a localised float – although the only case which he approved was that of Canada.[221] But he believed that the lessons of the 1930s were clearly against free rates – the negotiators at Bretton Woods had had 'the experience of nearly a decade of fluctuating rates and the consequent confusions'.[222] If the arguments for free exchange rates were really valid, there was a case for allowing every industry – even every parish – its own exchange rate.[223] Exchange fluctuations interfered with trade,[224] and they required money-illusion in order to be successful. This was not something which would persist in the long term.[225] Exchange fluctuations would feed through to wage and price inflation.[226] The exchange rate would then depreciate further – Robbins was an early advocate of the 'vicious circle hypothesis'.[227] As inflation proceeded, capital flight could take place,[228] depressing the exchange rate further and causing more vicious circle problems. So free rates were themselves destabilising. But in any case the discipline of the exchanges was necessary as a brake on domestic monetary expansion.[229] Without this discipline, monetary inflation in the domestic economy would be uncontrolled – 20 years before the Heath–Barber episode Robbins warned of the dangers of monetary inflation behind free rates, compounding the vicious circle dangers and validating the price increases which were taking place as the exchange rate depreciated and money illusion was eroded.[230] Drawing on the work of Bresciani-Turroni and of Mises,[231] Robbins argued that a sort of Gresham's Law in reverse would operate. Instead of bad money driving out good, which depends on money-illusion, transactors would cease to use their own national monies and instead resort to a stable outside currency, or gold. But this would undermine national monetary autonomy and so the authorities would prohibit the use of an outside money in contracts. Thus free exchange rates would lead to an illiberal solution – exchange control.[232]

Free exchange rates could not then last. The currencies for which there was only a thin market would have to stabilise against the major currency blocs. The blocs would then gradually stabilise in relation to each other and the world would gravitate back to fixity of exchange rates,[233] after experience of dirty floating involving competitive depreciation.[234]

8. CONCLUSION

Robbins's treatment of international trade was subtle, ingenious and wholly Classical. The underlying theory in dealing with the real aspects of trade was that of trade between areas of factor immobility; the underlying theory in relation to the monetary aspects was the Classical theory of the relationship between different centres of money supply. Using this basic analytical framework, Robbins provided nearly 50 years of penetrating discussion of international economics, appreciating, on this basis, the issues involved in customs unions well before the better-known modern literature had developed, while maintaining always the ideal (though it became steadily more distant) of international Federation and international liberalism as the way forward to a desirable world economic order.

10 Conclusion

In assessing Robbins's place in the history of economic thought it may be helpful to start by dividing leading economists into two broad categories: synthesisers, and those who start with a clean sheet of paper. In the first category may be placed writers like Alfred Marshall and Harry Johnson, and pre-eminent in the second category would be Ricardo and Keynes. Robbins is undoubtedly in the first category. But whereas Marshall and Harry Johnson tried to build new theory, developing the tools they inherited, Robbins was mainly concerned (despite his early phase of making ingenious use of the elasticity tool) with applying the old tools to solve existing problems without developing those tools further. The tools which he used were not always particularly old historically, but they had been developed by other writers and were not Robbins's own. He was perfectly clear about this, as he wrote in his *Autobiography*:

> I have no outstanding intellectual discoveries to my credit . . . My purpose in writing is not to suggest the importance of anything I have done, but rather to interpret the experiences I have had.[1]

Nonetheless, his achievement was substantial even though his aims were only partially achieved. One aim was undoubtedly to persuade economists to think in terms of a form of general equilibrium. In this he was not really successful. When general equilibrium finally became more widely accepted, it was in the Lausanne version (although this was to a considerable extent due to Hicks, and in the development of his work Robbins had considerable influence) and it was, moreover, a Lausanne version which was not really held together by a sort of marginal-utility cement as Walras had envisaged – and indeed as Robbins had envisaged in the first edition of *ENSES*[2] Nonetheless employment of a general equilibrium framework enabled Robbins to see how some of the lauded developments of the 1930s – notably Imperfect Competition – would lead nowhere, and to appreciate the illegitimacy of using partial equilibrium analysis for general equilibrium problems as had been done by Marshall, Pigou and Joan Robinson.[3] But his own insights were not influential.

In dealing with costs, Robbins endorsed the Wicksteed–Austrian approach. This has two particular aspects. Firstly, economists cannot use engineering cost data – costs had to be approached from the direction of general equilibrium. Secondly, opportunity cost is the basis of all costs of production – the value of foregone outputs. As a basis for a philosophical understanding of the economy as a whole, this approach undoubtedly has much to offer. But it is destructive of the whole technocratic, quasi-engineering, pretensions of economists, and of the partial equilibrium analysis on which a large part of these rests – it could not be accepted without destroying much of economic theory particularly in the form that has developed since *ENSES*. In particular, production functions in Robbins's view represented technology, if they represented anything, and not economics.

The general equilibrium approach, reflected in Robbins's treatment of costs, led in turn to the implicit aim of eliminating much of partial equilibrium analysis. Here, correspondingly, Robbins was unsuccessful. Instead of being eliminated, partial equilibrium analysis thrived, first in Joan Robinson's instalment of Cambridge welfare economics *Imperfect Competition* and then, post-war, in Cost-Benefit analysis which, despite the apparatus of shadow pricing, is basically a partial equilibrium approach. Whether Robbins's aim was right is a separate question. Personally, despite the absurd uses to which partial equilibrium analysis has sometimes been put, this author doubts whether we really want to replace it entirely with general equilibrium with the latter's very limited predictive content in the context of many problems. But Robbins was perfectly correct to insist that we should always ask general equilibrium questions when faced with policy conclusions based on partial equilibrium.

Robbins's opposition to quantitative economics was also unsuccessful. This is partly because as economists sought a technocratic role, they did so through applying econometric techniques and partly because of the monetarist counter-revolution. But Robbins's opposition was never absolute – indeed we have noted in Chapter 3 a number of points at which he approved of quantitative work, notably that by Bresciani-Turroni and, later, Phillips – and his own position shifted a little with the passing of time.

His own position may have shifted in part because of the monetarist counter-revolution, despite his reservations about some aspects of that. For it was precisely in the area of money that Robbins enjoyed one of his two greatest successes. His was a lonely voice in the late 1950s and even in the early 1960s as the Maudling boom, and its aftermath, gathered pace, while the Treasury was apparently controlled by people who thought that money could not be defined, could not be controlled and, in the last resort, did not matter. It was only with the Heath–Barber years of 1972–4 that Robbins's message was really absorbed by economists – the monetarist counter-revolution had struck home in Britain.[4]

Robbins's other great success was in persuading many economists (not all) of the necessity of the separation of value judgements from positive analysis and also, to some extent, a reduction in their use in economics. Essentially Robbins introduced a new demarcation criterion for science, as indicated in Chapter 3, and this was highly successful. Indeed it arguably remains Robbins's greatest single achievement. He attached great importance to the authority of 'economic science' and to the consensus of 'competent economists'. But at the time that he wrote *ENSES* this authority was being claimed for things which had no 'scientific' basis, and reflected particular (largely Cambridge) value judgements concerning equality. While Robbins was an egalitarian in his approach to many policy problems, he refused to accept that such a position could be arrived at within the boundaries of 'science'.

In contrast to these successes, Robbins's internationalism has come to seem more and more of a distant vision – as he himself came to realise. In the sphere of international money we have moved in an opposite direction from that which Robbins desired. Robbins insisted that free exchange rates were the opposite of a 'truly liberal' solution, fragmenting the world into areas of monetary nationalism. (He *may* have had a crucial role concerning the 1955 decision not to float the pound.) But we now live in a world of 'dirty-floating' and though many of his pessimistic predictions have been borne out (especially those concerning inflation-prone governments freed from the discipline of the exchanges, and the problems of short-run and long-run capital movements) the experience has not been the disaster that he might have anticipated. Indeed free exchange rates have coped with the oil price shocks with a smoothness inconceivable under fixed rates.

Robbins's vision of international liberalism and Federalism is even more distant. The only exception to this is in that area where he had the greatest doubts, and of which he initially opposed the unification – Western Europe. There is no sign of the Atlantic union which he favoured, and although we do not have the tariffs of the 1930s, we have experienced the multiplication of non-tariff barriers, and of barriers to migration. (The latter, however, are consistent with Robbins's own later forebodings, at times almost verging on panic, about the population explosion.) The IMF has not developed as the world central bank, and the United Nations remains as he described it. GATT, the post-war institution in the framing of which he had the largest hand, has survived and developed, and it has made substantial progress at least in dealing with tariff barriers. But Robbins's full vision remains still a distant vision. Despite his efforts, and those of many others, the world has moved only a little way towards an institutional framework of the kind which he believed would eliminate those national (and sectional) conflicts which concerned him so much throughout his life.

Robbins was a great teacher of economics, and more broadly a great educationist, and in this role he enjoyed substantial successes. In particular he enjoyed quite remarkable success in rescuing the history of economic thought in Britain, as witnessed by the two Prefaces to the two editions of his *Theory of Economic Policy*. But this picture must be qualified in that it is really only in *research* in the history of economic thought that Robbins's influence has been positive. The teaching of the subject has enjoyed very much less favour. While Robbins thought that courses in the subject should be compulsory, they have typically become at first optional and then non-existent. The teaching of the history of economic thought to economists, like the teaching of methodology and of the philosophy of science, is now at a very low ebb, and this has resulted in some quantitative work which, methodologically speaking, represents a revival of those things in pre-World War Two quantitative work which Robbins most deplored. Moreover, while Robbins advocated courses in the history of economic thought so as to make better economists – he believed, like Edgeworth, in a multiplication of authorities – economists have resisted this improvement. 'Subjective originality', as Schumpeter called it, is still very much in evidence, economists frequently appear to believe that economics started in about 1936, and important lessons (for instance the trade-diverting nature of customs unions) have had to be rediscovered though they were well-enough known to people like Jacob Viner and Robbins who knew their Classical literature. This is unfortunate: it was, not infrequently, precisely Robbins's knowledge of the wider literature which underlay his good judgement and sense of perspective in dealing with contemporary issues.

Nonetheless it is true to some extent that Robbins's ambition to open up British economics was achieved. The stifling influence of the 'one book' approach has, with the exception of some of the devotees of Keynes's *General Theory*, largely disappeared. But against that, the literature which economists know is now almost all in English – the language requirement was, despite Robbins's opposition, dropped at LSE itself, Moreover the opening up was largely due not to Robbins but to the influence of American economists, the English-language inheritors of the traditions of German scholarship. Even now, some may consider that there are differences in the degree of what is regarded as acceptable scholarly research between Britain and the United States, though they are nothing like so marked as in the 1930s.

In educational and arts administration Robbins achieved a good deal. The building up of LSE was a remarkable achievement, in which Robbins played a leading role. Ironically, as noted in Chapter 2, it was a development in the opposite direction to that envisaged by the founders of LSE. But it was nonetheless remarkable, and the Robbins Building of LSE library is a fitting tribute. In the field of university education more generally, Robbins's achievements have been mixed. The Robbins Report has not been followed directly. The postgraduate programme, to which Robbins attached such importance as a means of broadening excessively narrow English first degrees, blossomed at first but has since withered. University expansion itself has gone into reverse. Yet the Report, and Robbins's personal promotion of it – almost a personal crusade – have been, and are still, an important background influence. In the field of arts administration Robbins's achievements were considerable, though the freedom with which he argued for subsidy without considering the full economic consequences is another matter. But this is a subject for a full biography rather than for the present limited study.

By intelligence, erudition and force of personality, Robbins was a dominating figure in British economics. He was, as another great economist wrote, 'indisputably one of the most distinguished figures in the second golden age of British economics'.[5] He was not only a great public figure; he was also a great economist. As a British Nobel prize winner has written:

> the richness of his other lives and of his personality must not be allowed to overshadow the fact that he was by profession an economist and an economist of the first rank.[6]

He was a great economic essayist. It is to the credit of the profession that accorded him such deserved prestige that it is still able, implicitly at least, to recognise that a first class mind may be turned to something other than second-order conditions. As an economic essayist he drew upon an extraordinary range of sources, with a knowledge of economic literature which, in its span over time and over space, could be rivalled by his friend Jacob Viner but by very few others. This knowledge informed his work as an economic essayist. As he himself wrote of his own teacher, Edwin Cannan:

> he was deeply imbued with the spirit of the Classical outlook – its long views, its wide perspectives, the broad humanity and cosmopolitanism of its approach.[7]

Although he did not always agree with Cannan, there is no doubt that the influence of Cannan, as a great teacher, on Robbins was fundamental – it was Cannan whose sharpness of mind and knowledge of the literature excited Robbins and gave him a love for, and a fascination with, the whole subject. He in turn was to become a quite remarkable teacher. As Baumol has written:

> His extraordinary qualities as a teacher, his unstinting devotion to the professional development of his students, the special stimulating quality of his seminar which others have consciously sought to replicate, and, perhaps most of all, the thought and discussion which his powerful presence inspired in others, have undoubtedly enriched our literature profoundly. Thus he added much to our knowledge, both at first remove and at second. It is fair to say that among his many accomplishments

by no means the least was that of a great teacher in the broadest sense, and the group of persons who will be pleased to recognise themselves as his students in that sense is distinguished indeed.[8]

Perhaps it would be appropriate to end with something that Robbins himself wrote about John Stuart Mill. Robbins admired Mill perhaps above all economists, not for his economic writings taken on their own (though he certainly did admire these greatly and was imbued with their analysis) but for the qualities, both personal and philosophical, which surrounded, and indeed were interwoven with, the economics. Yet what he wrote about Mill could stand as a fitting conclusion to an essay on his own work:

for a generation disillusioned with systems, he once more appears as a highly admirable figure: a man with a firm hold on the ultimate values of truth and justice and liberty, with strong principles and a strong belief in their applicability; yet once the high spirits and arrogance of youth had been transcended, fair in argument, willing to learn from experience, empirical in practical judgement, experimental in action.[9]

Appendix: The Methods of Economic Observation and the Problems of Prediction in Economics[1]

The object of my lecture is two-fold. As its title implies, I hope to develop certain views on the method appropriate to economic prediction and certain criticisms of the methods which have been fashionable in the past; but I would not wish to develop these ideas so to speak *in abstracto*. As Professor at the London School of Economics I have had the good fortune to participate, for several years, in the bringing together of information on events, in the course of which one is led to predictions about future movements. Your President, M. Charles Rist, has suggested that I could combine, with my general discussion of the problem of prediction of events, a summary of the work which we carry out and of the methods which we employ in London. I propose therefore to commence with a brief summary of the research work undertaken at present at the London School of Economics. This will lead quite naturally to the more general problem of the prediction of events and will illustrate our account.

The London School of Economics, the centre of our studies, is part of the University of London; it fulfils a double function, it is a teaching institution and it is a research institution. The teaching side is not relevant here.

Although our special research, such as the new examination of life and work in London, offers as much of interest, for the problem that I have to discuss, as the methods practised by our permanent organisation (I allude to the London and Cambridge Economic Service) for the collection of economic data, my remarks refer principally to that organisation.

Strictly speaking, the London and Cambridge Economic Service is an organisation separate and distinct from the London School of Economics. It is managed by an executive committee composed in part of representatives of the Faculty of Political Economy at the University of Cambridge and of Sir Charles Addis, of the Bank of England, who fulfils the functions of Treasurer.

The bulletin published by this service is considered by a committee composed of representatives of the two institutions, but the work of collection and of analysis is carried out by the Department of Statistics at the London School of Economics and one can say that in reality it forms an integral part of the organisation of the School.

The work of this Service consists in bringing together economic data

170

and publishing them in a suitable form. The Service publishes a monthly bulletin on the general state of affairs, in the United Kingdom and the United States, and a monthly supplement for other countries, which covers France, Germany and Italy, with notes every three months on Holland and Belgium. The bulletin is published on the 23rd of each month and the supplement appears on the 7th of the following month. It thus provides a statistical service every fifteen days for the United Kingdom. From time to time, the Service publishes bulletins on special problems. During recent years, these special bulletins have comprised *Memoranda* on the restrictions on the supply of raw materials – rubber, sugar and coffee – a new index of prices, the railway industry in Great Britain, stocks of the principal commodities, a tabular guide to the external trade statistics of twenty-one large countries, the motor industry in England, and so on. These *Memoranda*, however, are of the same nature as the other investigations pursued at the School. The London and Cambridge Service having for its principal function the publication of the monthly bulletin, it is of that that I am going to talk about particularly.

The object of the bulletin is two-fold. First of all, it records the important statistical facts. In the second place, it puts forward a diagnosis of the general situation and attempts predictions. It is preferable to treat the two questions separately.

The principal statistical series published in the bulletin are grouped under four headings:

1. Finances;
2. Prices and wages;
3. Industry and Trade (including transport);
4. Unemployment.

The Service also publishes every three months a general index of output and supplementary tables concerning exchange rates, stocks and the principal commodities, the inclination and trend of trade. To these tables is joined every three months a detailed analysis of the most important trends. To the extent that current events require it, the editorial committee inserts, in this analysis, several supplementary tables to aid understanding of the situation.

I arrive now at the most interesting topic: the deductions and the predictions which are based on these facts; but firstly, it is necessary to examine the scientific bases of economic prediction.

Economic diagnosis and prediction were scarcely attempted until after the war. Without doubt, to predict the course of events has been the ambition of businessmen and of financial journalists since the existence of businesses and the financial press. But to bring together systematically the statistics and the analysis with a view to obtaining a general line of conduct for a future policy, is an entirely recent occupation. From before the war there existed in America a sort of barometer of business. But we can say that no serious work had been undertaken before the foundation of the Harvard Committee in 1916.

The movement began in a wave of enthusiasm. At first it was hoped to draw from past events, examined with the aid of new statistical apparatus, profitable lessons. Next, it was thought that businessmen would be able to predict further in advance their line of conduct and that even the administration of government, better instructed, would be able in time, by an appropriate policy, to reduce and perhaps to eliminate cyclical fluctuations.

Nowadays we have returned to a diametrically opposite opinion. The experience of the last fourteen years has not justified the hopes that we had formed. It is not from economic service to the world that these publications could justify the pretensions which were expressed. The methods employed have led, in many cases, to results so unfortunate that in betting constantly on the prediction opposite to that which had been published, one would have amassed a substantial fortune. The American experience in this matter must thus always be present in our mind. The consequence was a terrible disillusionment. Meanwhile, as the methodological knowledge developed, the field of possible prediction became more and more limited. In fact, many of sense and distinction refused to make any economic prognostications; they contended themselves with analysing the recorded facts and with making a simple diagnosis.

I am not in favour of either one of these extremes. I do not believe that the hopes that were expressed after the war are justified. But I do not believe either that it is necessary to arrive at a scepticism like that which my friend Dr Oscar Morgenstern has shown in *Wirtschaftsprognose*. If I had to choose between Dr Morgenstern and Harvard, I would be very embarrassed. In the matter of method, I would certainly follow Dr Morgenstern. But in order not to suppress all hope of the future of economic science, I would maintain Harvard in being. Happily, I do not believe it necessary to choose one or the other of these postures.

Let us then look at the first stage, the method of prediction of business with the aid of statistical correlations.

The attitude of partisans of this method can be summarised in two propositions. In the first place, they insist that the facts must be studied without any preconceived idea. In the second place, they pretend that with the aid of suitable statistical methods, notably correlation analysis and the analysis of time series, one could forecast future events. It is necessary to remember this double posture because it is only in keeping it in mind that one can discover the key to their lack of success. Only the second proposition has a constructive character. It is on this that rests all the work carried out. But it is the anti-theoretical position expressed in the first proposition which can explain the emptiness of the results obtained. It is not by accident that the work of the Harvard Committee has been directly inspired by the researches of Professor Wesley Mitchell. One knows that Professor Mitchell has been the leader of the anti-theoretical movement in America and one knows also that his influence has been preponderant on the studies of the Harvard Economic Service.

I have no desire in the world to play down the value of the statistical methods and of the presentations developed by Harvard, but neither of the two propositions on which these works depend is methodologically sound. Let us examine each of them separately.

It is not necessary, before an audience so experienced, to delay oneself in combating those who pretend that scientific investigations can develop without preconceived theory. The naivety of this scientific conception has been many times exposed. It is surprising that intelligent investigators should return to it. The evident truth is that we cannot draw any conclusions from facts if we do not bring to their examination a preconceived theory. The facts, as facts, only have significance for us as we have ideas about them. It is not the man of science, it is the village idiot, who considers all facts equally important. Whatever selection the mind may make in the continuity of the data, this choice implies a principle of selection, a conscious or unconscious theory. What distinguishes the man of science from the layman is not that he has a theory but that he submits his theory to certain logical and objective tests. That amounts to saying that his theory is a hypothesis and not a dogma. Not to recognise this indicates that we are the victims of an unconscious theory – that our analysis is not scientific.

If we examine the works of the leading prophets, we find that this is exactly what has happened to them. When they talk of method, when they talk of the results of their analyses, they conform constantly to a kind of theory – the theory that the other theories are bad.

We arrive thus at the second proposition which requires that forecasts may be guided satisfactorily by the unaided results of statistical analysis. But this theory does not withstand examination. In practice it has failed lamentably and even in theory it appears inconsistent and deceitful.

The essence of the method which I am discussing is that certain sequences of movement, observed in previous periods, make it possible to predict similar sequences for the future. An upward movement in a series is deemed to predict an upward movement in another series. The rule of prediction can be qualitative or quantitative – we can say that an upward movement in the first series will be followed at any moment by an upward movement in the second, – or we can try to give a numerical estimate of the change which should be expected. In either case, the method remains the same. It is believed that past sequences furnish the bases for predicting future sequences.

It is not necessary to be a great logician to bring out the weakness of this proceeding. The sequences which the analysis of statistics reveals can certainly appear very regularly in the past. But unless we are capable of explaining why they appear, of discerning their prime cause, we have no reason to be convinced that they will reproduce themselves necessarily in the future. Unless we are able to explain the relations of causality we are at the mercy of what could have been merely a simple accident; we are not in a state to discern the accidental from the inevitable. It may well be that the continuity of certain relations over a very long period may be due to the persistence of some accidental element sufficient to transform entirely the effect of hidden trends. The discovery of uniformity in the statistics is without doubt an important discovery; but it is the discovery of a problem, and not of a solution.

A simple example will clarify the problem. During many years before the war, the development of a 'boom' – I employ this word to indicate the high level of industrial activity which precedes a crisis – was accompanied by a rise in prices. Statistical analysis brought this connection to light; but if this connection is treated like a law, from which one draws predictions, one is in grave risk of error. We know, from economic theory, that it is possible to conceive a boom with a stable level of prices. Recent experience has shown that this can in practice be the case. It is very clear that the relationship between the increase in prices and a boom, in the past, has been due to the accidental coexistence of certain ratios in the alterations of monetary and technical factors. In the last boom, this coexistence did not appear, and the forecasts founded on crude inductions from statistics proved thus completely false. Here we have a typical example of the mistakes to which the anti-theoretical methods of prediction lead.

But, moreover, it is for more fundamental reasons that methods of this type lead to erroneous results. Economic phenomena, of all kinds, result in the last analysis, from the play of diverse factors which give birth to scarcity. We have, on the one side, the tastes of diverse individuals and on the other the technical and legal constraints of the environment within which they operate. If we suppose that these fundamental data are unalterable, we can arrive at important conclusions on the diverse relations which result from them. This is the domain of 'economic law'. When the data are modified, we can discover the result of these changes. There are uniformities here, but this is no reason to suppose that they retain their meaning during the several changes of the data – changes in tastes, technique, the legal framework of economic activity. The correspondence and the series which emerge from the study of statistics are correspondences which can very well be derived from changes of this sort.

Once more, I am going to appeal to a simple example. Given certain information about prices, it is possible, by the employment of subtle statistical methods, to discover the coefficients which depict the conditions of the demand for products. The studies of statisticians, such as Professor Schultz, have done much for the progress of knowledge in this matter. One of the results of their efforts is to inform us, up to a point, about the elasticity of demand for agricultural products, important in America, during the last ten years. But what is the significance of these results. If one proves that the elasticity of demand for sugar was, from 1880 to 1925, 0.85, what does this signify? In the last analysis, simply this: it is a compact formula, in practice, to record past events. If we suppose that customs do not change, it can serve as a guide for approximate prediction in the immediate future. But it is quite arbitrary if this hypothesis asserts that the numbers should have anything other than an historic meaning. There does not exist a 'law' which says that the elasticity of demand for sugar must be of such a size. And if we reflect on the diversity of influences which determine the demand for sugar or any other commodity, it is certainly apparent that the idea of obtaining permanent and constant quantitative laws, in talking of a single historical period, is entirely illusory. Changes of religion, changes of composition, changes in the availability of substitutes, changes in the technical conditions of production of other goods – all these changes can affect the demand conditions for sugar. It is clear that to hope to obtain quantitative laws in such matters, is to hope to obtain not quantitative *economic* laws but quantitative *historical* laws.

I have chosen as an example a statistical induction relating to a single commodity because I do not believe that for such a simple case there can be any divergence of opinion. Professor Schultz will not contradict me. But if we agree here on the limits of the significance of statistical induction, we could be in disagreement on the position of this induction in a more complex field, in that of the prediction of business. Certainly, nothing is more futile than the attempts to establish the duration of what is called 'the business cycle' in taking the average of statistics which correspond to different conditions of time and space. The mountains of statistical analysis prepared since the war constitute an economic history of value. They offer a useful starting point for the verification of particular theories, but that in themselves they can provide anything else seems a pure illusion.

From considerations of this sort, coupled with the breakdown of the principal American apparatus of prediction, one passes to the attitude of complete scepticism, of which Dr Morgenstern is the most striking example. Attention is drawn to the deserved failure, the abuse to which correlation analyses have given rise, the evident impossibility of developing quantitative and objective laws, the complexity of tastes, the legal and technical obstacles which they meet. It is concluded that the statistical institutes should renounce all prediction. They have no other object, it is said, than the verification of facts. As I have said, I have a considerable sympathy for the attitude of these authors. I share their repulsion for what often seems to be the charlatanism of the so-called experts in statistics. I share completely their scepticism about the possibility of deriving laws, concerning changes in the heterogeneous data, and I think that the statistical services have for their principal object the development of precise and verifiable statistics. Nevertheless, I believe that to disown all power of diagnosis and of prediction is to exhibit a truly superfluous austerity. This austerity would deprive economic science of one of its most useful applications and it is not at all necessary according to the demands of economic science.

Allow me to emphasise the grounds of my opinion. The principal argument of the school whose opinions I am discussing, has referred to quantitative laws. No such laws, they insist, can be established. It follows that no forecasting is possible. The argument does not seem to me conclusive. We can admit that quantitative laws, of the kind which they have in mind, cannot be established. I have insisted myself already, in the course of this lecture, that this is indeed the case. But the possibility of making forecasts is not, as a result, excluded. Quantitative laws, such as the American statisticians hoped to formulate, are not the only kind of law possible. What this argument does not take into account is that the laws on which the principal deductions of analytical economics depend –

and consequently its capacity to make predictions – are not of this kind. They depend on facts universally recognised: our preferences are of a certain kind; output varies with the variations of the factors of production . . .[2] They are empirical because they are dependent on certain conditions of fact, but these conditions are of a kind so general that they are the most often operational and consequently the predictions which one arrives at are not subject to the same restrictions as those which one draws from fortuitous results of correlation analysis. Again a simple example here will show what I have in mind. I have maintained that the numerical coefficient of the elasticity of demand for sugar is necessarily the result of historical forces, of which the effect can be very singular. Given that, in normal times, when habits do not change, they may serve as a basis for a limited prediction, they are not of a necessary character. The 'laws' of this kind must be continually revised, but the law of demand which says that, all other things being equal, the quantities consumed vary inversely with the price, is not of this kind. It is derived from studies of subjective value, which have led to what is called the law of diminishing marginal utility. We can conceive of exceptions to this rule. Observation should be employed to verify that sugar does not prove to be one of these exceptions. But the considerations which lead us to conclude that demand, for the majority of commodities, falls under this law, have a more general character than the considerations which establish the temporary elasticity.

The example which I have given is simple and one could claim that we do not need complicated scientific apparatus to predict a reaction as simple as a fall in demand due to an increase in price. I am in agreement with that, but if one starts from very simple commonplaces, it does not follow that one arrives at conclusions as simple. Starting from facts as simple as the law of demand, as the laws of the diminishing marginal productivity of capital, we can reach very complex conclusions on the changes in capital and the periodical oscillations of business. The conclusions are not apparent immediately to the layman. However I am convinced that, correctly employed, they are of great assistance in making forecasts.

But the question then inevitably arises of knowing in what sense conclusions of this sort permit interpretation of situations of fact. It is here that statistical observation is applicable. It indicates to us what are the forces in operation in the case examined. The structure of our theoretical apparatus is hypothetical; its characteristic generalisations tell us that, if certain conditions are present, all other things besides being equal, one can expect that certain consequences will follow. The function of our statistical services is to keep us informed of the existing conditions. Our theory must tell us what effects one can expect to observe to ensue. Thus general theoretical reasoning tells us that if a currency is significantly over-valued compared with others, the phenomena which one can call deflation appear in the country of relative over-valuation. That is not certain in the sense that, if some other cause acts on the initial influence, the method of operation is no longer the same; but it is certain in the sense that, if nothing else operates, the consequences are those which would be expected from the initial influence. Thus, if statistical observation informs us of the presence of such a disparity, the prediction is justified. But a prediction of this kind is essentially qualitative. It does not tell us the amplitude or the timing of the expected reactions. Is it not possible to give it a quantitative character? I see no objection.

I have emphasised already the impossibility of establishing quantitative laws, in the sense of numerical formulae applicable at all times and places. But that does not prevent belief in the possibility of collecting, during periods of relative stability, quantitative information concerning the immediate past, information which can greatly aid prediction of the immediate future. The elasticity of demand for sugar can, as I have claimed, require to be continually recalculated, but that does not mean that it may be without value at the moment at which it is calculated. Statistical analysis cannot furnish 'laws' but it can aid materially in the formulation of forecasts.

I thus conclude that there are no methodological reasons to prevent the development of the technique of forecasting, in economic matters, in similar ways to those which I have already discussed. A double lesson emerges from this analysis of past experience, coupled with the statement of present theory. Firstly, it is futile to attempt forecasts, or rather, all kinds of statistical investigation, without the assistance of general economic theory. Secondly, it is always necessary to keep in mind that all quantitative results obtained by this kind of analysis have a very limited application and cannot be employed except in conjunction with what, for lack of a better expression, I will call the 'common sense' of the general situation. The error in prediction of business in the past has been to fail to observe these elementary rules. It has been forgotten that the technique of prediction cannot proceed in advance of the technique of general theory, and attempts have been made, in a way that was too rigid, to apply quantitative methods to the analysis of situations in which qualitative factors were also important. In the last analysis, the error is inherent in the environment in which the forecasting of business was first developed. It is regrettable that the application of this marvellous new technique, statistical analysis, was in the hands of men who had fallen victim to a series of mistaken ideas concerning the general methods of the social sciences. From these mistaken ideas Europe, after half a century of controversies, is only beginning to escape. Hence a loss of credit for methods which, in themselves, were entirely excellent. With the perspective from which we profit today, let us be careful that in rejecting the errors of the past we do not reject at the same time genuine progress.

Let us return to our experience in London, which has provided moreover the majority of my arguments. The history of the London and Cambridge Economic Service, with regard to the matter of prediction, illustrates the change of opinion which I have already attempted to trace. When we began, in 1923, we were, to some extent, under the influence of the methods of Harvard. Our introductory number dwelt on the sequences of the general series of indexes of business. I do not think that this was much use. The particular economic conditions, which developed in Great Britain after the return to the gold standard in 1925, were such that one could evidently not apply rules based on pre-war experience or on American experience. In the excellent book by M. Lacombe, written in 1926, our graphs of business are still given much weight. I was not a member of the editorial committee before the end of 1929. Since then, I cannot remember a single occasion when we used these graphs in our deliberations on prediction. If the graphs are always printed at the head of the bulletin, it is a kind of atavistic survival – like so many of the elements of the practical English constitution. They had the power to be our tyrant – knowing Professor Bowley, I doubt it however, – now they hardly fulfil the very limited functions of a constitutional monarch. It is from a sense of continuity that they are always printed in the same place.

I cannot better give you an idea of our methods than describe to you one of the meetings of our editorial committee. The meetings are completely without ceremony, the meeting of a half dozen friends seated around a table, following almost always the same procedure. They begin by reading out loud the diagnosis and the prediction of the previous bulletin; then, the available materials are examined to see what errors have been committed and to what extent the most important changes have been indicated. This exercise habitually introduces a certain spirit of humility which is suitable for the principal objective of the meeting. Then we scrutinise one by one the changes that we have discovered. The quantitative methods of seasonal analysis are of great help here. I do not remember having employed very seriously the analysis of trends. Our conclusions, up to this point, are contained in the article of detailed analysis to which I have made allusion above.

At last the task arrives of preparing a short diagnosis and prediction. The investigations, which I have detailed this afternoon, find their role here; but the role played by general theoretical considerations and qualitative factors in the situation becomes much larger. One after the other, the members of the committee state what they believe to be the most significant elements in the situation. A discussion takes place and the different opinions are recorded by the editor. A draft is circulated and usually corrections are made to it before publication.

The results are not as brilliant as one could wish, for our knowledge is not sufficiently advanced for our predictions to be other than limited attempts. At the beginning of the crisis, in the autumn of 1927, we made a serious error. I do not wish to discuss it now, because it is better not to criticise decisions in which I had no responsibility; but, generally speaking, I do not think that since the spring of 1930, our collection would suffer by comparison with that of all other services. A businessman or a statesman who reads our bulletin will not find there material on which to base long-term projects, but I do not think that he could make much mistake and, in one case at least, if he has found us against the majority of opinions, events have justified us.

It remains only, gentlemen, to transmit to you and to your Institute, the best wishes of my colleagues in London. English work on the theory of the business cycle already owes much to French authors. We await, with impatience, the increase of this debt by this centralisation of your facilities of research and thought.

Notes and References

2 Biography

1. (1971a).
2. (1971a) p. 1.
3. (1968a) p. 1.
4. For instances of this see (1971a) pp. 29, 68; Baumol (1984) p. 10; Moser (1984) p. 14 (concerning Robbins's overwhelmed reaction to a Rembrandt painting).
5. Johnson (1972) p. 835.
6. See Robbins (1971a) pp. 58–9. For his father's public activities see, for example, *The Times*, 15 January 1931 (8g), 15 May 1931 (12c), 7 and 18 November 1929 (10a, 18f) – this is a controversy involving Cannan – 28 May (16d), 11 July (12c), 13 July (10d) 1928.
7. (1934g, h); (1939a) contains the two articles referred to: the quotation is at p. 178. See also (1932c), (1937f).
8. (1971a) p. 20.
9. See for instance (1980a) p. 106.
10. (1971a) p. 20; see also (1970d) p. 424.
11. (1980a) pp. 7, 35.
12. (1955b) pp. 10–12.
13. (1971a) pp. 24–5.
14. (1971a) pp. 36–53.
15. (1925/6) pp. 55–7.
16. (1971a) p. 56.
17. (1971a) p. 65. The anecdote is one which quotation would spoil.
18. (1971a) pp. 70–1.
19. (1971a) pp. 74–5.
20. A useful indication of some of this reading will be found in (1925/6) p. 91, which contains an interesting tribute to Sidgwick.
21. (1971a) pp. 80–3, 93–5; see also Gregory (1921).
22. (1971a) p. 75. See also Robbins's obituary of Gregory (1971d).
23. (1971a) pp. 83–6.
24. (1925/6) p. 94. Robbins referred to Cannan 'to whose teaching and inspiration the writer [LCR] owes whatever knowledge he has of Economic Science and its application to the complex and bewildering problems of our day'.
25. Hicks (1982) pp. 4–5.
26. 1935c. See also (1929d) p. 411 and p. 414 referring to 'a high standard and a shining example'.
27. (1937b) is dedicated to the memory of Edwin Cannan; see also ibid pp. 37, 232 and (1963a) p. 123.
28. (1929b) p. 71; (1939d) p. 291n.
29. Coats (1982) p. 23. On this question see also Robbins (1929d) pp. 411–12.

30. Coase (1982) p. 33.
31. Cannan (1932) p. 426. Although Cannan puts these words into the mouth of a hypothetical complainant, they seem to reflect his own sentiments.
32. On the Scottish writers see Robbins (1968a) p. 2; on Wallas see (1971a) pp. 86–9; (1965a) p. 5; (1963b). On Robbins's attitude to the Utilitarians see Chapter 5 of this book.
33. (1971a) p. 76.
34. (1971a) p. 96.
35. Grimmond (1985).
36. Pimlott (1985) p. 137.
37. Pimlott (1985) pp. 160–3. See also Dalton (1986a) p. 520 for a revealing comment on his view of Robbins's debt to him, and (1986b) p. 53 on the resistance to Robbins's appointment.
38. Pimlott (1985) pp. 161, 215; Coats (1982) p. 24 and n. 27; Dalton (1986a) pp. 467, 522, 525, 618; (1986b) p. 165; Robbins (1962c).
39. Young (1928b) p. 115.
40. (1971a) pp. 116–18, 193.
41. Meade (1984) p. 5.
42. (1966b) pp. 8–9.
43. Hicks (1982) p. 3, (1979) p. 356, (1963a) pp. xii, 306. (See also Robbins (1930c) p. 129 for a neat footnote contributed by Hicks.)
44. Hicks (1963) p. 306; see also Hicks (1967) p. x; Coase (1982) p. 32; Coats (1982) p. 21; Koot (1982); Wiseman (1985).
45. See *The Times* obituary 17 May 1985, 4f: 'It is difficult to describe his love for, and his contribution to, the London School of Economics. Suffice it to say that the preeminence of that college was in a large part due to him.' See also *Annual Register* (1984), Levy (1984), and Norman (1986).
46. (1971a) p. 296. See for example, *The Times*, 12 May 1969 (10a), 5 December 1969 (1d), 27 June 1970 (2a), 23 October 1971 (12d). See also Dunworth (1980).
47. Coase (1982) p. 33.
48. (1971a) p. 278n; (1966c), p. 25; see also Peston (1981) p. 183.
49. (1954) pp. 18–40; (1971a) pp. 75, 96, 135–42, 157–8, 189–90, 230; see also Harris (1977) pp. 288–9, 296–9, 317–19, 322–4, 409–12, 429; Dalton (1986a) p. 538.
50. Beveridge (1937); the quotation is from p. 466. See also Robbins (1971a) pp. 81–2, 94–5; Harris (1977) pp. 292–303, 309.
51. (1971a) p. 134.
52. Moser (1984) p. 14. See also Robbins (1928b), (1930g).
53. (1966a).
54. (1971a) p. 124.
55. Muggeridge (1973) pp. 262–3.
56. (1962a) p. 204, and cf. Muggeridge (1966) p. 62. See also Baumol (1984) p. 10.
57. (1971a) p. 111. But LSE was such a central part of his life that he took the title for his peerage from Clare Market beside it – Corry (1978) p. 61.

58. See also Coats (1982) p. 20.
59. Robbins [Chairman] (1963c) for example pp. 177–8.
60. (1947c) pp. 10, 30–1, 75.
61. (1932a) p. 119; (1935a) p. 108. See also (1927c, d), (1931e, f), (1936h), (1937e). As a reviewer his range of interests was exceptionally wide – see also (1926b, c, d).
62. (1971a) pp. 107, 143.
63. (1937b) pp. 235–7.
64. (1970a) especially pp. 1–2, 6–7; (1971a) pp. 132, 163, 217, 219–20; (1980c). See also Robbins (1966g) which refers to 'the unrivalled knowledge of the [Classical] period and the deep historical insight of which, for so many years, Professor Viner has given so freely to those who have had the privilege of his friendship and conversation'.
65. Baumol (1984).
66. (1954) p. viii.
67. (1963a) pp. 225–6n.
68. 'Professor Robbins writes so as to ask for trouble, and he will always get it, but his courageous pen is one of our assets' – MacGregor (1939) p. 493. See also Robbins (1971a) ch. 10 especially p. 229; Peacock (1982) p. 40.
69. (1971a) p. 234. See (1932h), (1934g), (1935d), (1935f), (1937d), (1939c, d), (1949b) as examples of this.
70. (1971a) p. 234. See also Robertson (1937), Henderson (1937), Keynes (1935), Henderson (1935b), Shone (1935), Rist (1935a), Brand (1935).
71. (1929a).
72. (1971a) pp. 151–2. See also (1978c) p. 114.
73. See notes 69 and 70 above. See also (1932e, f, g); (1932c); (1971a) pp. 155–9; (1931d); (1936e); Cannon (1936); Wise (1931a, b).
74. Peacock (1982) pp. 35, 36. For a tribute to Robbins's courage in (1937b) see Morrow (1937).
75. (1947c) pp. 32, 34. Robbins's own courage is evident in his accepting the Chairmanship of the LSE governors – (1971a) pp. 294–5.
76. Hayek (1931a, b), (1932); Keynes (1931); Sraffa (1932a, b). See also Coats (1982) p. 28n.
77. (1934d) pp. 20, 64; (1974b) p. 25; (1958a) p. 21; (1971a) p. 153; (1949b) pp. 19–24; (1979a) pp. x, 38, 44; (1937d) p. 239.
78. (1971a) pp. 154–5; see also (1979a) p. 14.
79. (1971b) p. 6; (1954) pp. 69–70.
80. (1971b) p. 2; (1958c).
81. (1970b) pp. 244–5. See also (1959) pp. 36–8.
82. (1976) p. 84. This is hardly surprising given the intervening macro-economic experience.
83. (1953b) especially pp. 105, 111; (1970b) pp. 248–52. Robertson (1955). Robertson treated his macroeconomic writings with respect, and shared Robbins's disappointment at the Radcliffe Report. See Robertson (1937), (1959).
84. Robertson (1935) especially p. 104.
85. Johnson and Johnson (1978) pp. 92, 130–1, 136–9.
86. (1971a) pp. 193, 208–12.

87. (1949a) p. 104; (1954) p. 104; (1973a) p. 3.
88. Meade (1984).
89. Harrod (1952) p. 567. Robbins recounted that he fought for the Keynes plan rather than the White plan at Bretton Woods – *Hansard*, vol. 277, col. 89, 29 March 1961.
90. Harrod (1951) p. 567.
91. Harrod (1951) pp. 426–7, 429–30; Winch (1969) pp. 150, 160.
92. Pimlott (1985) p. 162; Dalton (1986b) pp. 122–4.
93. Robbins (1925).
94. Robbins (1929d) p. 412.
95. Cannan (1924); Keynes (1924).
96. Cannan (1921); Robbins (1926d).
97. Robbins (1927b) p. 131n. See however (1926c) for a compliment to Keynes.
98. (1931b) p. 100. On Keynes as conscientious objector see Moggridge (1976) pp. 17–19, 168 (n 7); Skidelsky (1983) pp. 315–27.
99. (1931b) p. 100.
100. (1931a) pp. 57–62.
101. (1932d) pp. 178–80.
102. (1937b) pp. 298, 319–24.
103. Dalton (1986b) p. 165, entry for 6–8 January 1932.
104. Robbins (1930f), (1962b). Robbins's opening review after more than 30 years contained a dig at Keynes's vacillations over the importance of the rate of interest.
105. (1971a) pp. 155–6.
106. (1976a) p. 177n. However Robbins reviewed the reprint of *Essays in Biography* in a complimentary manner (1973c).
107. (1971a) pp. 168, 176, 184.
108. Meade (1984).
109. Robbins (1944). I am most grateful to Denys Gribbin for bringing this document to my attention. I am also grateful to Dr Elizabeth Hallam Smith for further help in connection with this document.
110. (1971a) p. 190.
111. Harrod (1952) pp. 608–9.
112. (1947c) p. 1.
113. Robbins (1971b) p. 6; (1958c) qq. 10205, 10228.
114. Robertson (1959) p. 719.
115. (1971a) pp. 54–5.
116. Harrod (1952) pp. 608–12.
117. Drogheda (1984).
118. Johnson (1972) p. 835.
119. (1971a) p. 290.
120. *Economist*, 19 May 1984, p. 38.
121. (1971a) p. 234.
122. (1971a) pp. 283–4.
123. (1966b) pp. 138–57.
124. (1979a). The peerage was seen as non-political – *The Times*, 23 January 1959 (10d). See also *The Times*, 17 June 1959 (16g), 16 July 1959 (3f).

125. For example, (1951a); (1949b) p. 12.
126. (1971a) ch. 11.
127. (1963a) pp. 53–72. See also Peston (1984). It is arguable that in this context Robbins the economist was rather overshadowed by Robbins the public figure. See Wilson (1965).
128. (1974b) pp. 14–15.
129. (1966c) pp. 27–8.
130. (1963a) p. viii; (1971a) pp. 268–71, 283; Corry (1986).
131. (1971a) pp. 271–3.
132. Moser (1984).
133. *The Times*, 17 May 1984.
134. (1966b) p. 52; (1980a) p. 50.
135. See the dedication of Layard, King and Moser (1969).
136. Robbins [Chairman] (1963a) pp. 49–54; see also Blaug (1970) p. 43.
137. Layard, King and Moser (1969) p. 26.
138. 26 honours are listed in *Who's Who*.
139. (1971a) p. 160.
140. (1971a) p. 188.
141. See especially Robertson (1935); Rist (1935b); the *Banker*, 1934; see also Henderson (1935), Tom (1935). Where the reviewers disagreed, they did so with respect. The book did not find such favour with all reviewers. Ryan (1935) considered it 'quite nineteenth century' in its 'flavor'.
142. The quotations are contained in (1937b) after the end of the text. See also the *Banker*, 1934.
143. (1929b).
144. (1971a) p. 145.
145. (1971a) p. 78.
146. (1963a) p. 27.
147. (1965a) p. 5; (1947c) *passim*; (1963a) p. 20.
148. For example, (1949b) p. 1, 'informed opinion'.
149. Knight (1938) p. 259. See also Staley (1943). Knight was less enthusiastic about the book's contents. Robbins himself admired Knight – Robbins (1957c).
150. (1974b) p. 4.
151. Moser (1984).
152. Coase (1982) pp. 32–4; Coats (1982) p. 29. For a recognition of this during the 1930s see the *Banker*, 1939.
153. Peacock (1982) pp. 39–40; Corry (1978); Wiseman (1985) p. 157; Prest (1972).
154. Dahrendorf (1984). See also Robbins (1979c) p. 90; *The Times*, 11 May 1965 (13d).
155. Pimlott (1985) p. 479. See also Robbins (1938d); Balogh (1938); Hobson (1938); Dalton (1986a) p. 538; *The Times*, 14 February 1947 (5e), 18 February 1947 (5e), 28 February 1947 (5e).
156. (1966b) pp. 38, 48. See also Balogh's maliciously-toned review of Robbins (1971a) – Balogh (1971).
157. Coats (1982) p. 25; see also Moser's account of Robbins's reaction to a Rembrandt in the Hermitage – Moser (1984).

158. (1971a) p. 148.
159. (1971a) p. 236.
160. (1935c).
161. (1937b) pp. 324–6.
162. (1971a) pp. 168–9.
163. (1953a) pp. 1–2. See also note 89 above. Robbins's pre-war internationalism is discussed in Chapter 9 of this book.
164. (1949b) pp. 3, 9.
165. (1949b) p. 30; (1953a) p. 24.
166. (1949b) p. 1.
167. (1949b) p. 31; (1971a) p. 239; (1975b) p. 145; (1979a) pp. 85, 90, 97.
168. (1963a) p. 111.
169. (1976a) p. 192.
170. Baumol (1984b); see also Baumol (1984a).
171. Dahrendorf (1984).
172. See Meade, Drogheda, Baumol, Moser (1984).
173. Meade (1984).

3 Methodology

1. Friedman (1953); Blaug (1980) p. 87; Stewart (1979) p. 126.
2. (1971a) p. 146; see also (1953b) p. 104; (1935a) p. 129 (throughout the pagination of the second edition of *ENSES* will be cited); (1929c) p. 249.
3. (1927a).
4. (1935a) pp. 147–8, 151.
5. (1938c) pp. 635–7; see also (1963a) pp. 12–19.
6. Young (1913); Robbins (1934a).
7. Preface to second edition of *ENSES*, (1935a) p. viii; (1963a) pp. 7–12; (1949a) p. 103; (1971a) pp. 147–8.
8. Baumol (1987).
9. (1938a).
10. (1930b) pp. 23–4.
11. (1947c) p. 54: 'The economic problem is essentially a problem of regulating the quantities which go to different uses and securing some rough equality of yield at the margin. It is a problem not of priority but of allocation.'
12. Hutchison (1981) p. 189.
13. A better idea of Robbins's sources can be obtained from the first edition of *ENSES* rather than from the more widely available second edition. In particular, seven of the Mises references in the first edition are missing from the second edition.
14. Blaug (1980) p. 87.
15. (1968a); (1981) pp. xiii, xxviii–xxix.
16. (1963a) pp. 12–19; (1981) p. xxii.
17. (1935a) pp. 74, 82, 96, 105; see also Blaug (1980) pp. 87–9; Mill (1825), (1844) pp. 25, 312, 314–17, 325, 329, 332.

18. (1981) p. xx; Jevons (1871) p. 85; Robbins (1934b) p. 95; (1953b) p. 108; (1933) p. xvi.
19. (1934b) p. 95; (1936a) pp. 6–7; (1970b) p. 176; see also Wicksteed (1910) pp. 766–7; Jevons (1871) pp. 84–6, 94–121; Blaug (1962) pp. 309, 334.
20. (1935a) pp. xii, xv–xvi, 55, 96; (1970b) pp. 189–209 especially p. 209.
21. (1930d); Coase (1982) p. 33.
22. Robbins (1933) p. xiv.
23. Blaug (1962) p. 488.
24. Wicksteed (1910) chs. 1, 2, 6.
25. (1935a) p. 55; Wicksteed (1910) pp. 212–400.
26. Robbins (1933) p. xvii.
27. See especially Wicksteed (1910) Book III.
28. Weber (1949) p. 52; Robbins (1935a) p. 148; see also p. xii – when Souter (1933) attacked Robbins's positivism, Robbins referred him to Weber. See also Kirzner (1976) p. 209 n.12 for Weber's use of scarcity.
29. (1935a) pp. 90, 148; Weber (1949) pp. 1–47 especially p. 11; Hutchison (1979); Bendix (1968) p. 495.
30. Weber (1949) p. 162; see also Lachman (1976).
31. (1934d) p. 57; (1937b) p. 237; (1939a) pp. 128–30.
32. (1939b) pp. 52–3, 73n.
33. See especially (1930a); (1934a).
34. (1970b) pp. 210–14; (1933) p. xx.
35. In (1934c) Robbins refers to 'goods of first order' – cf. Menger (1871) pp. 92–109 and Wieser (1889) Books III and IV.
36. See Addleson (1984). See also Knight (1934) p. 661 (who identified Wicksteed with the Austrians) and Hicks (1979) p. 358.
37. Robbins has indeed been criticised by some of the modern 'Austrians' but as Hutchison has shown, the correspondence of modern 'Austrians' with the older Austrians is less than complete (1981) pp. 187–9. See also Kirzner (1976) p. 161.
38. (1935a) pp. xv–xvi. See also (1930b) and Addleson (1984).
39. (1935a) p. 77n; (1971a) p. 107.
40. (1935a) pp. 16, 18, 39, 54, 77, 78, 83, 89. Most of the references in (1935a) are to Mises's *Gemeinwirtschaft* (1932) which was translated as *Socialism*. See also (1930b).
41. (1935a) p. 83.
42. (1935a) p. 145.
43. The contrast is evident in the discussion of Kirzner (1976) pp. 159–63; see also Stewart (1979) p. 154. On Mises's *a priorism* see also Rothbard (1968); Mises (1949) pp. 31, 55, 350–7.
44. (1971a) p. 16. The famous definition refers to Menger, Mises, Fetter, Strigl and Mayer.
45. (1935a) p. 96; (1934a); (1933) p. xvi; (1981) p. xiii; see also Addleson (1984); Hutchison (1981) pp. 187–9. But there is an important question here, raised by Wiseman (1985); the later Austrians, such as Mayer, emphasised a more passive form of subjectivism than had Menger and Wieser – the consumer now responded, computationally, to data. It is an open question how far Robbins himself accepted this

shift of emphasis though the present writer believes that, for the most part, he did do so.

46. (1935a) p. 16.
47. (1935a) p. 16. See also Hutchison (1981) p. 226n.
48. (1930d) p. 257. The work which has never been translated into English is Schumpeter (1908). Pp. 521–626 of it deal with methodological questions and the role of pure theory. See also Lachman (1976); Hutchison (1981) p. 205; Kirzner (1976) pp. 68–70.
49. Menger (1871) pp. 58–9, 129–30; Wieser (1889) p. 176.
50. (1935a) pp. 67–8. But Robbins later became much more critical of the Austrians – see (1966f).
51. (1935a) pp. 55, 67; Wicksteed (1910) pp. 212–400; Robbins (1933) p. xvi; (1934a) pp. 11, 14–15; (1930a); see also J. M. Buchanan (1973).
52. See especially (1934c) p. 465. There are also general equilibrium considerations in (1927b) pp. 124–9 – labour-saving inventions may indicate a larger rather than a small optimum population, in contrast to the partial equilibrium conclusions derived from looking at individual industries.
53. (1971a) p. 160 ('the *the*-industry fallacy'); (1954) pp. 201–25; (1947c).
54. (1934a).
55. (1929a); (1930c).
56. Kirzner (1974) pp. 38, 94–6, 147–8. See also note 45 above.
57. (1939a) p. 42.
58. (1930d) p. 257.
59. J. M. Buchanan (1968) p. 425.
60. J. M. Buchanan (1968) p. 426 sees Knight as the economist as philosopher rather than scientist. However, both Knight and Robbins (1957e) p. 399, agreed that economics differed from natural science because people *learn*.
61. (1935a) pp. 16, 83.
62. Young (1925b).
63. Cannan (1914) ch. 1.
64. (1971a) p. 105. See also (1926c).
65. (1971a) p. 146.
66. (1935a) pp. 20, 87, 88.
67. Cassel (1925) pp. 28–9.
68. Cassel (1925) pp. 30–1, 46–7.
69. Cassel (1925) pp. 88–9.
70. Wicksteed (1910) p. 766.
71. Robbins (1932a) p. 96.
72. Addleson (1984) p. 520; Blaug (1980) p. 90; see also Stewart (1979) pp. 121–6; Hicks (1983). Cooter and Rappoport (1984) p. 521 assert that 'much of Robbins's argument was anticipated by Frederic Benham (1930)'. Benham's article is certainly valuable, and it is indeed unfortunate that it should have been so completely overshadowed by *ENSES* as to become more or less completely forgotten. However the limited content of Benham's short article, the wealth of other sources on which Robbins drew, and had been drawing for some time before the appearance of Benham's paper, the

nature of Robbins's 1927 review of Hawtrey – which in fact Benham acknowledged (p. 174n) as making his central point – and Robbins's own account of the genesis of *ENSES* (1971a pp. 146–7) all combine to make Benham an unlikely source, particularly as he went so far as to reject the subjective elements in value theory and to describe (p. 187) marginal utility as a 'question-begging term' – Robbins in *ENSES* (1935a) pp. 20, 87, 88 was to be critical of similar elements in Cassel's work.

73. Cannan (1932).
74. (1914) ch. 1.
75. (1935a) pp. 4–11.
76. Beveridge (1937).
77. Knight (1934a) p. 225n. Other reviews are by James (1933) who regarded the work as 'too metaphysical and subjective' and by Peck (1936) who argued that the book represented an outdated individualism. See also Kaufman (1933), who criticises Robbins by implication.
78. Souter (1933).
79. Parsons (1934) p. 516.
80. Parsons (1934) p. 515.
81. Parsons (1934) p. 516.
82. Harrod (1938).
83. Robbins (1938c); see also (1938a).
84. Fraser (1932) p. 558.
85. Fraser (1932) pp. 566, 569.
86. Robbins (1935a) p. viii. See also (1939d) p. 295. It is rather puzzling that Robbins seems neither to have reviewed nor referred to Hutchison (1938) which Wiseman (1985) p. 149 refers to as a 'point by point critique' of *ENSES*. The review by Pirou (1936) was sufficiently non-committal, though it recognised the importance of the work, to make reply unnecessary.
87. (1935a) p. 1; see also (1959) pp. 32–5.
88. (1934a) p. 1.
89. See Meade (1984) on Robbins's Oxford lectures.
90. (1935a) pp. 2–3; (1930b) pp. 16, 24; (1930a) p. 194; see also Hutchison (1979).
91. (1949a).
92. (1927a); see also (1935a) p. 91; Weber (1949) p. 11.
93. (1935a) p. 151; (1927a) p. 177.
94. (1963a) pp. 12–19.
95. (1976a) pp. 2–3 and n.
96. (1938c) p. 638; (1934c) p. 464–5; (1971a) pp. 147–8; (1935a) p. 87; (1939a) p. 164; (1959) p. 45; (1932d) pp. 173–4; (1953b) pp. 107–8.
97. (1935a) pp. 88–90, 106; (1981) p. xviii; (1963a) pp. 6–7, 19; (1938c) p. 639; (1927a); (1971a) pp. 147–8; Hutchison (1964) pp. 18–19; Weber (1949) p. 52; Menger (1883) p. 46; Kirzner (1976) p. 137; see also Mill's science/art distinction (1844) p. 312.
98. (1934b) p. 100.
99. (1935a) pp. 4–6; (1953b) p. 104; see also Hutchison (1964) p. 172.

100. (1935a) p. 96. See also (1926c) pp. 224–5 for a defence of Robinson Crusoe methodology.
101. (1934b) p. 100; (1935a) pp. 90–4.
102. (1935a) pp. 92–4; cf. Mises (1949) p. 103 and n; Wicksteed (1910) pp. 32–4.
103. Wicksteed (1910) pp. 75, 212–65; Wieser (1889) Bk I; Robbins (1935a) p. 56 citing Menger.
104. For example (1932a) p. 56 (omitted from 1935a p. 56); (1935a) p. 93; Mises (1932) p. 93; Robbins (1934) p. 41; (1936) pp. 113–22; (1953b) pp. 102–4.
105. (1953b) pp. 103–4. However Robbins introduced elements of cardinality by recognising degrees of difference – see Robertson (1954) pp. 668, 677 and (1955).
106. (1935a) pp. 7, 12, 14, 30.
107. (1935a) pp. 16, 30, 152–3; (1930b) p. 24; (1954) pp. 201–25; (1934c) p. 465; see also Menger (1871a) pp. 52–3, (1871b) pp. 94–5.
108. Robbins (1935a) pp. 87–8; (1971a) p. 147.
109. (1935a) pp. 32, 67–8, 70–1, 73, 76–7; (1971a) p. 147.
110. J. S. Mill could be *one* of the sources for this distinction (1844) pp. 314–17. However Weber is the main source – (1949) p. 162 and cf. Robbins (1934c) p. 465.
111. (1935a) p. 16; (1963a) p. 28. Cf. Weber (1949) p. 52.
112. (1935a) p. 24. See also (1931e) p. 470.
113. (1935a) pp. 24–5, 30, 145; see also Blaug (1980) p. 149.
114. (1974b) pp. 9–10.
115. (1938c) p. 638.
116. (1954) pp. 201–2; cf. Mises (1933) p. 89: 'Wenn jemand für nationale Autarkie eintritt, sein Volk vom Verkehr mit den übringen Völkern abschliessen will und bereit ist, alle materiellen und ideellen Folgen solcher Politik zu tragen, um das angestrebte Ziel zu erreichen, dann ist das eine Wertung, die man als solch mit Argumenten nicht zu widerlegen vermag.'
117. (1963a) p. 22.
118. (1971a) p. 147; (1935a) p. 31 citing Wicksteed (1910) pp. 155–7; (1939b) pp. 116–17; cf. Wieser (1914) p. 5; Weber (1949) pp. 67–8. Fraser (1932) p. 557 charged that Robbins had in fact smuggled in an economic *end* in the form of rational, maximising behaviour, only to concede this on p. 141 (1932a) and p. 157 of (1935a).
119. (1971a) p. 147.
120. (1935a) pp. 73–5, 78, 104–6; (1938a) pp. 347–9; (1971a) p. 149.
121. Mises (1933), (1949). The whole tone of Wieser (1889) is *a priori*.
122. Blaug (1962) pp. 697–8; see also Stewart (1979) pp. 118–23 for a discussion of *a priorism*.
123. Mill (1844) p. 325.
124. Cairnes (1875) pp. 5–6, 48.
125. See in particular Hicks (1935), Lavington (1921) pp. 29–35 cited by Robbins (1935a) p. 78. It is ironic that one reviewer of the first edition of *ENSES* (James 1933) interpreted the book to be an attack on the English methodological tradition.

126. On the *verstehen* doctrine see Blaug (1980) pp. 47–9 and (in relation to Robbins) p. 88.
127. (1935a) pp. 89, 104–5; Cairnes (1875) pp. 75–6; Mill (1844) p. 329; see also Wieser (1914) pp. 4, 8; Hutchison (1981) p. 227n.
128. (1935a) pp. 73–5.
129. (1935a) p. 140; (1938c) p. 637.
130. (1935a) pp. 106–9, 132; (1981) p. xvi; (1938a) pp. 349–51; see also (1930d) p. 258; (1929b) p. 82; (1972a) p. 134; Addleson (1984) p. 517.
131. (1957e) p. 399; (1981) pp. xvi–xvii.
132. (1935a) p. 109.
133. See in particular Leamer (1983).
134. (1935a) pp. 131–5.
135. Lipsey (1963) pp. 158–61.
136. See Stewart (1979) pp. 50–69; Lakatos and Musgrave (1970) pp. 91–132.
137. Popper (1934) pp. 252–4.
138. (1935a) pp. 73–5. Fraser, whose critique has recently been endorsed by Cooter and Rappoport (1984) believed not only that induction was necessary (1932 pp. 564–5) but that 'The certainty of many of the best attested laws of physics is rather a matter of high inductive probability than of necessity.' (1932 p. 560).
139. Robbins (1928a) pp. 390–1.
140. (1935a) p. 111; (1971a) p. 149; (1966b) p. 27; (1979a) p. 81; (1971b) pp. 149, 166; (1963a) p. 162; cf. Mises (1949) pp. 55–6; Cairnes (1875) pp. 115–16.
141. (1935a) p. 111.
142. (1981) p. xvii.
143. (1935a) p. 121.
144. (1935a) p. 112.
145. (1935a) pp. 114–15. (1938a) is however less overtly hostile to empirical work. Fraser (1932 p. 565n) accused Robbins of unfairness to the Institutionalists – unfortunately supporting his claim with a reference which is clearly inaccurate.
146. (1981) p. xvii; (1934b) p. 99.
147. Beveridge (1937) p. 467.
148. Beveridge (1937) p. 464.
149. Beveridge (1937) pp. 463, 465.
150. Robbins (1938b) pp. 12–13.
151. Robbins (1928b) p. 250; Young (1925a) pp. 240–5, 250–9. Robbins (1938b) which is relevant here is translated in an Appendix to this volume.
152. Robbins (1938b) pp. 18–19.
153. (1935a) pp. 56–7.
154. In his famous article on the elasticity of demand for income in terms of effort Robbins, having established that it was not possible to decide from *a priori* reasoning whether the individual supply curve of labour was positively or negatively sloped, concluded that 'any attempt to predict the effect of change in the terms on which income is earned must proceed by inductive investigation of elasticities. The

attempt to narrow the limit of possible elasticities by *a priori* reasoning must be held to have broken down.' (1930c) p. 129. See also, on observation (1930b) pp. 20–1.

155. (1937a); (1959) p. 44.
156. (1934d) has a substantial Appendix (pp. 201–38) containing 36 statistical tables.
157. (1970b) p. 80.
158. Peston (1984).
159. Blaug (1980) p. 91.
160. (1935a) pp. 116–19 (and cf. 1959 p. 44); (1937a); (1934c) p. 465; (1971b) pp. 188–9; (1938a) p. 352.
161. (1938b) p. 161.
162. Cairnes (1875) p. 85; Weber (1949) p. 148; Mises (1960) pp. 86–8. See also Mill (1844) pp. 326–30.
163. (1963a) p. 43.
164. (1971a) pp. 149–50; cf. (1932b) p. 428 and p. 429; (1934d) contains elements of 'verification' and 'testing' though Henderson (1935) saw it as engaging in 'verification'.
165. Cairnes (1875) pp. 91–2 and cf. pp. 150–1.
166. (1939b). This was perceived by one contemporary reviewer – Staley (1939).
167. (1932b) especially p. 428.
168. (1981) pp. xiv–xv; (1939b) p. 121; (1932b) pp. 428–9.
169. (1959) pp. 43–4. This seems to have confused some later commentators who regarded Robbins as having adopted a Popperian position – see in particular Peston (1981) pp. 185–6; see also Lipsey (1963) p. 158n.
170. (1929b) p. 73; (1929a) p. 27. See also Hutchison (1938) p. 106 for criticism of this.
171. Notes 127, 132, 152 above. This is again consistent with the work of Cairnes and some of the Austrians – see Cairnes (1875) pp. 77, 108–9; Mises (1949) p. 31; and contrast Hutchison (1981) pp. 187–9 (on Menger), 203–4 (on Böhm-Bawerk) and 205 (on Wieser).
172. (1963a) p. 43.
173. (1932a) p. 81. This was however omitted in the second edition of *ENSES* (1935a). Mises (1949) pp. 350–2. See also Lachman (1976) and Cairnes (1875) pp. v–vii.
174. (1971a) p. 118.
175. Samuelson (1972) p. 8; Baumol (1972) pp. 14–15; see also Baumol and Seiler (1979).
176. (1935a) pp. 83–6; (1934b) especially pp. 95, 98–9; see also (1927a) p. 175.
177. (1934b) pp. 97–8; see also (1953b) p. 102. Behaviourism could not cope with expectations and analyse speculation. Moreover it was necessary to be able to contrast plans and realisations.
178. (1981) pp. xiv–xv.
179. The reference is to Young (1925a).
180. (1975a) p. ix.
181. (1947c) pp. 20–2, 85; (1963a) p. 112; (1976a) p. 21.

182. Koot (1982) especially p. 16; see also Coase (1982) p. 33.
183. See also the preface to the second edition of *ENSES* – (1935a) p. vii, and (1932b) pp. 420–1.
184. (1963a) pp. 12–19.
185. (1935a) pp. 140–1.
186. (1938c) p. 646; (1971a) p. 148.
187. (1953b) pp. 108–9; (1970b) p. 204; Wicksteed (1910) pp. 777–8; Mises (1936) p. 115.
188. (1938c) p. 635; (1935a) p. 140; (1932b) pp. 420–1; see also (1934a) p. 10; (1935a) p. 141.
189. (1938c) p. 635.
190. (1935a) pp. 142–3.
191. (1981) p. xxiii.
192. (1971a) p. 147.
193. Lipsey (1963) p. xiii.
194. Baumol (1984a) p. vii.

4 History of Economic Thought

1. (1939e); (1969); (1953b) p. 111; (1929d) p. 410; (1935a) p. ix; see also the reference in (1976b) to 'those who do not regard the contemporary as the all'.
2. (1955c) p. 589.
3. Coats (1982) p. 29.
4. Robbins (1952) p. vii.
5. (1970b) p. 228.
6. (1968c) pp. xi–xii.
7. (1952) p. 1.
8. (1978a) p. xiii.
9. While Classical influences can be found on many pages of Robbins's writings, a few examples may help to reinforce the point, for example (1971b) pp. 14–16 (application of the Ricardian definition of excess); (1937b) pp. 159–66 (price levels dependent on relative international productivity, as Senior had argued); (1968c) pp. 74–5 (investment in education). In truth Robbins, like Viner, *was* to some extent a Classical economist.
10. (1951a) pp. 17–18.
11. (1963a) p. 209.
12. (1970b) p. 54. See however (1980c) p. 489. He was not overly enthusiastic about the Physiocrats – (1966e). However his range was otherwise remarkably wide from an early age – see for example *The Times*, 15 October 1929 (12d).
13. (1976a) p. 39.
14. Cannan (1932) p. 426. Cannan put the words into the mouth of a hypothetical complainant – but the implication is clearly that he did not dissent from them.
15. Hicks (1963) p. 306; J. M. Buchanan (1968) p. 425. However he later became more critical of the Austrians – (1966f).

16. Hutchison (1979) pp. 660–1.
17. (1930e) p. ix.
18. The knowledge of German language literature is particularly evident in (1932a) – cf. note 14 above.
19. (1947c) p. 21. He doubted some of the claims for Marx's originality – see (1940b) p. 94.
20. (1926a); see (1940c) for a particularly strong statement.
21. (1937b) pp. 188–91.
22. (1937b) p. 236.
23. (1935a) pp. 42–3.
24. Cf. also Knight's point that a theory has to work within an institutional framework but that does not equate the theory with the framework. (1924a) pp. 137–9.
25. (1975a) p. xi.
26. (1975a) p. x.
27. Seckler (1975) pp. xiii–xiv.
28. A good example of this is the grand overview in (1970b) pp. 11–46.
29. (1958e) pp. vii–viii.
30. (1952) p. xvi.
31. (1958e) pp. 259–347. The only mistake in this appendix that has come to light is demonstrated in Thweatt (1981). One reviewer commented: 'Robbins' mode of presentation might well serve as an examplar to economists doing books on a single economics author' – Spengler (1959).
32. (1975a) p. xi; see also (1958d) for a particular example of the vigour and interest of Robbins's style.
33. (1970b) p. 104. Robbins seems to have objected strongly to Packe's 'factionalised' biography of Mill – (1970b) pp. 97–117.
34. (1970b) p. 108.
35. But see (1970b) p. 140 – he had no illusions about the sharpness of Gladstone's intellect. On Overstone see (1972c).
36. (1958e) pp. 161–4.
37. Again, (1958d) provides a good example.
38. See (1929b) p. 77 for a reference to 'my spiritual parentage in *Dogmengeschichte*'. As befitted a Cannan pupil, he dismissed historical relativism as an interpretation of economic theory (1935a) p. 80.
39. (1970b) p. 60; (1968c) pp. 83–94. See also Spiegel's comparison of Robbins with Cannan in Spiegel (1953).
40. Young (1928b) p. 114.
41. Robbins (1965c); (1970a); (1971a) pp. 132, 163, 217, 219–20; (1980c). Viner was 'easily the most eminent all-rounder of this century in the history of economic ideas'.
42. Robbins's review is reprinted in (1970b) pp. 47–72.
43. (1934e) pp. xiv–xvi; compare Schumpeter (1954) p. 837.
44. See for example (1937b) pp. 225–6n on Keynes's caricature of Classicism, and (1965a) p. 7. Spiegel (1953) noted Robbins's success in combating the caricature.
45. (1971a) pp. 226–7. See also Robbins's reference to 'the great multitude who now acquire cheap notoriety by denunciation of the classical economists' – (1927e).

46. (1968a) pp. 1–2; (1963a) p. 96.
47. (1935a) pp. 50, 68–9.
48. Young (1928a).
49. (1966b) p. 119; see also (1968c) pp. 74–5 on Smith's endorsement of investment in education.
50. See for example (1932b) pp. 424–5 where the influence *inter alia* of Hume is apparent in the concept of new money flowing to producers.
51. See for example (1971b) p. 190 where Hume's balance of payments essay is seen as destroying the case for mercantilism.
52. (1963a) pp. 97–8.
53. (1970b) pp. 57n, 74, 80–1; (1938c) p. 635; (1963a) pp. 97–8.
54. (1963a) pp. 100–1.
55. (1963a) p. 104.
56. (1965a) p. 6.
57. (1963a) p. 103.
58. (1963a) pp. 104–6.
59. The tone of (1965a) illustrates this point. See also (1963b) 'I personally place him [Bentham] among the great intellects of history'.
60. Burns (1984), (1985).
61. (1956); (1958e) passim especially p. 258; (1961b). Of course he delighted in scholarship more generally – see for example (1932i).
62. (1970b) p. 91.
63. (1967a); (1970b) p. 91; James (1979).
64. (1969) p. 443; (1970b) p. 83; (1975c); (1980b). Professor J. Creedy has pointed out to me that there is a link here with Robbins's regard for Wicksell, who was also very concerned with the matter of population.
65. (1935a) pp. 56, 60–2; Bowley (1937); Rauner (1956). Robbins admired Senior; and his dismay at Levi's compilation (Robbins 1930f) may also have influenced him as supervisor.
66. (1958e) p. 154.
67. (1958e) p. vii.
68. (1971a) pp. 227–8.
69. (1939a) p. 235.
70. (1935a) pp. 116–17.
71. (1970b) pp. 118–63. At times his tone in discussing Mill in this essay can be quite harsh, see for example pp. 127–8. See also (1976b). On the Saint-Simonians see Robbins (1960d).
72. (1970b) p. 110. For Robbins's admiration of Mill see also (1962a), (1965c), (1967d) ('one of the finest minds that ever addressed themselves to the problems of social improvement'), (1970c), (1974c), (1979c), (1980d).
73. (1939b) p. 99. He also had a great regard for John Rae's intellectual contribution – (1967e).
74. (1970b) pp. 169–88. The essay dates from 1936. See also ch. 3 n. 19 above.
75. (1925/6) pp. 91, 93. See also (1927b) p. 113.
76. (1934e) p. ix.
77. (1963a) pp. 223–4.
78. (1934e) p. xi; (1954) pp. 76, 96–7.
79. (1927b) p. 112 reflects Cannan's critical tone.

80. (1928a) p. 387n.
81. (1976a) pp. 47–9; (1970b) pp. 30–1.
82. (1970b) p. 209.
83. (1970b) p. 64. See also (1977b).
84. (1970b) p. 64–9.
85. (1933) p. xiv; see also pp. xv–xvi where Wicksteed and the Austrians are favourably contrasted with the Cambridge tradition; (1970b) pp. 189–209 (this dated from 1930d and 1933); (1934e) pp. xvii–xix.
86. (1934e) especially p. vii; (1970b) pp. 223–8. D. H. Robertson shared this admiration (1937) p. 506.
87. (1970b) p. 225. See Note 64 above.
88. (1934e) pp. xin, xviii–xix.
89. (1934e) pp. xiii–xiv.
90. (1934e) p. xvii.
91. (1958c) q. 10219.
92. (1978a) p. xiii.

5 Economic Welfare

1. (1938c) p. 635.
2. (1965a); (1963b).
3. (1970b) p. 80; see also (1963b); (1965a) pp. 11–12; (1966b) p. 15.
4. (1963a) p. 15; (1981) p. xxii. See also (1953b) p. 109.
5. (1970b) p. 81; (1965) p. 12. See also (1979d) p. 684. As one of his critics noted, there were differences between the Utilitarianism of Robbins's various historical sources which he did not explore. Macfie (1953).
6. (1976a) pp. 2–3; (1963a) pp. 20–1; (1981) p. xxii. See (1979d) p. 683 for his aversion to Pareto optimality.
7. (1953b) p. 110; (1981) pp. xxiii–xxiv.
8. (1947c) pp. 8, 22.
9. (1947c) pp. 44–6, 50. See also note 125 below, and Hayek (1935), (1940).
10. (1935a) p. 16; (1971a) p. 146.
11. On the relation between the ends/means distinction and the economist as technocrat see Blaug (1980) p. 149. For insight into Robbins's leadership of the Economic Section I am indebted to an unpublished paper by J. D. Gribbin (1977b).
12. (1947c) p. 5.
13. (1947c) p. 7.
14. (1947c) pp. 41–2.
15. (1947c) p. 44; (1954) pp. 201–25.
16. (1954) p. 210.
17. (1947c) p. 53.
18. (1954) p. 213.
19. (1947c) p. 54.
20. (1954) pp. 203–4.

21. (1954) pp. 216–17.
22. (1954) p. 218.
23. (1976a) pp. 125–7.
24. (1963a) p. 37.
25. (1947c) pp. 12–14.
26. (1947c) p. 15.
27. 'I hold that there is an essential arrogance – a sin of pride if you wish – in believing that we are so competent to decide for others the way of life they should follow that we should wish to assume to ourselves compulsory powers of control.' (1947c) p. 18.
28. (1976a) p. 17.
29. (1976a) p. 18; (1947c) p. 18.
30. (1963a) pp. 29–30; (1966a) p. 16; (1976a) p. 175; (1977a) p. 8.
31. (1935a) pp. 143–4.
32. (1965a) p. 13.
33. (1976a) pp. 190–2.
34. (1976a) pp. 14–15, 17.
35. (1947c) p. 21; (1976a) p. 21.
36. (1968c) p. 71. See also (1940c).
37. (1966b) pp. 14, 33.
38. (1971b) pp. 352–3.
39. (1963a) pp. 93–4; (1976a) pp. 180–1.
40. (1972a) p. 25: 'Inflations of a greater order of magnitude are not only incompatible with orderly economic arrangements but also are incompatible with political democracy and the decency and culture which go with it.'
41. (1963a) p. 38; (1977a) p. 21; (1976a) pp. 28, 173–5; (1937b) pp. 221–4.
42. (1963a) p. 93.
43. (1938c) pp. 635, 637; (1970d) p. 423.
44. (1963a) pp. 77–81.
45. (1963a) pp. 73–90.
46. (1963a) pp. 45–7, 74–6; (1976a) p. 108; (1977a) p. 12.
47. (1963a) pp. 76–7; (1976a) p. 109; (1977a) pp. 13–14.
48. (1977a) p. 15.
49. (1963a) pp. 77–81.
50. (1976a) p. 116.
51. (1976a) pp. 141–2.
52. (1955b) pp. 16–18.
53. (1963a) pp. 77–81.
54. (1963a) p. 47.
55. (1963a) p. 80; (1937b) pp. 266–8.
56. (1963a) p. 80.
57. (1963a) p. 81.
58. (1955b) p. 9.
59. (1976a) p. 110.
60. (1955b) p. 10.
61. (1955b) pp. 13–15.
62. (1955b) p. 18.
63. (1955b) p. 14.

64. (1955b) p. 14; (1977a) p. 21; (1963a) pp. 63–4, 87; (1976a) p. 117; see also (1939a) pp. 23–4.
65. (1955b) pp. 14–15.
66. (1963a) pp. 94–5.
67. (1963a) p. 9; (1976a) p. 6; (1947c) p. 83; (1935a) pp. 143–4.
68. (1976a) p. 8.
69. (1977a) p. 8.
70. (1939a) p. 6.
71. (1966b) p. 134.
72. (1971b) p. 253.
73. (1937b) pp. 223–32.
74. (1963a) pp. 34–6; (1979d) p. 684.
75. (1976a) pp. 12–14.
76. (1976a) pp. 42–6.
77. (1963a) p. 81.
78. (1963a) p. 109.
79. (1976a) pp. 119–34 at p. 120; see also ibid. p. 136.
80. (1939a) p. 275.
81. (1963a) pp. 42–3. Robbins was of course particularly concerned with the importance of State patronage in the arts – see (1963a) pp. 53–72.
82. (1976a) pp. 7–8.
83. (1937b) pp. 230–2.
84. (1934d) p. 191.
85. (1965a) pp. 6–7.
86. (1976a) p. 134.
87. (1947c) p. 11.
88. (1976a) p. 136.
89. (1976a) p. 180.
90. (1976a) pp. 176–8.
91. (1947c) pp. 22–3.
92. (1947c) pp. 25–6.
93. (1976a) pp. 178–9.
94. (1976a) pp. 176–80.
95. (1976a) p. 179. The objection to simple majority decision was the disregarding of minority preferences. See also (1979c).
96. (1976a) p. 110; see also (1966b) p. 103.
97. (1925/6) p. 88.
98. (1976a) pp. 103–7.
99. (1966b) p. 136; (1949b) p. 15; (1979a) pp. 31–2.
100. (1935a) pp. 136–8, 150–1; (1979a) pp. 31–2.
101. (1935a) p. 141; (1953b) pp. 108–9. See also Robertson (1955).
102. (1935a) pp. 58–9.
103. (1963a) p. 22.
104. (1930c).
105. (1976a) pp. 110, 115–16.
106. (1963a) pp. 105 (citing Smith), 109.
107. (1963a) pp. 81–3.
108. (1963a) pp. 88–90; (1955b) pp. 10–12.
109. (1974b) pp. 10–11.

110. (1963a) p. 85; (1976a) p. 116; (1974b) pp. 10–11; (1979a) p. 32.
111. (1974b) pp. 10–12.
112. (1955b) p. 8.
113. (1963a) pp. 84–5.
114. (1939a) p. 267n.
115. (1976a) p. 146.
116. (1971a) pp. 191–2.
117. (1947c) p. 80; (1963a) p. 104.
118. (1963a) p. 40. See also (1940c) p. 95 and ibid. p. 96: 'One feels that one is listening in to the gibber of a collection of robots wound up by the village imbecile. Talk about the "opium of the people . . .".'
119. (1939a) pp. 185–7.
120. (1947c) pp. 77–8.
121. (1939a) p. 189.
122. (1963a) p. 38.
123. (1939a) p. 192. Robbins believed that Stalin was the natural outcome of collectivism – (1940c) p. 96.
124. (1939a) pp. 194–202.
125. (1934d) pp. 148–56; (1935a) pp. 17–18; Mises (1932) especially pp. 86–138.
126. (1976a) pp. 142–5.
127. (1947c) pp. 22–3; (1966c) pp. 28–9.
128. (1934d) p. 146. See also (1935d) p. 92.
129. (1934d) pp. 146–7.
130. (1934d) pp. 148–56.
131. (1937b) pp. 194–205.
132. (1937b) pp. 205–18.
133. (1937b) pp. 130–4.
134. (1937b) pp. 141–54.
135. (1976a) pp. 146–50; (1971a) pp. 55–6, 61–2, 64, 67.
136. (1976a) pp. 146–9.
137. (1976a) p. 150.
138. (1976a) pp. 29–31.
139. (1939a) pp. 27–8.
140. (1963a) p. 107.
141. (1976a) pp. 111–13; (1947a) p. 28; (1974b) pp. 23–5.
142. (1947c) pp. 9–10.
143. (1974b) pp. 13–14.
144. (1966c) pp. 28–9; (1976a) pp. 137–8.
145. (1976a) pp. 137–8. However Robbins does not make explicit reference to Hayek's book.
146. (1939a) p. 43.
147. (1943) p. 14.
148. (1976a) pp. 55–8.
149. (1943) p. 14; (1939c) pp. 424–5; (1937b) pp. 144–54.
150. (1939a) p. 44; see also ibid. pp. 29–32, 157.
151. (1939a) p. 35.
152. (1939a) pp. 36–7.
153. (1934d) pp. 130–45.
154. (1934d) p. 142.

155. (1939a) p. 38.
156. (1939a) pp. 136, 173–9; (1934g).
157. (1939a) pp. 41–2.
158. (1939a) p. 43.
159. (1939a) pp. 176–7; see also ibid. p. 79–80n; (1934g); (1976a) pp. 49–51.
160. (1947c) p. 80.
161. (1939a) pp. 45–80; (1939b) p. 43n; (1976a) p. 48; (1943); (1937b) pp. 154–7.
162. (1947c) p. 75.
163. (1939a) pp. 51, 135–6; (1934h).
164. (1939a) pp. 63–76.
165. (1937b) pp. 154–7.
166. (1934) p. 139.
167. (1953a) pp. 20–1. This presumably derived from Robbins's wartime experiences.
168. (1939a) pp. 41–2.
169. (1939a) p. 42n.
170. (1943).
171. (1943); (1976a) pp. 53–5, 57–8, 113–14, 137–8; (1947c) pp. 83–4; Gribbin (1977a) is illuminating on the ambitions of the trade associations to control the economy, and Gribbin (1985) shows Robbins's strong support for G. C. Allen's insistence on the need to control monopoly and promote competition.
172. (1973b) pp. 83–4.
173. (1976a) pp. 58–62, 113–14; (1974b) pp. 14–17; (1971a) p. 231; (1934d) p. 188.
174. See also (1971b) p. 214.
175. (1976a) pp. 103–7; (1966b) p. 137.
176. (1966b) p. 22.
177. (1972b) p. 3.
178. (1972b) pp. 11–13. His willingness to use hypothetical compensation here probably springs from his acceptance of Kaldor's distinction between a change in productive power and its distributive consequences – (1953b) p. 110; Kaldor (1939).
179. (1972b) pp. 23–4.
180. (1966b) pp. 104–5; (1980a) p. 8.
181. (1947c) pp. 18–22; (1976a) pp. 19–20.
182. (1976a) pp. 38–9; (1972b) p. 18; see also (1935a) pp. 133–4.
183. (1972b) pp. 16–17.
184. (1932c) pp. 167–9.
185. (1972b) pp. 20–1.
186. (1927b).
187. (1970b) p. 232.
188. (1929b) pp. 74–5.
189. (1929b) p. 74; see also (1925/6) p. 85, and compare (1939d) pp. 289–91. Robbins later admitted to having been, in the 1930s, a victim of the 'delusion, so fashionable' at that time of a prospective fall in the population. (1970b) p. 188n.
190. (1965a) pp. 14–15; (1966b) p. 121; (1969) p. 443; (1980b).

191. (1976a) p. 107; (1965a) pp. 14–15; Pimlott p. 136.
192. (1971a) p. 158.
193. (1931a) especially pp. 49–50.
194. (1939a) p. 81–106, 207; (1977a) pp. 10–11.
195. (1939a) p. 210.
196. (1939a) pp. 81–106; see also Chapter 9 in this book.

6 Education

1. Cmnd 2154, cited as (1963c).
2. (1971a) pp. 271–3.
3. (1971a) p. 273.
4. See also (1966b) p. xiii: 'I would also like . . . [to declare] my embarrassment at the prevalent habit of describing the report . . . as the Robbins Report . . . as a participant with less experience than others of some of the most important problems, I certainly learnt much more than I gave.'
5. (1971a) p. 283: the result was (1966b).
6. *Times Higher Education Supplement*, 18 May 1984, p. 36.
7. Robbins's essay on Montagu Norman (1970b) pp. 234–42 is a testimony to Robbins's belief in the value of public discussion.
8. (1966b) pp. 19–20, 29–30; (1980a). See Blaug (1967) for a discussion of the issues involved.
9. (1966b) p. 21; (1971a) pp. 275–6; (1980a) p. 106.
10. (1980a) pp. 39–40; (1966a) p. 4.
11. (1976a) pp. 125–7.
12. (1955c) pp. 582–3.
13. (1980a) p. 108.
14. (1980a) p. 44.
15. (1980a) pp. 52–63.
16. (1980a) p. 25. But he hesitated at the corollary – some 'weeding out' at the end of the first year (ibid, pp. 26–7).
17. (1971a) pp. 275–6.
18. (1971a) p. 275.
19. (1966b) pp. 2–3, 40–1, 138; (1980a) p. 25; (1971a) p. 282.
20. (1966b) pp. 45–6.
21. (1966b) p. 40; (1980a) p. 109; (1968c) pp. 72–3.
22. (1966b) p. 156; (1976a) pp. 20–6, 120–3; (1968c) p. 81. Robbins was worried by the totalitarian dangers inherent in a monolithic State educational system – like J. S. Mill he believed in public provision of education but not a public monopoly.
23. (1968a) p. 8; (1980a) p. 18; (1955c) pp. 580–1.
24. (1955c) p. 580.
25. (1966b) p. 95. See also (1968a) p. 7; (1980a) pp. 38–9; (1971a) pp. 276–7.
26. (1966b) p. 64.
27. (1980a) pp. 95–6. Indeed this was one reason why Robbins was unhappy with DES management of higher education.

28. (1966b) pp. 12–13.
29. (1968a) p. 6.
30. (1955c) p. 591; (1966b) p. 95.
31. (1966b) pp. 97.
32. (1968a) pp. 9–10.
33. (1966b) p. 90.
34. (1968a) pp. 8–9.
35. (1980a) pp. 106–7.
36. (1955c) p. 585.
37. (1955c) p. 585; (1971a) p. 215.
38. (1955c) pp. 583–4, 586–7, 589; (1971a) p. 215. See also (1966b) pp. 126–34.
39. (1955c) pp. 589—90.
40. (1966b) pp. 106–7, 116–17; (1968a) pp. 4–5; (1980a) p. 14.
41. (1968a) p. 1.
42. (1971a) pp. 276–7; (1968a) pp. 9–10.
43. (1966b) pp. 24, 43–4; (1968a) p. 8; (1980a) pp. 102, 107.
44. (1971a) p. 276; (1966b) pp. 42–3.
45. (1980a) p. 41.
46. (1971a) p. 276; (1966b) pp. 42–3.
47. (1966b) pp. 34–5, 48–9, 55–6, 154; (1980a) pp. 91–2; (1966a) pp. 10–12.
48. (1971a) p. 280; (1966b) pp. x–xi, 48, 53–4, 139.
49. (1980a) pp. 94–5.
50. (1971a) p. 281; (1966b) pp. 138–57.
51. (1966b) pp. 149–50.
52. (1980a) pp. 101–2.
53. (1966b) pp. 148–9.
54. (1966b) p. 32; (1980a) p. 32; (1966a) p. 9; (1976a) p. 136.
55. (1966b) p. 30.
56. (1966a) pp. 9–10.
57. (1963c) pp. 211–12. This part of the report, which bears the imprint of the Chairman's pen, regarded the arguments for and against loans as 'very evenly balanced' (para. 647).
58. (1966b) pp. 46–7.
59. (1966b) p. 29; (1968c) pp. 79–80.
60. (1976a) p. 124; (1977a) p. 15; (1980a) p. 33.
61. (1980a) p. 34.
62. (1980a) p. 34.
63. (1976a) p. 125; (1980a) pp. 35–6, 88–9, 108. He paid no attention to possible marginal disincentive effects.
64. (1980a) p. 37.
65. (1966b) pp. 44–5.
66. (1966b) p. 44.
67. (1966b) pp. 45–6.
68. (1980a) p. 65.
69. (1980a) p. 110.
70. (1966b) pp. 139–40; see also (1980a) p. 98.
71. (1980a) pp. 45–51.
72. (1980a) pp. 49–51.

73. (1966b) pp. 8–9, 70, 110–11.
74. (1966b) pp. 10–11.
75. (1980a) pp. 48–9.
76. (1966b) pp. 57–100.
77. (1966b) p. 103.
78. (1966b) p. 140–1.
79. (1980a) pp. 5–6. Italics in original.
80. (1971a) p. 282.
81. (1971a) p. 282.
82. (1966b) pp. 141–6, 153; *The Times*, 15 December 1964 (11e). See also Carter (1967).
83. (1966b) pp. 33–4.
84. (1966a) p. 2.
85. (1966a) p. 5.
86. (1966a) pp. 7–8.
87. (1966a) pp. 5–6.
88. Peacock (1982) p. 40.
89. (1966a) p. 6.
90. (1966b) pp. 6, 50–1; (1980a) pp. 6–7.
91. (1966b) p. 51.
92. (1980a) pp. 66–7.
93. (1980a) pp. 40–1.
94. (1980a) pp. 68–71.
95. (1980a) pp. 8–9, 71–3; see also (1966b) p. 15.
96. (1968c) pp. 74–5.
97. (1966b) pp. 121–2.
98. (1966b) p. 28.
99. (1971a) p. 276; (1966b) p. 27.
100. (1980a) p. 10.
101. (1980a) p. 32.
102. (1971a) p. 276.
103. (1966b) pp. 4–5.
104. (1966a) pp. 8–9; see also (1968a) pp. 3–4; (1972b) pp. 11–13; (1980a) p. 9.
105. (1971a) p. 282.
106. (1971a) p. 283.
107. *The Times*, 1981 (3 July 4e; 21 July 7a; 16 October 2g). *Times Higher Education Supplement*, 1981 (16 October 13a). *Times Educational Supplement*, 1982 (7 May 5c).
108. See also Carter (1967) for a similar view.

7 Microeconomics

1. (1930a) p. 194.
2. Addleson (1984) p. 508 distinguishes between Austrian and Lausanne general equilibrium.
3. (1933) p. xv; (1970b) pp. 201–2.
4. (1927b) pp. 124–9.

5. (1935a) pp. 67–8.
6. (1935a) pp. 70–1.
7. (1928a).
8. (1928a) pp. 395–7.
9. O'Brien (1981) p. 44; (1984) pp. 32–3, 46.
10. (1934a) p. 16.
11. Ibid.
12. (1930a). See section 5.2 below.
13. (1930a) pp. 207–8.
14. (1930a) p. 208.
15. (1930a) p. 209.
16. (1930a) pp. 212–14.
17. Blaug (1962) p. 422. Robbins's argument concerning business statistics is in (1928a) pp. 390–1.
18. (1928a) pp. 393–5. He thus preferred to talk of an equalised reward for a given factor quality rather than assuming that all factors were homogeneous.
19. (1934a) pp. 8–9.
20. (1933) p. xvn.
21. Sraffa (1926).
22. (1934a) pp. 6–8.
23. (1926a) p. 543.
24. (1934a) p. 11.
25. Young (1913) pp. 676–86. Young had pointed out the confusion between pecuniary and real diseconomies (and the distinction is one which is relevant to a general equilibrium approach). Edgeworth (1925) in a surprisingly acid review of the second edition of Pigou's *Economics of Welfare* (Pigou 1924) had also criticised Pigou's argument although in a typically allusive and incomplete manner, while Knight (1924b) had pointed out that Pigou's argument failed to take account of private ownership charges for the use of resources, which would result in rents which would, in turn, prevent over-expansion of increasing cost industries. Pigou in (1924) pp. vi, 194, made some retreat in the face of Young's critique. See also Robbins (1931e) p. 472.
26. (1934a) p. 10.
27. (1929a); (1930).
28. (1934a) pp. 2–3.
29. (1934a) p. 3: Robbins said that the work of Mayer as one of Wieser's successors had 'brought home to us all' the concept of opportunity cost 'as a unifying principle in the structure of modern analysis'.
30. (1935a) p. 35; Weber (1949) pp. 34–5; Weber (1947) pp. 147, 201, 207; Kirzner (1976) pp. 127, 131.
31. (1934c); see especially p. 463.
32. Robbins (1934a) pp. 2–3; Wieser (1889) pp. 171–3, 176.
33. Wicksteed (1910) Book I, ch. ix.
34. Wicksteed (1910) p. 732.
35. Robbins (1933) p. xv.
36. (1930d) pp. 253–4; (1970b) pp. 204–5.

37. Note 25 above and Young (1928a) pp. 527, 531.
38. (1970b) p. 218; (1934e) pp. xiii–xvi.
39. (1970b) p. 218.
40. (1976a) pp. 58–62; (1978b).
41. (1929a).
42. Marshall (1890) vol. I, pp. 822–9; see also vol. II, pp. 822–7.
43. (1929a) p. 25.
44. (1934a) pp. 2–6; (1930d) pp. 253–4; see also Hutchison (1979) p. 661; Wicksteed (1910) p. 788.
45. (1934a) pp. 2–3.
46. (1934a) p. 3; Wicksteed (1910) Book I, ch. ix.
47. (1972b) p. 7.
48. (1934a) p. 6.
49. (1930a) pp. 207–8.
50. (1934a) p. 3.
51. (1934a) pp. 3–4.
52. Knight (1928).
53. Robbins (1934a) pp. 4–5.
54. (1934a) p. 5.
55. In (1933) Robbins had written that 'The conception of real costs as displaced alternatives is now accepted by the majority of theoretical economists' (p. xviii). But when he reprinted this in (1970b) he added: 'I now think this paragraph to be too cocksure' (1970b) p. 205n. See Buchanan, J. M. (1973) pp. 7–8, 10–13 for further discussion of this point.
56. (1934c) pp. 463–5; (1934a) p. 11; (1935a) p. 65; (1972b) pp. 4–5; (1966b) p. 125; see also Wicksteed (1910) p. 767; Kirzner (1976) pp. 127, 131; Weber (1947) p. 147; Wieser (1914) p. 100.
57. (1934c) p. 463.
58. (1934c) p. 466.
59. (1934c) pp. 464–5; (1935a) pp. 67–8; see also Buchanan, J. M. (1973) p. 3.
60. (1935a) pp. 76–7.
61. (1927b) pp. 107–8 – here Robbins removed the time dimension from 'diminishing returns'.
62. (1934a) pp. 14–15.
63. Young (1928a) p. 539.
64. Kirzner (1973) p. 31. See also pp. 33–4 for a contrast with Mises. On Robbins's treatment of competition see Chapter 5 above and Notes 157–60, 171 in particular. See also (1927c). But the matter is not entirely clear-cut. Firstly, entrepreneurial expectations are important in Robbins (1934d). Secondly, there is the question raised by Wiseman (Chapter 3, n. 45 above).
65. Cassel (1925); Robbins (1935a) pp. 87–8. On Robbins and Cassel see Chapter 3, section 2 of this book.
66. Robbins (1934c) p. 463.
67. (1972b) pp. 8, 10.
68. (1976a) p. 17.
69. Ibid.

70. See Robbins (1930d) p. 254.
71. A reference to the marginal utility of money in the first edition of *ENSES* (1932a) p. 82 is replaced in the second edition (1935a) p. 78.
72. (1935a) pp. 90–3.
73. Cf. Mises (1936) p. 115.
74. (1930) p. 255.
75. (1928a) pp. 397–8.
76. (1935a) pp. 88–9.
77. Kirzner (1973) p. 38.
78. (1930a) pp. 209–11.
79. Buchanan, D. H. (1929) had explained the nature of the confusion clearly.
80. This, it would appear from the references cited by Robbins, was arrived at via an attempt to clarify Marshall's rather evasive discussion of the issue, rather than as a direct result of borrowing from D. H. Buchanan (n. 79 above), though Robbins can hardly have been unaware of Buchanan's article which appeared in the LSE's own journal.
81. (1930a) pp. 211–14.
82. (1930a) p. 212.
83. (1930a) p. 213.
84. See O'Brien (1975) p. 120.
85. Robbins (1930a) p. 213.
86. Robbins (1925/6).
87. 'Sidgwicks's "Principles of Political Economy" though greatly neglected to-day, still provides a more intelligible explanation of the causes governing general wages than is to be found in most modern text-books.' Robbins (1925/6) p. 91.
88. Robbins cites Dalton (1929) and Robertson (1926) – Robbins (1930c) p. 123. The reference to Robertson is not precise: but the relevant material is on p. 13 and is not very fully developed. However Dalton's account, which clearly forms the starting point for Robbins's article, and which contains the essential analysis, is admirably explicit. The various editions of Dalton's work are confused by the inclusion of reprints, but the genuine second edition (1929) contains the relevant material at p. 106.
89. Robbins (1929a) p. 25. The reference is to Chapman (1909).
90. (1929a) pp. 29–30 citing Marshall (1890); (1978b) p. 9. The latter reference cited Marshall (1892) pp. 362–403 and Pigou (1925) p. 398.
91. Robbins (1925/6) pp. 18–19.
92. (1930a) pp. 204, 209.
93. (1925/6) pp. 61–2; (1929a) p. 30. Robbins was following Marshall here; he later encouraged Hicks in the exploration of the theoretical issues involved, as noted in Chapter 2.
94. (1929a).
95. (1930c).
96. (1929a) pp. 39–40. This is a basic assumption even though it is only spelled out at the end of the article.
97. (1929a) pp. 30–3.

98. (1929a) pp. 32–3.
99. See Bowley (1937) p. 256; O'Brien (1975) pp. 278, 297.
100. (1929a) pp. 26–7. This was a central point of Chapman (1909) which, as already noted, Robbins cited.
101. (1929a) pp. 28–30, 32–3.
102. (1929a) p. 34.
103. Ibid.
104. (1929a) pp. 34–5.
105. (1929a) pp. 36–7.
106. (1929a) p. 37.
107. (1930c) p. 123. See Note 88 above.
108. Knight (1921) pp. 117–18. See also Blaug (1962) pp. 314–16.
109. (1930c) pp. 123–4.
110. See the discussion in Marshall, R. and Perlman (1972); see also Peston (1981).
111. Robbins (1925/6) pp. 28–33.
112. (1927b) pp. 120–1.
113. (1925/6) p. 22.
114. (1925/6) pp. 24–5; for J. S. Mill see O'Brien (1975) p. 223 and n. 62.
115. (1974b) p. 15. 'I would like this lecture to be printed and distributed: I therefore refrain from giving actual examples [of restrictive labour practices] from my own experience in business.'
116. (1925/6) pp. 59–61, 68–9.
117. (1976a) pp. 58–62; (1978b) pp. 6–7.
118. (1925/6) pp. 70–4.
119. (1925/6) pp. 51–5.
120. (1925/6) pp. 51–2.
121. (1925/6) pp. 33–8.
122. (1925/6) pp. 51–2.
123. (1925/6) pp. 41–51.

8 Macroeconomics

1. (1935b) pp. vii, xvi. On the long lasting nature of Classical trade and monetary theory see (1939e).
2. (1932b) pp. 422, 427. Cassel's trade cycle theory itself however is not Austrian (1923) II pp. 537–47, because of its emphasis on real factors in over-investment, though Haberler (1937) pp. 68–70 points out similarities in the treatment of the (subordinate) monetary factors and also stresses the role in the analysis of shortages of real savings and of a reduction in the rate of interest.
3. Hayek (1931c) ch. 2.
4. See (1932b) p. 429.
5. Mises (1934) pp. 339–66; Robbins (1931c) p. ix; (1932a) p. 53; (1935a) p. 54. Robbins also acknowledged Machlup's *Borsenkredit, Industriekredit und Kapitalbildung* as helpful in the application of Mises's theory – Robbins (1931f).

6. Robbins contributed an introduction (1935b) to the translation which was made by H. E. Batson, a lecturer in the Department of Economics at LSE and the author of *A Select Bibliography of Modern Economic Theory* (1930).

7. (1935b) p. xvii–xviii.

8. Hayek (1931c) p. 25.

9. Robbins (1935b) p. xviii. It is however interesting that a lack of attention to term-structure was one of W. C. Mitchell's criticisms when reviewing Robbins's *The Great Depression*. Mitchell (1935).

10. Robbins (1935a) p. 62.

11. Hayek (1931a), especially pp. 270, 272, 279–80, 294.

12. Haberler (1937) pp. 30, 31, 44n, 54n, 56, 57n, 76.

13. Robbins (1934d) pp. 30–54; see also (1932b, h).

14. (1932b) pp. 424–9; (1934d) pp. 30–7.

15. Haberler (1937) p. 54.

16. (1932b) p. 429.

17. (1934d) p. 39.

18. (1934d) p. 129.

19. See the material on Tout and Hansen in Hayek (1931c) pp. 132–5.

20. Robbins (1934d) p. 39. Hayek's (1931c) also seems unclear on this point.

21. Robbins (1934d) pp. 38–41. Hicks (1982) relates that he was unable to produce a formal model of Hayek's macroeconomic theory because of uncertainties over the concept of equilibrium which it involved.

22. See Machlup (1979).

23. (1932b) p. 428.

24. (1934b) pp. 44–52; (1931c) p. xi; (1932e): 'The traveller in the countries of the great inflations at any time during the last seven years has seen lying idle and devoid of return the great works and concerns erected with inflationary capital'; Hayek (1931c) p. 162.

25. Robbins (1934d) pp. 4–8, 18.

26. (1932b) pp. 414–17, 419–23, 427. Douglas replied in his (1936).

27. Robbins (1934d) pp. 4–8, 18.

28. (1934d) pp. 160–1; (1939a) pp. 242–4.

29. (1934d) pp. 185–9.

30. (1932b) pp. 429–30; (1934d) pp. 69–71, 82–3, 107, 186–9; (1931a) pp. 51–2.

31. (1934d) p. 187; see also (1932h) p. 437.

32. (1931b) p. 100.

33. (1934d) pp. 117–18.

34. (1934d) p. 55–67.

35. (1937b) pp. 134–41; (1934d) pp. 72–3; (1939a) pp. 222–8.

36. (1934d) pp. 112–17.

37. (1934d) pp. 171; see also (1932h) p. 431; (1935f) pp. 211–12; (1937d); (1939a) pp. 235, 238. The similarity with the position held by the members of the Currency School amongst the Classical economists is notable.

38. (1934d) pp. 78–81, 165–72; see also (1932h) p. 436.

39. (1934d) p. 77.

40. Robbins (1932e, f, g, h); (1938d) pp. 165–6; see also Harrod (1932); Henderson (1937). Robbins also wrote a letter to *The Times*, with Hayek, Gregory and Plant, attacking public expenditure as a remedy for depression – Hutchison (1968) p. 21. Keynes paid tribute to the consistency between Robbins's theoretical position and his policy recommendations – (1936) p. 20n.

41. (1939a) pp. 216–22.
42. (1939a) pp. 231–4.
43. (1932e).
44. (1939a) pp. 272–4.
45. (1932b) p. 415; see also (1972a) p. 20; (1939a) pp. 272–4; (1937a).
46. (1932b) pp. 418–19, 423; (1934d) pp. 20–1.
47. (1958b) p. 212.
48. (1939a) pp. 269–71; see also (1938d) pp. 161–4.
49. (1939a) pp. 217, 251–4; (1937d) pp. 242–3.
50. (1934d) pp. 58, 63–4, 91–2; Hutchison (1978) p. 185.
51. (1934d) p. 125.
52. (1934d) pp. 190, 192–4, 197; (1937b) pp. 261–2.
53. (1934d) pp. 125, 130–1, 135–6, 141, 144.
54. (1939a) pp. 173–9; (1937b) pp. 39–41.
55. (1939a) pp. 238–9; (1937d).
56. (1939a) pp. 263–8; (1938d) pp. 161–2.
57. (1939a) pp. 272–4; (1938d) pp. 165–6.
58. (1939a) pp. 217–22; (1937d) pp. 239–41.
59. (1939a) pp. 224–5; (1941) pp. 24–5; see also (1976a) p. 26.
60. (1939a) pp. 256–77.
61. (1939a) pp. 225–6.
62. (1939a) pp. 226–7.
63. (1939a) pp. 228–30.
64. (1972a) p. 24.
65. (1971a) p. 153.
66. (1971a) p. 154. See also (1979a) p. 14.
67. (1971a) pp. 188–9.
68. (1971a) pp. 186–8.
69. (1971a) p. 188.
70. (1947c) pp. 67–8.
71. (1971a) p. 224.
72. (1971a) p. 161; this continuity was also noted by Harry Johnson (1972) p. 835.
73. Howson and Winch (1977) p. 152n.
74. (1979a) pp. 14–15; (1974b) pp. 20–1.
75. 'But the exact nature of his achievement is not so easy to summarise. Much of his most striking work was concerned with particular applications, where the uniqueness of his contribution consists, not so much in new theory, as in the revelation of how existing theory can be applied; and the status of the *General Theory*, where his concern was with the widest type of generalisation and where his claims to far-reaching innovation were emphatic, is still a matter of some dispute. It must be admitted, I think, that a case, which is not

intellectually negligible, can be made for the view that his claims in
this respect were overstated; that some of what he thought to be
novel was in fact in line with developments of the past, and some of
what was truly novel was one-sided in its emphasis.' (1951b)
reprinted in (1970b) p. 244.
76. (1976a) p. 26.
77. (1954) pp. 18–40; (1978b) p. 10.
78. (1971a) p. 188.
79. (1958a); (1974a); see also (1976a) pp. 98–9.
80. (1979a).
81. (1971b) p. 2.
82. (1958b) pp. 217–18; Dacey (1956).
83. (1958b) p. 212 shows evidence of the influence of the Davidson–
    Wicksell debate on price stability.
84. (1958c) q. 10219.
85. (1972a) pp. 13–14; (1958b) pp. 217–19.
86. (1958b) p. 211; (1951a) pp. 10–11; (1976a) p. 162; (1971b) pp. 164–5;
    (1979a) pp. 97–100.
87. (1972a) pp. 20–1; see however (1982) pp. 29–30.
88. (1971a) pp. 230–1; (1954) pp. 18–40; (1976a) pp. 86–94, 97; (1949b)
    p. 11; (1978b) pp. 11–12. Perhaps not surprisingly there were
    similarities with the position of H. C. Simons – see Bronfenbrenner
    (1955) p. 536.
89. (1974b) pp. 20–2; (1979a) pp. 3, 33, 39, 49; (1982) pp. 10–11.
90. (1958a) p. 23; (1971b) p. 4; (1947c) p. 71; (1974b) p. 21.
91. (1979a) p. 104; (1976a) p. 85.
92. (1971b) p. 2; (1958b) p. 213; (1976a) p. 84n; see also Hutchison (1981)
    p. 127. Nurkse (1955) had complained that Robbins's critique of
    Beveridge had not mentioned the latter's unemployment target of 3
    per cent which was greater than the 2 per cent or less actually
    prevailing in Britain.
93. (1947b) p. 31. See also *The Times*, 14 February (5e) and 28 February
    (5e) 1947.
94. (1974b) pp. 12–14, 19–20; (1958b) p. 213; (1972a) pp. 18, 132. See also
    Pemberton (1979).
95. (1947b) pp. 26–7.
96. (1958a) pp. 22–3.
97. (1974b) p. 20; (1972a) p. 19; (1958a) p. 6.
98. (1974a) p. 3; (1979a) pp. 62, 66, 86.
99. (1979a) pp. 80, 86–7; (1972a) p. 13.
100. (1976a) pp. 91–4; (1972a) p. 135.
101. (1974a) pp. 5–6.
102. (1972a) p. 133.
103. (1958b) p. 213.
104. (1974b) p. 23.
105. (1978b) pp. 12–13; (1971a) p. 231; (1982) p. 13.
106. (1947b) pp. 22–3.
107. (1979a) pp. xi, 18–19, 32–3, 107; see also (1971b) p. 3; (1982) p. 14.

108. (1979a) pp. 32–3, 45, 50; (1982) pp. 7–8.
109. (1979a) pp. 68–9.
110. (1958a) p. 24.
111. (1954) p. 71.
112. (1976a) p. 95.
113. (1979a) p. 9.
114. (1974b) p. 23; (1954) p. 67.
115. (1974b) p. 24.
116. (1979a) p. 50.
117. (1979a) p. 84.
118. (1972a) p. 140.
119. (1974a) pp. 104–5; (1979a) p. 37.
120. (1979a) p. 50.
121. (1972a) pp. 138–9.
122. (1976a) pp. 94–6.
123. (1974b) p. 24. See also *The Times*, 29 November 1972 (17f).
124. (1972a) p. 138; (1971a) p. 231; (1979a) pp. 62–5, 75, 105–6; (1974b) pp. 23–4.
125. (1979a) p. xi.
126. (1979a) p. 71.
127. (1974b) pp. 24–5.
128. (1976a) pp. 94–6; (1974a) pp. 3–4.
129. (1979a) p. 38.
130. (1951a) p. 32.
131. (1979a) pp. 83, 90, 97.
132. (1979a) p. 85.
133. (1972a) p. 25; (1954) p. 60.
134. (1979a) pp. 41–2.
135. (1966b) pp. 135–6.
136. (1979a) pp. x, 32, 35–6, 41, 56.
137. (1976a) p. 94.
138. (1974b) pp. 18–19; (1974a) p. 3.
139. (1979a) p. 61.
140. (1976a) pp. 93–4.
141. Hayek (1931c) pp. 151–2.
142. (1972a) pp. 12, 14; (1979a) pp. 35–6, 78; (1982) p. 4.
143. (1979a) p. 42.
144. (1976a) p. 94.
145. (1972a) p. 15.
146. (1976a) p. 94.
147. (1958b) p. 211; (1976a) pp. 83, 97.
148. (1971b) p. 164.
149. (1966) p. 31.
150. (1979a) pp. 35, 70.
151. (1971b) p. 10.
152. (1958a) p. 24; (1971b) pp. 13–14; (1958b) p. 212. Cf. Friedman (1968); Hayek (1978).
153. (1971b) p. 12; (1979a) pp. 28–9.

154. (1958c) q. 10190.
155. (1979a) p. 32. This point does not appear to have been appreciated by all his readers – see Pemberton (1979).
156. (1972b) p. 3.
157. (1974b) pp. 7, 20; (1974a) p. 5; (1979a) pp. 46–8.
158. (1972a) p. 18; (1954) pp. 61–3; (1958a) p. 5.
159. (1958a) p. 6.
160. (1979a) p. x; (1974a) p. 7.
161. (1974b) p. 19.
162. (1947c) pp. 34–5; (1954) pp. 216–17.
163. (1947c) pp. 40–1.
164. (1974b) pp. 19–23.
165. (1971a) p. 225; (1976a) p. 91; (1951a) p. 19; (1949b) p. 10.
166. (1972a) p. 14.
167. (1974b) p. 12.
168. (1979a) pp. 28–9, 57.
169. (1951a) p. 20.
170. (1979a) p. 29. It would appear however from a reference at this point to 'an excellent book by Mr Nicholas Kaldor' that Robbins had in mind the Mill version of the argument, which is endorsed by Kaldor – (1955) pp. 79–82.
171. (1947b) pp. 12–13.
172. (1974b) p. 17; (1958b) p. 213; (1947b) p. 11; (1947c) p. 215.
173. (1974a) p. 8.
174. (1972a) pp. 13–14.
175. (1951a) pp. 10–11.
176. (1971b) pp. 158–9.
177. (1972a) p. 19.
178. (1974b) pp. 17, 19; (1972a) p. 18; (1979a) p. 91. See also *Hansard*, 29 March 1961 col. 85.
179. (1979a) p. 87.
180. (1955b) pp. 4–7; (1958a) pp. 17–18; (1979a) pp. 20–1, 28.
181. (1949b) pp. 19–21; (1947b) p. 21; (1947c) p. 62.
182. (1955b) pp. 47; (1949b) pp. 19–21.
183. (1979a) p. xii; (1976a) p. 97.
184. (1979a) pp. 72, 76, 80, 81, 91; (1974b) pp. 24–5.
185. (1972a) p. 24.
186. (1958a) p. 11.
187. (1972a) p. 20. See also the *Hansard* reference in Note 178 above.
188. (1955b) p. 1.
189. (1979a) pp. 38, 49; (1954) pp. 77–8.
190. (1963a) p. 213.
191. (1958b) pp. 217–19; (1958c) q. 10205; (1963a) p. 213.
192. (1947c) pp. 72–3.
193. (1947b) p. 21; (1949b) p. 22.
194. (1947c) p. 62; (1947b) p. 21.
195. (1954) pp. 222–3.
196. (1958a) pp. 18–19.
197. (1972a) pp. 141–2.

198. (1954) p. 69. His Marshall Lectures had caused misunderstanding on this score in the mind of at least one reader – Heflebower (1948).
199. (1954) pp. 70–1.
200. (1954) p. 73.
201. (1976a) p. 99; (1979a) p. x.
202. (1955b) pp. 1–2.
203. (1971a) p. 233.
204. (1951a) pp. 31–2.
205. (1955b) p. 1.
206. (1951a) pp. 17–18, 20–1.
207. (1954) pp. 73–4.
208. (1971a) p. 233.
209. (1971a) p. 233.
210. (1954) pp. 74, 76.
211. (1954) p. 76.
212. (1955b) pp. 1–2; (1971a) p. 233; (1971b) pp. 5–6.
213. (1929a) pp. x, 38.
214. (1979a) p. 80.
215. (1958c) q. 10228; see also (1947c) pp. 61–2.
216. (1958b) p. 219.
217. (1958a) p. 8.
218. (1971a) p. 233.
219. (1971a) p. 234; (1971b) p. 6. See also *Hansard* vol. 291, 10 April 1968, col. 399. Interestingly this material, similar to (1971a) p. 234, was omitted when the speech was republished in (1979a) pp. 20–5.
220. (1979a) p. ix; (1971b) p. 7.
221. (1971b) p. 6.
222. (1958c) q. 10205.
223. See Addleson p. 517 on this non-determinism and cf. Cairnes (1875) pp. 108–15 on the character of economic laws.
224. (1971a) p. 235.
225. (1963a) pp. 200–2; Robbins cites Sayers (1957) pp. 92–107. See also ibid. pp. 54–5.
226. (1963a) pp. 204–5.
227. (1971b) p. 9.
228. (1963a) pp. 205–10.
229. (1971b) p. 8.
230. (1963a) pp. 207–8.
231. (1963a) pp. 216–17.
232. (1979a) p. 57.
233. (1963a) pp. 214–15.
234. (1963a) p. 215.
235. (1963a) pp. 215–16.
236. (1979a) p. 40.
237. (1963a) pp. 220–2.
238. Robertson (1959) p. 719; for a striking example of the change of mood referred to in the text see Little (1974).
239. (1958a) pp. 8–9; (1963a) pp. 200–2; (1958b) pp. 217–18; Dacey (1956); Dacey (1960) pp. 82–6.

240. (1958a) p. 15.
241. (1958b) p. 218.
242. (1963a) p. 220.
243. (1958a) p. 14.
244. (1958a) pp. 15–16; (1958b) p. 218.
245. (1958b) pp. 217–18.
246. (1954) p. 76; (1979a) pp. 19, 36–7, 58, 96; (1976a) p. 98; (1971) p. 9; (1958b) pp. 217–19; (1949b) p. 21.
247. (1954) pp. 78–80.
248. (1958b) pp. 217–19.
249. (1979a) pp. 66, 76.
250. (1963a) pp. 208–10.
251. (1976a) p. 77.
252. (1963a) pp. 210–21.
253. (1958b) p. 218; (1958c) qq. 10207, 10236.
254. (1963a) pp. 225–6.
255. (1974b) p. 25; (1974a) p. 5; (1972a) pp. 25, 141; (1979a) pp. xi, 43–4, 49, 57–8, 62–3, 85.
256. (1972a) pp. 130–1; see also (1954) pp. 75–6; (1963a) pp. 216–17.
257. (1953a) pp. 15–16; (1958b) pp. 217–19.
258. (1958a) pp. 12–14.
259. (1958b) p. 218; (1958c) q. 10219.
260. (1963a) p. 217; see also Dacey (1960) p. 121. It is instructive that the same charge has more recently been levelled against Keynes's reading of the economic events of the 1930s; Mishkin (1986) pp. 526–7; Darby and Lothian (1986) pp. 74–5.

9 International Economics

1. (1937b) pp. 9–10, 41n, 55, 60; (1971a) p. 158–9.
2. (1937b) pp. 68–73.
3. (1971a) pp. 155–65.
4. (1971a) pp. 163–5; (1971b) pp. 34–5; (1939b) p. 99; (1947c) p. 65; (1936b, g).
5. (1976a) p. 168; (1939a) pp. 116–17; (1936f) pp. 33–4.
6. (1937b) pp. 100–2; (1936g) pp. 473–4.
7. (1937b) pp. 102–11; (1936g) p. 474.
8. (1971b) pp. 214–16.
9. (1937b) pp. 22–3; (1936d).
10. (1937b) pp. 39–41; (1936g) pp. 467–8; (1935e) p. 25; (1936b) pp. 228–9.
11. (1937b) pp. 60–8, 76–8.
12. (1937b) pp. 80–96.
13. (1939a) pp. 203–6; (1931d).
14. (1939b) pp. 95–8; (1934d) p. 196. Keynes, for instance, believed as late as August 1939 that war was very unlikely – (1978) p. 3.
15. (1937b) pp. 238–46.
16. (1937b) pp. 221–68; (1971b) p. 269.

17. (1937b) pp. 302–27; (1931a) p. 49.
18. (1937b) pp. 309–10.
19. (1971a) p. 239.
20. (1971b) p. 184.
21. (1937b) pp. 242–3, 250–6.
22. (1965a) p. 9.
23. (1957b).
24. (1937b) pp. 166–73; (1931a) pp. 48–9; (1958b) p. 214.
25. (1932c) p. 153.
26. (1971b) p. 193.
27. (1971b) p. 22; (1931a) pp. 55–6.
28. (1971b) p. 190; (1971a) pp. 232–3.
29. (1971b) p. 209.
30. (1971b) pp. 30, 194–5, 197–9.
31. (1939a) pp. 81–106; see also (1939d) pp. 293–4; (1937c).
32. (1939b).
33. (1937b).
34. (1971b) p. 268n.
35. (1940a); (1941); see also (1939a) pp. 276–7.
36. (1971b) pp. 248–51; (1941) p. 3.
37. (1939a) pp. 81–106; (1937c).
38. (1971b) pp. 267–72.
39. Harrod (1951) pp. 192–3.
40. (1971a) pp. 161–2.
41. See also (1972a) pp. 145–6.
42. (1976a) pp. 186–9.
43. (1937b) pp. 238–46.
44. (1941) pp. 4–7; (1937b) pp. 244–5.
45. (1941) pp. 23–4. See however his concern about this proposal after the Second World War in *The Times*, 23 July 1950 (7e).
46. (1941) pp. 24–5.
47. (1941) pp. 25–6.
48. (1941) pp. 29–32.
49. (1941) pp. 31–2.
50. (1941) pp. 12–16, 28; (1976a) p. 167; (1937b) p. 246; (1963a) pp. 120–1.
51. (1941) pp. 26–9.
52. (1963a) pp. 128–9; (1941) pp. 23–6.
53. (1941) pp. 7–12; (1939b) pp. 94–8; (1937b) pp. 92–6.
54. (1937b) pp. 323–4.
55. (1931a) p. 46.
56. (1937b) pp. 80–90, 246–7; (1941) pp. 26–7; (1963a) pp. 122–3.
57. (1941) pp. 17–23; (1937b) pp. 299–301; (1954) pp. 176–7.
58. (1937b) pp. 270–80; (1936e).
59. (1963a) pp. 124–8.
60. (1941) p. 20n.
61. (1971b) p. 24; (1973a) p. 19; (1976a) p. 190n.
62. (1971a) p. 160; see also (1939c) pp. 217–18; (1937b) pp. 87–96; (1936g) pp. 476–7; (1936b) pp. 23–8.
63. (1971b) pp. 31–3, 211–12.

64. (1971b) pp. 235–51.
65. (1939a) pp. 81–106; (1937c).
66. (1937b) pp. 116–23.
67. (1971b) p. 245; (1939b) p. 77; (1937b) pp. 123–8.
68. (1971b) p. 247.
69. (1939b); (1971a) p. 160; (1939a) pp. 81–106; (1971b) pp. 235–51; (1937c).
70. (1939b) pp. 34–7, 67–8; see also (1939a) pp. 1–28.
71. (1939b) pp. 119–20.
72. (1939b) p. 120.
73. (1939b) pp. 40–59, 92.
74. (1939b) pp. 56–7.
75. (1939b) p. 74; (1971b) pp. 240–2.
76. (1971b) p. 242.
77. (1937b) pp. 17–19; (1936d).
78. (1954) pp. 173–4.
79. (1939b) p. 90.
80. (1939b) pp. 92–3.
81. (1971b) p. 214; (1971a) p. 156.
82. (1939a) pp. 132–4; (1936f) p. 43.
83. (1976a) pp. 152–3.
84. (1971b) pp. 210–11.
85. (1971b) p. 211.
86. (1976a) pp. 156–7; (1971b) pp. 29–30, 254, 259–62.
87. (1976a) p. 164.
88. (1971b) p. 217.
89. (1971a) pp. 156–8; Harrod (1952) pp. 429–30; Robbins (1932b) pp. 178–83; (1931a) pp. 57–62; (1937b) pp. 315–16, 319–24; (1975b) pp. 155–6; (1931b); (1971b) p. 213.
90. (1937b) pp. 17, 24–8, 41–5; (1971b) pp. 204–6; (1936d).
91. (1971b) p. 208.
92. (1937b) pp. 25–32.
93. (1934d) pp. 65, 68, 115, 181; (1937b) pp. 39–40, 48.
94. (1931a) pp. 45–51.
95. (1931a) pp. 56–7.
96. (1932c) pp. 153–5.
97. (1949b) pp. 28–30; (1953a) pp. 1–5.
98. (1971a) pp. 100–1.
99. (1971b) p. 231.
100. (1941) p. 13; (1971b) pp. 27–8, 194–8, 222, 260–1; (1932) pp. 170–3; (1939a) p. 91; (1939b) p. 89.
101. (1958e) pp. 197–231.
102. (1971b) pp. 27–8, 193; (1937b) pp. 17–18; (1963a) p. 120.
103. (1931a) pp. 47–8.
104. (1976a) pp. 40–2.
105. (1947b) pp. 23–4; (1971b) pp. 159–62; (1949b) p. 29; (1934d) p. 115.
106. (1937b) pp. 55–60; (1934d) pp. 115, 182–5; (1939a) pp. 169–73.
107. (1937b) pp. 111–16, 134–41.
108. (1937b) p. 121.
109. (1954) p. 197n; Viner (1953).

110. (1954) pp. 174–6.
111. (1971b) pp. 226–7.
112. (1963a) pp. 115–16, originally (1958).
113. (1954) pp. 170–97.
114. (1954) p. 191.
115. (1954) pp. 194–5.
116. (1947b) pp. 26–7.
117. (1953a) pp. 7–8.
118. (1939b) p. 102.
119. (1954) ch. 9; (1953a) pp. 10–14; (1971b) p. v, 36–8, 170–1, 177–82; (1949b) p. 30. See also *The Times*, 23 July 1950 (7e).
120. (1971a) pp. 237–8, 240; (1968d); see also (1971a) pp. 207–8 for his deep personal commitment to the success of the Anglo-American negotiations.
121. (1971a) pp. 238–9; (1971b) pp. v, 36–8, 271.
122. (1963a) p. 154.
123. (1971b) pp. 37–8; see also (1973a) pp. 18–21; (1975b) pp. 20–1.
124. (1971b) p. 36.
125. (1954) pp. 183–9.
126. (1954) pp. 188–9.
127. (1954) pp. 184–5.
128. O'Brien (1976).
129. (1968b) pp. 676–7.
130. (1954) p. 193.
131. (1967b) p. 25.
132. (1937b) pp. 292n, 298; see also (1932h) pp. 423–5, 436; (1935f) pp. 208–9, 213–17; Henderson (1935b).
133. (1934d) pp. 9–10, 22–9, 49–53.
134. (1934d) pp. 78–81, 84–5, 86–90, 94–8, 107, 112–14, 117, 165–72.
135. (1934d) pp. 171–82.
136. (1971b) pp. 131–2.
137. (1973a) pp. 4–6.
138. In particular his version of the history of gold and silver as monetary precious metals ignores Gresham's Law and asserts that gold displaced silver because it was thought to be more stable whereas (i) gold displaced silver only after a change in Mint parities caused it to be relatively over-valued; (ii) government intervened to demonetise silver after the 1870s discoveries. Cf. Robbins (1973a) p. 9 and Yeager (1976) pp. 296–7.
139. (1976a) p. 81.
140. (1976a) pp. 157–60.
141. (1976a) p. 166; (1971b) pp. 20, 124–33, 180–1, 257.
142. (1967b) pp. 7–12.
143. (1975b) pp. 18–19; see also (1963a) pp. 164–5.
144. (1971b) p. 257; (1973a) pp. 16–18; (1975b) p. 17.
145. (1951a) pp. 18–19.
146. (1979a) pp. 22–3; see however (1982) pp. 29–30.
147. (1975b) p. 17.
148. (1972a) pp. 143–4.

149. (1967b) p. 23.
150. (1975b) p. 155.
151. (1967b) pp. 18–22; (1971b) pp. 174–6; (1979a) pp. 22–3; (1973a) p. 16.
152. (1971b) pp. 151–3.
153. (1951a) p. 14; (1971b) pp. 155–6; (1953a) p. 14; (1971a) p. 233.
154. (1949b) pp. 24–8.
155. (1951a) pp. 15–16.
156. (1949b) pp. 9–10; (1954) pp. 25–8.
157. (1953a) pp. 6–7.
158. (1971b) pp. 16–17.
159. (1971b) pp. 14–16; (1958b) pp. 214–15; see also (1954) p. 28.
160. (1971b) pp. 156–7.
161. (1958a) pp. 4–5, 25.
162. (1953a) p. 13.
163. (1951a) p. 14.
164. (1951a) p. 17; see also (1971b) pp. 14–16, 153–9.
165. (1951a) p. 18.
166. (1951a) p. 16.
167. (1951a) pp. 27–8, 31–2; (1979a) pp. 28, 30.
168. (1972a) pp. 141–2.
169. (1951a) pp. 20–1.
170. (1971b) pp. 14–17; for an exposition of the principle of 'metallic fluctuation' see (1958e) pp. 97–100.
171. (1971b) pp. 18–19; (1968b) p. 673.
172. (1958b) p. 218.
173. (1951a) pp. 22–3.
174. (1937b) pp. 159–73; (1931a) pp. 48–9.
175. (1947b) pp. 18–19; (1971b) pp. 168–70; (1953a) pp. 17–19.
176. (1951a) pp. 24–5; (1979a) pp. 108–11; (1958a) p. 11; (1934d) pp. 100–2.
177. (1951a) p. 24.
178. (1951a) pp. 25–6.
179. (1971b) pp. 127–33, 171–3; (1967b) p. 17; (1968b) pp. 671–4; (1953a) p. 18; (1958a) pp. 3, 25; (1958b) p. 219.
180. (1971b) p. 143; (1973a) p. 10; (1958a) p. 10.
181. Harrod (1951) p. 557; Robbins (1971a) p. 190.
182. (1972a) p. 21. See also *Hansard*, 29 March 1961, cols 79–82, where Robbins recounts having fought for the Keynes plan at Bretton Woods, only later deciding that it would have been inflationary.
183. (1973a) pp. 12–14.
184. (1973a) pp. 14–18.
185. (1937b) pp. 296–9.
186. (1971b) pp. 133–6; (1975b) p. 23; (1958a) p. 10; (1979a) pp. 5, 13–14; (1968b) pp. 674, 677.
187. (1947b) pp. 25–6; (1951a) pp. 28–9; (1971b) pp. 28–9, 159–60, 229; (1954) pp. 189–90; (1979a) pp. 17–19, 54–5; (1949b) pp. 17–19; (1953a) p. 16; (1972a) pp. 22–3; (1958a) p. 20; (1958b) p. 215.
188. (1934d) pp. 104–7, 112–13, 117–18, 161, 178–81; (1939a) p. 232.
189. (1972a) p. 23.
190. (1958b) p. 216.

191. (1979a) pp. 93–6.
192. (1968b) pp. 674–7.
193. (1937b) pp. 290–9.
194. (1958a) p. 10.
195. (1971b) p. 19; (1979a) pp. xi, 5, 13.
196. (1963a) pp. 127–8; (1971b) p. 177.
197. (1979a) pp. 20–1, 26–9; (1949b) p. 31.
198. (1979a) pp. 21–2, 149.
199. (1971b) pp. 166–7.
200. (1971b) p. 178; (1973a) p. 11.
201. (1971a) pp. 196–7. See also *Hansard*, 29 March 1961, cols 82–3; (1982) p. 25.
202. (1971b) pp. 182–3; (1967b) p. 23; (1968b) pp. 673–7; (1973a) p. 12; (1958a) p. 216.
203. (1967b) pp. 12–14.
204. (1975b) pp. 24–5.
205. (1975b) pp. 25–6; (1982) p. 29.
206. (1972a) pp. 21–2, 145–6.
207. (1958b) p. 219 (Robbins did not object at that date to the idea that there was a need for more international liquidity in general); (1971b) pp. 174–6; (1979a) pp. 22–3; (1967b) pp. 16–22; (1973a) pp. 16–17; (1968b) p. 676. See also *Hansard*, 29 March 1961, cols 77–85; 9 November 1966, col. 927.
208. (1979a) pp. 22–4.
209. (1967b) p. 18.
210. Yeager (1976) pp. 589–94.
211. (1971b) pp. 17, 144–62. See also Robertson (1955) p. 107.
212. (1963a) pp. 159–65; (1953a) pp. 2–7, 14.
213. (1972a) p. 23.
214. Yeager (1976) pp. 592–3.
215. (1951a) pp. 28–9; (1982) pp. 27–8.
216. (1971b) p. 138; (1968b) p. 669; (1973a) p. 9; (1967b) p. 11.
217. (1963a) pp. 124–8.
218. (1979a) p. 54.
219. (1976a) p. 161; (1971b) pp. 20–1, 170–2; (1967b) p. 11; (1968b) pp. 667–71, 674–7; (1972a) p. 7; (1953a) pp. 16–17; (1979a) p. 5; (1958) p. 216.
220. (1972) pp. 22–3.
221. (1971b) pp. 21, 141.
222. (1971b) p. 20; see also (1973a) pp. 7–8; (1935f) pp. 208–10.
223. (1941) pp. 18–20; (1971b) pp. 24, 136–43; (1968b) p. 669.
224. (1941) p. 21; (1937b) pp. 280–90; (1958b) p. 216.
225. (1976a) p. 162; (1937b) pp. 280–90.
226. (1976a) p. 162; (1939b) pp. 280–90; (1979a) pp. 53–4; (1967b) p. 11.
227. (1939b) pp. 280–90; (1979a) p. 82; (1975b) p. 15; (1968b) pp. 669–71; (1953a) pp. 16–17; (1974b) p. 19; (1958a) p. 216. It is possible that Robbins derived this from Bresciani-Turroni's account of the German inflation although Bond (1980) credits Haberler (1936) with an appreciation of the problem.

228. (1974a) p. 7; (1958a) p. 10.
229. (1971b) p. 142; (1958b) p. 216.
230. (1971b) pp. 140–1; (1963a) pp. 124–8; (1979a) pp. 54–5, 82; (1975b) p. 15; (1968b) pp. 669–71.
231. Bresciani-Turroni (1937) p. 174; see also Mises (1934) pp. 200–3.
232. (1976a) p. 163; (1971b) pp. 22, 138–9; (1937b) pp. 280–90; (1963a) pp. 124–8; (1975b) pp. 15–16, 19; (1968b) pp. 669–71; (1973a) pp. 8–9; (1958b) p. 216.
233. (1971b) pp. 23, 143; (1975b) p. 20; Baumol (1987) p. 7; (1979a) pp. xi, 24; (1967b) p. 12; (1968b) pp. 669–71.
234. (1973a) p. 9.

10 Conclusion

1. (1971a) p. 11.
2. (1932a) pp. 78–83.
3. See especially (1934a) p. 10. See also O'Brien (1983) pp. 32, 36–7.
4. For a striking example of this see Little (1974).
5. Johnson (1972) p. 835.
6. Meade (1984) p. 5.
7. Robbins (1970b) p. 231.
8. Baumol (1988).
9. Robbins (1970b) p. 163.

Notes to Appendix

1. Translated by D. P. O'Brien. Translated from 'Les méthodes d'observation économique et les problèmes de la prévision en matière économique' delivered at the Institut de Recherches Économiques et Sociales, 1934, and published in *Cinq Conférences sur la Méthode dans les recherches économiques* (Paris: Recueil Sirey, 1938) with a preface by Charles Rist. The other contributors were Wagemann (Germany), Dupriez (Belgium), Vandellós (Spain) and Stuart (Holland). In translating Robbins's lecture I have as far as possible avoided the temptation to paraphrase the French so as to produce something closer to Robbins's own rolling English style.
2. This sequence break is in the original French version and does not indicate the omission of material by the translator.

Bibliography

Works by Robbins cited in this study

(1925) Review of T. E. Gregory, *The Present Position of Banking in America*, *Economica* 5, pp. 358–9.

(1925/6) *Wages. An Introductory Analysis of the Wage System under Modern Capitalism* (London: Jarrolds). [The work is undated: but the Nat. U. Cat. gives [1925] and the B.M. Cat. gives [1926].]

(1926a) 'The Dynamics of Capitalism', *Economica* 6, pp. 31–9.

(1926b) Review of S. Mills, *Taxation in Australia* and A. Ramaiya, *A National System of Taxation*, *Economica* 6, pp. 111–12.

(1926c) Review of G. Cassel, *Fundamental Thoughts in Economics*, *Economica* 6, pp. 223–5.

(1926d) Review of R. Mills and F. Benham, *Lectures on The Principles of Money, Banking and Foreign Exchange*, *Economica* 6, pp. 359–60.

(1927a) 'Mr Hawtrey on the Scope of Economics', *Economica* 7, pp. 172–8.

(1927b) 'The Optimum Theory of Population' (pp. 103–34) in T. E. Gregory and H. Dalton (eds), *London Essays in Economics: in Honour of Edwin Cannan* (London: Routledge).

(1927c) Review of M. J. Bonn, *Das Schicksal des Deutschen Kapitalismus*, *Economic Journal* 37, pp. 613–16.

(1927d) Review of E. Mahaim, *L'Organisation Permanente du Travail*, *Economic Journal* 37, pp. 638–9.

(1927e) Review of J. Bonar, *The Tables Turned*, *Economica* 7, pp. 391–2.

(1928a) 'The Representative Firm', *Economic Journal* 38, pp. 387–404.

(1928b) Review of Sir A. Mond, *Industry and Politics*, *Economic Journal* 38, pp. 442–4.

(1929a) 'The Economic Effects of Variations of Hours of Labour', *Economic Journal* 39, pp. 25–40.

(1929b) 'Notes on Some Probable Consequences of the Advent of a Stationary Population in Great Britain', *Economica* 9, pp. 71–82.

(1929c) Review of Sir J. Stamp, *Some Economic Factors in Modern Life*, *Economic Journal* 39, pp. 248–50.

(1929d) Review of E. Cannan, *A Review of Economic Theory*, *Economic Journal* 39, pp. 409–14.

(1930a) 'On a Certain Ambiguity in the Conception of Stationary Equilibrium', *Economic Journal* 40, pp. 194–214.

(1930b) 'The Present Position of Economic Science', *Economica* 10, pp. 14–24.

(1930c) 'On the Elasticity of Demand for Income in Terms of Effort', *Economica* 10, pp. 123–9.

(1930d) 'The Economic Works of Phillip Wicksteed', *Economica* 10, pp. 245–58. Provides the basis of (1933).

(1930e) Introduction (pp. vii–ix) to H. E. Batson, *A Select Bibliography of*

219

Modern Economic Theory 1870–1929 (London: Routledge & Kegan Paul, 1930) Reprinted 1967/8.

(1930f) Review of N. W. Senior (ed.) S. L. Levi, *Industrial Efficiency and Social Economy*, *Economic Journal* 40, pp. 272–5.

(1930g) Review of O. Spann, *Types of Economic Theory*, *Economica* 10, pp. 200–202.

(1931a) 'Economic Notes on Some Arguments for Protection', *Economica* 11, pp. 45–62.

(1931b) 'A Reply to Mr. Keynes', *New Statesman and Nation*, 14 March 1931, pp. 98–100.

(1931c) Preface to 1st edition of Hayek (1931c).

(1931d) 'The Economics of Import Boards', *Political Quarterly* 2, pp. 204–23. Reproduced in (1939a) pp. 182–210.

(1931e) Review of M. S. Braun, *Theorie der Staatlichen Wirtschaftspolitik*, *Economica* 11, pp. 469–72.

(1931f) Review of F. Machlup, *Börsenkredit, Industriekredit und Kapitalbildung*, *Economica* 11, pp. 472–5.

(1932a) *An Essay on the Nature and Significance of Economic Science*, 1st edition (London: Macmillan).

(1932b) 'Consumption and the Trade Cycle', *Economica* 12, pp. 413–30.

(1932c) 'The Case of Agriculture' (pp. 148–69) in Sir W. Beveridge et al., *Tariffs: The Case Examined* (London: Longmans) (with G. L. Schwartz).

(1932d) 'Tariffs for Revenue' (pp. 170–84) in Sir W. Beveridge et al., *Tariffs: The Case Examined* (London: Longmans).

(1932e) Letter to the *Economist*, 14 May 1932, p. 1081.

(1932f) Letter to the *Economist*, 28 May 1932, pp. 1118–19.

(1932g) Letter to the *Economist*, 11 June 1932, p. 1295.

(1932h) 'The Ottawa Resolutions on Finance and the Future of Monetary Policy', *Lloyds Bank Review* N.S., vol. 3, no. 32, October 1932, pp. 422–38.

(1932i) Review of J. Bonar, *A Catalogue of the Library of Adam Smith*, *Economica* 12, p. 365.

(1933) 'Introduction' in *Philip H. Wicksteed: The Commonsense of Political Economy* (1910) (London: Routledge). Corrected and expanded version of (1930d). Reprinted in (1970b) pp. 189–209.

(1934a) 'Remarks upon Certain Aspects of the Theory of Costs', *Economic Journal* 44, pp. 1–18.

(1934b) 'Remarks on the Relationship between Economics and Psychology', *Manchester School* 5, pp. 89–101.

(1934c) 'Production', *Encyclopaedia of the Social Sciences* (ed. E. R. A. Seligman) vol. 12, pp. 462–7 (New York: Macmillan).

(1934d) *The Great Depression* (London: Macmillan).

(1934e) 'Introduction' (pp. 11–13) in L. v. Mises, *The Theory of Money and Credit*, 2nd edition, trans. H. E. Batson (London: Jonathan Cape, 1934).

(1934f) 'The Planning of British Agriculture', *Lloyds Bank Review* 5, pp. 458–69. Reprinted in (1939a) pp. 161–81 with insignificant changes.

(1934g) 'L'Agriculture Dirigée', *Revue d'Economie Politique* 48, pp. 1503–20. Reprinted in (1939a) pp. 135–60.

(1935a) *An Essay on the Nature and Significance of Economic Science*, 2nd edition (London: Macmillan).

(1935b) 'Introduction' (pp. vii–xix) in K. Wicksell, *Lectures on Political Economy*, trans. E. Classen (London: Routledge). Reprinted in (1970b) pp. 210–22.

(1935c) 'A Student's Recollections of Edwin Cannan', *Economic Journal* 45, pp. 393–8.

(1935d) 'The Planning of British Agriculture – A Rejoinder', *Lloyds Bank Review* N.S., 6, pp. 89–92.

(1935e) 'The Economics of Restrictionism', *Banker* 33, pp. 19–25. Reproduced in (1937b) pp. 29–37, 39–41, with final paragraph omitted.

(1935f) 'The Problem of Stabilisation', *Lloyds Bank Monthly Review* 6, pp. 207–18.

(1936a) 'The Place of Jevons in the History of Economic Thought', *Manchester School* 7, pp. 1–17. Reprinted in (1970b) pp. 169–88.

(1936b) 'The Consequences of Economic Nationalism', *Lloyds Bank Review* N.S. 7, pp. 226–39. Reprinted in (1936g) and partially in (1937b) chs 3 and 4.

(1936c) 'Międzynarodowe regulowanie plac i czasu pracy' ['International Organisation of Wages and Hours of Work'] trans. J. Drewnowski, *Ekonomista* 36, no. 4, pp. 3–15. Reprinted in (1937b) pp. 158–83.

(1936d) 'The Nature of National Planning in the Sphere of International Business', *Financial and Economic Review of the Statistical Department, Amsterdamsche Bank*, no. 47, pp. 1–9. Reproduced (with omissions) in (1937b) pp. 13–20, 22–38.

(1936e) 'Economic Nationalism and Monetary Policy', *Banker* 38, pp. 192–7. Reprinted (with alterations) in (1937b) pp. 271–5, 277, 278–9.

(1936f) 'Memorandum on the fundamental reasons for increased protectionism' (pp. 27–43) in Carnegie Endowment for International Peace – International Chamber of Commerce, *Memoranda . . . on the Improvement of Commercial Relations between Nations and the Problems of Monetary Stabilisation* (Paris: International Chamber of Commerce, 1936). Reprinted in (1939a) pp. 107–34.

(1936g) 'The Consequences of Economic Nationalism' (pp. 466–78) in *International Conciliation. Documents for the Year 1936* (New York: Carnegie Endowment for International Peace). Reprint of (1936b). Partially incorporated into (1937b) chs 3 and 4.

(1936h) Review of R. Nurkse, *Internationale Kapitalbewegungen*, *Economica* N.S. 3, pp. 108–9.

(1937a) Foreword to C. Bresciani-Turroni, *The Economics of Inflation*, 1931 trans. M. E. Sayers (London: Allen & Unwin).

(1937b) *Economic Planning and International Order* (London: Macmillan).

(1937c) 'The Economics of Territorial Sovereignty' (pp. 41–60) in C. A. W. Manning (ed.), *Peaceful Change* (London: Macmillan). Reprinted in Robbins (1939a) pp. 81–106 and in (1971b) pp. 235–51.

(1937d) 'How to Mitigate the Next Slump', *Lloyds Bank Review* N.S., vol. 8, no. 87, pp. 234–44. Reprinted in (1939a) pp. 237–55.

(1937e) Review of G. Haberler, *Der Internationale Handel* and *The Theory of*

International Trade, trans. A. Stonier and F. Benham, *Economica* N.S. 4, pp. 102–5.

(1937f) Review of *The Agricultural Dilemma. A Report of an Inquiry organised by Viscount Astor and Mr. B. Seebohm Rowntree*, *Economica* N.S. 4, pp. 113–14.

(1938a) 'Live and Dead Issues in the Methodology of Economics', *Economica* N.S. 5, pp. 342–52.

(1938b) 'Les méthodes d'observation économique et les problemes de la prévision en matière économique' [delivered 1934] in L. Robbins et al., *Cinq conferences sur la Méthode dans les recherches économiques* (Paris: Librairie du Recueil Sirey).

(1938c) 'Interpersonal Comparisons of Utility: A Comment', *Economic Journal* 48, pp. 635–41.

(1938d) 'The Long-term Budget Problem', *Lloyds Bank Review* N.S., vol. 9, no. 98, April 1938, pp. 158–67.

(1939a) *The Economic Basis of Class Conflict* (London: Macmillan).

(1939b) *The Economic Causes of War* (London: Jonathan Cape).

(1939c) 'The Export Problem', *Lloyds Bank Review* N.S., vol. 10, no. 113, July 1939, pp. 214–27.

(1939d) 'The Export Problem: A Reply to Mr. Glenday', *Lloyds Bank Review* N.S., vol. 10, no. 115, pp. 286–95.

(1939e) 'Preface' (pp. xi–xii) in Chi-Yuen Wu, *An Outline of International Price Theories* (London: Routledge).

(1940a) 'Economic Aspects of Federation' (pp. 167–86) in M. Chaning Pearce (ed.), *Federal Union. A Symposium* (London: Jonathan Cape, 1940). Reprinted in (1941).

(1940b) Review of I. Berlin, *Karl Marx: His Life and Environment*, *Economica* N.S. 7, pp. 93–4.

(1940c) Review of B. Souvarine, *Stalin: A Critical Survey of Bolshevism*, *Economica* N.S. 7, pp. 94–6.

(1941) *Economic Aspects of Federation* (London: Macmillan for the Federal Research Institute). Reprint of (1940a).

(1944) 'Restrictive Developments in Industry' (appendix to a report of the War Cabinet Reconstruction Committee, pp. 66–78). Public Record Office CAB 87/70, R(44), 6.

(1947a) 'Economic Prospects', *Lloyds Bank Review* 3 (January) pp. 21–32.

(1947b) 'Inquest on the Crisis', *Lloyds Bank Review* 6 (October) pp. 1–27.

(1947c) *The Economic Problem in Peace and War* (London: Macmillan).

(1949a) 'The Economist in the Twentieth Century', *Economica* N.S. 16, pp. 93–105. Reprinted in (1954) pp. 1–17.

(1949b) 'The Sterling Problem', *Lloyds Bank Review* 14 (October) pp. 1–31.

(1949c) 'Full Employment as an Objective', *Comptes-rendus des Travaux de la Société d'Economie Politique de Belgique*, no. 192 (December), pp. 6–22. Reprinted in (1954) pp. 18–40 and in (1971b) pp. 41–65.

(1949d) 'Cannan, Edwin', *Dictionary of National Biography*, Supplement 1931–1940, L. G. W. Legg (ed.) (Oxford: Oxford University Press) pp. 141–3. Reprinted in (1970b) pp. 229–33.

(1950) 'Towards the Atlantic Community', *Lloyds Bank Review* 17 (July) pp. 1–24. Reprinted in (1954) pp. 170–97.

(1951a) *The Balance of Payments*, Stamp Memorial Lecture (London: Athlone Press).

(1951b) Review of R. F. Harrod, *The Life of John Maynard Keynes*, *The Times*, 26 January 1951, 7f–g. Reprinted in (1970b) pp. 243–7.

(1952) *The Theory of Economic Policy in English Classical Political Economy* (London: Macmillan).

(1953a) 'The International Economic Problem', *Lloyds Bank Review* 17 (January) pp. 1–24.

(1953b) 'Robertson on Utility and Scope', *Economica* N.S. 20, pp. 99–111.

(1954) *The Economist in the Twentieth Century and Other Lectures in Political Economy* (London: Macmillan). Chapters III–VIII reprinted in (1971b).

(1955a) 'Schumpeter's History of Economic Analysis', *Quarterly Journal of Economics* 69, pp. 1–22. Reprinted in (1970b) pp. 47–72.

(1955b) 'Notes on Public Finance', *Lloyds Bank Review* 38 (October) pp. 1–18. Partially reprinted in (1963) pp. 88–90.

(1955c) 'The Teaching of Economics in Schools and Universities', *Economic Journal* 65, pp. 579–93.

(1956) 'A Letter from David Ricardo', *Economica* N.S. 23, pp. 172–4.

(1957a) 'Packe on Mill', *Economica* N.S. 24, pp. 250–9. Reprinted in (1970b) pp. 97–117.

(1957b) 'A Note on the Formal Content of the Traditional Theory of International Trade' (pp. 267–71) in *Contribuicões à Análise do Desenvolvimento Econômico (Escrito em Homagem a Eugenio Gudin)* (Rio de Janeiro: Agir).

(1957c) 'Montagu Norman: A "Monarch" in the City' (BBC Third Programme talk) *The Listener*, 6 June 1957, pp. 913–14. Reprinted in (1970b) pp. 234–42.

(1957d) 'Equality as a Social Objective', *Crossbow* 1, Part 1, pp. 18–22. Reprinted in (1963) pp. 73–90 in extended form.

(1957e) Review of F. H. Knight, *On the History and Method of Economics*, *American Economic Review* 47, pp. 397–9.

(1958a) 'Thoughts on the Crisis', *Lloyds Bank Review* 48 (April) pp. 1–26. Reprinted in (1963) pp. 166–96.

(1958b) *The Aims of Monetary Policy and the Means of Achieving Them.* Memorandum to the Committee on the Working of the Monetary System (Radcliffe Committee) (London: HMSO 1960) pp. 211–19.

(1958c) Evidence to the Committee on the Working of the Monetary System (Radcliffe Committee) 24 July 1958 (London: HMSO 1960) pp. 673–8 qq. 10190–254.

(1958d) 'Introduction', in *R. Torrens: Letters on Commercial Policy* (1833) (London: LSE). Reprinted in (1970b) pp. 92–6.

(1958e) *Robert Torrens and the Evolution of Classical Economics* (London: Macmillan).

(1958f) 'MacDougall on the Dollar Problem', *Crossbow* (January). Reprinted in (1963) pp. 159–65.

(1959) 'The Present Position of Economics', *Rivista di Politica Economica* (reprinted pp. 31–46) in E. Henderson and L. Spaventa (eds), *Guest Lectures in Economics* (Milan: Giuffrè, 1962).

(1960a) 'Monetary Theory and the Radcliffe Report' (reprinted pp. 87–109) in E. Henderson and L. Spaventa (eds) *Guest Lectures in Economics*

(Milan: Giuffrè, 1962) and, with minor changes and an additional final section, in Robbins (1963) pp. 197–226 and (1971b) pp. 90–119.

(1960b) Review of K. Wicksell, *Selected Papers on Economic Theory* and T. Gårdlund, *The Life of Knut Wicksell, Economica* N.S. 27, pp. 173–7. Reprinted in (1970b) pp. 223–8.

(1960c) Review of D. H. Robertson, *Lectures on Economic Principles, Economica* N.S. 27, pp. 71–4. Reprinted in (1970b) pp. 248–52.

(1960d) Review of R. Pankhurst, *The Saint Simonians, Mill and Carlyle, Economica* N.S. 27, pp. 278–9.

(1961a) 'Hayek on Liberty', *Economica* N.S. 28, pp. 66–81. Reprinted in (1963) pp. 91–112.

(1961b) Review of C. S. Shoup, *Ricardo on Taxation, Economica* N.S. 28, pp. 326–8.

(1962a) Review of J. Stillinger (ed.), *The Early Draft of John Stuart Mill's Autobiography, Economica* N.S. 29, pp. 202–4. Reprinted in (1970b) pp. 110–13.

(1962b) Review of G. S. L. Tucker, *Progress and Profits in British Economic Thought, Economic Journal* 72, pp. 374–6.

(1962c) 'Lord Dalton. An Outstanding Teacher', *The Times*, 20 February 1962 (15b).

(1963a) *Politics and Economics* (London: Macmillan). Chs 7, 10 reprinted in (1971b).

(1963b) Review of M. P. Mack, *Jeremy Bentham: An Odyssey of Ideas, 1748–1792, Economica* N.S. 30, pp. 196–7.

(1963c) [Chairman] *Committee on Higher Education. Report* (London: HMSO, Cmnd 2154).

(1965a) *Bentham in the Twentieth Century.* An Address to the Assembly of Faculties, University College London on 16 June 1964 (London: Athlone Press). Reprinted in (1970b) pp. 73–84.

(1965b) 'Recent Discussion of the Problems of Higher Education in Great Britain', *Public Policy* 14, pp. 203–20. Reprinted in (1966b) pp. 17–39.

(1965c) Review of *The Collected Works of John Stuart Mill*, vols 12–13, *The Earlier Letters, Economica* N.S. 32, pp. 458–60. Reprinted in (1970b) pp. 113–17.

(1966a) *On Academic Freedom.* An Inaugural Lecture under the 'Thank-Offering to Britain Fund', 6 July 1966 (London: Oxford University Press for the British Academy).

(1966b) *The University in the Modern World* (London: Macmillan).

(1966c) 'An Economist Looks at Business' (pp. 25–31) in *Economics, Business and Government* (London: I.E.A.).

(1966d) Review of *The Collected Works of John Stuart Mill*, vols II–III, *Economica* N.S. 33, pp. 92–4. Reprinted in (1970b) pp. 164–8.

(1966e) Review of R. L. Meek, *Economics of Physiocracy, Economica* N.S. 33, pp. 94–6.

(1966f) Review of E. Kauder, *A History of Marginal Utility Theory, Economica* N.S. 33, pp. 347–8.

(1966g) Review of J. Rae, *Life of Adam Smith* with introduction by Jacob Viner, *Economica* N.S. 33, pp. 348–9.

(1967a) 'Malthus as an Economist', *Economic Journal* 77, pp. 256–61. Reprinted in (1970b) pp. 85–91.

(1967b) 'Issues and Alternatives' (pp. 7–25) and 'Concluding Observations' (pp. 143–50) in R. Hinshaw (ed.), *Monetary Reform and the Price of Gold* (Baltimore: Johns Hopkins University Press).

(1967c) 'Introduction' (pp. vii–xli) in J. S. Mill, *Essays on Economics and Society*, ed. J. M. Robson (Toronto: University of Toronto Press). Reprinted in (1970b) pp. 118–63.

(1967d) Review of J. S. Mill, *On the Logic of the Moral Sciences*, *Economica* N.S. 34, p. 90.

(1967e) Review of R. W. James (ed.), *John Rae, Political Economist*, *Economica* N.S. 34, pp. 335–7.

(1968a) *Address . . . on the Occasion of . . . Installation as Chancellor of the University of Stirling* (Stirling: University of Stirling). Reprinted in (1980) pp. 12–22.

(1968b) 'The International Monetary Problem', *Journal of Political Economy* 76, pp. 664–77.

(1968c) *The Theory of Economic Development in the History of Economic Thought* (London: Macmillan).

(1968d) Preface (pp. 5–8) to the 1968 Edition of *The Economic Causes of War* (New York: Howard Fertig).

(1969) Review of M. Blaug, *Economic Theory in Retrospect*, 2nd edition, *Economica* N.S. 36, pp. 442–3.

(1970a) *Jacob Viner. A Tribute* (Princeton, New Jersey: Princeton University Press).

(1970b) *The Evolution of Modern Economic Theory* (London: Macmillan).

(1970c) Review of J. M. Robson, *The Improvement of Mankind: The Social and Political Thought of John Stuart Mill*, *Economica* N.S. 37, pp. 194–5.

(1970d) Review of *The Collected Works of John Stuart Mill*, vol. 10, *Essays on Ethics, Religion and Society*, *Economica* N.S. 37, pp. 422–4.

(1971a) *Autobiography of an Economist* (London: Macmillan).

(1971b) *Money, Trade and International Relations* (London: Macmillan).

(1971c) Review of D. P. O'Brien, *J. R. McCulloch*, *Economica* N.S. 38, p. 321.

(1971d) 'Sir T. Gregory. Gifted Teacher of Economics', *The Times*, 23 February 1971 (14g).

(1971e) 'Inflation: The Position Now', *Financial Times*, 23 June 1971.

(1972a) 'Inflation: An International Problem' (pp. 10–25) and 'Concluding Observations' (pp. 128–46) in R. Hinshaw (ed.), *Inflation as a Global Problem* (Baltimore: Johns Hopkins University Press).

(1972b) *Technology and Social Welfare*, Joseph Wunsch Lecture 1972 (Technion, Israel Institute of Technology: Haifa).

(1972c) Review of D. P. O'Brien (ed.), *The Correspondence of Lord Overstone*, *Financial Times*, 6 January 1972, p. 20.

(1973a) *The International Monetary Problem*. Second Keynes Lecture in Economics, 26 October 1972 (London: Oxford University Press for the British Academy, 1973).

(1973b) 'Summing Up: Mergers and the Legal Framework' (pp. 83–4) in *Mergers, Take-overs and the Structure of Industry* (London: I.E.A.).

(1973c) Review of J. M. Keynes, *Essays in Biography. Collected Works*, vol. x, *Economic Journal* 83, pp. 530–1.

(1974a) 'Causes, Effects, Developments' (pp. 1–9) and 'Summing Up' (pp. 104–5 and *passim*) in *Inflation: Causes, Consequences, Cures* (London: I.E.A.) 1974.

(1974b) *Aspects of Post-war Economic Policy*. 5th Wincott Memorial Lecture (London: I.E.A.).

(1974c) Review of *The Collected Works of John Stuart Mill*, vols 14–17. *The Later Letters of John Stuart Mill, 1849–1873, Economica* N.S. 41, pp. 336–8.

(1975a) 'Foreword' (pp. ix–xi) in D. Seckler, *Thorstein Veblen and the Institutionalists* (London: Macmillan).

(1975b) 'Issues and Choices' (pp. 11–27) and 'Concluding Reflections' (pp. 145–57) in R. Hinshaw (ed.), *Key Issues in International Monetary Reform* (New York: Marcel Dekker).

(1975c) Review of D. P. O'Brien, *The Classical Economists* and T. Sowell, *Classical Economics Reconsidered, Times Literary Supplement*, 1 August 1975.

(1976a) *Political Economy Past and Present* (London: Macmillan).

(1976b) Review of J. S. Mill, *A System of Logic. Collected Works*, vols 7 and 8, *Economica* N.S. 43, p. 446.

(1977a) *Liberty and Equality* (London: I.E.A.).

(1977b) Review of J. K. Whitaker (ed.), *The Early Economic Writings of Alfred Marshall, Economica* N.S. 44, pp. 91–2.

(1978a) *Preface to the Second Edition of The Theory of Economic Policy in English Classical Political Economy* (London: Macmillan).

(1978b) 'Economists and Trade Unions, 1776–1977' (pp. 5–16, 19–20) in *Trade Unions: Public Goods or Public 'Bads'?* (London: I.E.A.).

(1978c) Review of S. Howson and D. Winch, *The Economic Advisory Council, 1930–1939, Journal of Economic Literature* 16, pp. 114–15.

(1979a) *Against Inflation* (London: Macmillan).

(1979b) 'On Latsis's Method and Appraisal in Economics: A Review Essay', *Journal of Economic Literature* 17, pp. 996–1004.

(1979c) Review of *The Collected Works of John Stuart Mill*, vols 18 and 19, *Essays on Politics and Society, Economica* N.S. 46, pp. 89–90.

(1979d) Review of J. M. Buchanan, *Freedom in Constitutional Contract, Economic Journal* 89, pp. 683–4.

(1980a) *Higher Education Revisited* (London: Macmillan).

(1980b) Review of P. James, *Population Malthus: His Life and Times, Economica* N.S. 47, p. 471.

(1980c) Review of J. Viner (op. posth.), *Religious Thought and Economic Society, Economica* N.S. 47, pp. 489–90.

(1980d) Review of *The Collected Works of John Stuart Mill*, vol. 11, *Essays on Philosophy and the Classics, Economica* N.S. 47, pp. 490–1.

(1981) 'Economics and Political Economy', Richard T. Ely Lecture. *American Economic Review* 71 (May Suppt) pp. 1–10. Reprinted in *An Essay on the Nature and Significance of Economic Science*, 3rd edition (London: Macmillan, 1984) pp. xi–xxxiii.

(1982) *Stagflation. International Economic Relations* (Nankang, Taipei, Taiwan: Institute of Economics, Academia Sinica).

(1984) *An Essay on the Nature and Significance of Economic Science*, 3rd edition (London: Macmillan).

Works by other authors cited in this book

ADDLESON, MARK (1984) 'Robbins's Essay in Retrospect: on Subjectivism and an "Economics of Choice" ', *Rivista Internazionale Die Scienze Economiche e Commerciali* 31, pp. 506–23.

ANNUAL REGISTER (1984) Obituary of Lord Robbins, vol. 226, p. 535.

BALOGH, T. (1938) 'The Short-term Budget Problem', *Lloyds Bank Review* N.S., vol. 9, no. 97, March 1938, pp. 106–17.

BALOGH, T. (1971) 'The Lion in Winter', *New Statesman*, 24 September, pp. 388–9.

BANKER (1934) Review of Robbins (1934d) 31, pp. 172–9.

BANKER (1939) 'Some British Economists', 49, pp. 215–26.

BAUMOL, W. J. (1972) 'Jacob Viner at Princeton', *Journal of Political Economy* 80, pp. 12–15.

BAUMOL, W. J. and SEILER, E. V. (1979) 'Viner, Jacob', *International Encyclopaedia of the Social Sciences*, ed. D. Sills, vol. 18, pp. 783–7 (New York: Free Press).

BAUMOL, W. J. (1984a) 'Foreword' (pp. vii–ix) in L. C. Robbins, *An Essay on the Nature and Significance of Economic Science*, 3rd edition (London: Macmillan).

BAUMOL, W. J. (1984b) pp. 10–11 in *Tributes in Memory of Lord Robbins* (London: L.S.E.).

BAUMOL, W. J. (1988) 'On the Work of Lionel Robbins' in D. Greenaway and J. R. Presley (eds), *Pioneers of British Economics*, vol. II (London: Macmillan).

BENDIX, R. (1968) 'Max Weber', *International Encyclopaedia of the Social Sciences*, ed. D. Sills (New York: Crowell Collier and Macmillan) vol. 16, pp. 493–503.

BENHAM, F. (1930) 'Economic Welfare', *Economica* 10, pp. 173–87.

BEVERIDGE, W. (1937) 'The Place of the Social Sciences in Human Knowledge', *Politica* 2, pp. 459–79.

BLAUG, M. (1962) *Economic Theory in Retrospect*, 4th edition (Cambridge: Cambridge University Press, 1985).

BLAUG, M. (1967) 'Approaches to Educational Planning', *Economic Journal* 77, pp. 262–87.

BLAUG, M. (1970) *An Introduction to the Economics of Education* (Harmondsworth: Penguin).

BLAUG, M. (1980) *The Methodology of Economics* (Cambridge: Cambridge University Press, reprinted 1982).

BOND. M. E. (1980) 'Exchange Rates, Inflation, and Vicious Circles', *I.M.F. Staff Papers* 27, pp. 679–711.

BOWLEY, M. E. A. (1937) *Nassau Senior and Classical Economics* (London: George Allen & Unwin).

BRAND, R. H. (1935) 'Stabilisation', *Lloyds Bank Review* N.S. 6, pp. 642–59.

BRESCIANI-TURRONI, C. (1937) *The Economics of Inflation* (1931) trans. M. E. Sayers (London: George Allen & Unwin).

BRONFENBRENNER, M. (1955) Review of Robbins (1954). *Journal of Political Economy*, 63, pp. 536–7.

BUCHANAN, D. H. (1929) 'The Historical Approach to Rent and Price Theory', *Economica* 9, pp. 123–55.

BUCHANAN, J. M. (1968) 'Knight, Frank H.', *International Encyclopaedia of the Social Sciences*, ed. D. L. Sills, vol. 8, pp. 424–8 (New York: Free Press).

BUCHANAN, J. M. (1973) 'Introduction: L.S.E. cost theory in retrospect' (pp. 3–16) in J. M. Buchan and G. F. Thirlby (eds) *L.S.E. Essays on Cost* (London: Weidenfeld & Nicolson for L.S.E.).

BURNS, J. H. (1984) 'Lord Robbins', *The Bentham Newsletter*, no. 8, June, p. 63.

BURNS, J. H. (1985) 'Lord Robbins: A Tribute', *The Bentham Newsletter*, no. 9, June, pp. 4–6.

CAIRNES, J. E. (1875) *The Character and Logical Method of Political Economy* (London: Macmillan).

CANNAN, E. (1914) *Wealth*, 3rd edition (London: P. S. King, 1928).

CANNAN, E. (1921) 'The Meaning of Bank Deposits', *Economica* 1, pp. 28–36.

CANNAN, E. (1924) 'Limitation of Currency or Limitation of Credit', *Economic Journal* 34, pp. 52–64.

CANNAN, E. (1932) Review of Robbins (1932a) *Economic Journal* 42, pp. 424–7.

CANNON, D. H. (1936) 'Money and the State', *Banker* 39, pp. 194–9.

CARTER, C. F. (1967) Review of Robbins (1966b) *Economic Journal* 77, pp. 638–40.

CASSEL, G. (1923) *The Theory of Social Economy*, 2 vols trans. J. McCabe (London: Fisher Unwin).

CASSEL, G. (1925) *Fundamental Thoughts in Economics* (reprinted Port Washington: Kennikat Press, 1971).

CHAPMAN, S. J. (1909) 'Hours of Labour', *Economic Journal* 19, pp. 353–73.

CLAYTON, G. C. (1934) 'The Planning of British Agriculture', *Lloyds Bank Review* N.S. 5, pp. 540–7.

COASE, R. H. (1982) 'Economics at LSE in the 1930s: a personal view', *Atlantic Economic Journal* 10, pp. 31–4.

COATS, A. W. (1982) 'The Distinctive LSE Ethos in the Inter-War Years', *Atlantic Economic Journal* 10, pp. 18–30.

COOTER, R. and RAPPOPORT, P. (1984) 'Were the Ordinalists Wrong about Welfare Economics?', *Journal of Economic Literature* 22, pp. 507–30.

CORRY, B. A. (1978) 'Lord Robbins', *Challenge*, January–February, pp. 61–2.

CORRY, B. A. (1986) 'Robbins, Lionel', in *The New Palgrave*, vol. 4 (London: Macmillan).

DACEY, W. M. (1956) 'The Floating Debt Problem', *Lloyds Bank Review*, April, pp. 24–38.

DACEY, W. M. (1960) *Money under Review* (London: Hutchison).

DAHRENDORF, R. (1984) 'The true Renaissance man', *Financial Times*, 17 May 1984 (27a–f).

DALTON, H. (1929) *Principles of Public Finance* (revised edition, London: Routledge).

DALTON, H. (1986a) *The Second World War Diary of Hugh Dalton 1940–1945* (ed.) B. Pimlott (London: Jonathan Cape).

DALTON, H. (1986b) *The Political Diary of Hugh Dalton 1918–40, 1945–60* (ed.) B. Pimlott (London: Jonathan Cape).

DARBY, M. R. and LOTHIAN, J. R. (1986) 'Economic Events and Keynesian Ideas: The 1930s and the 1970s' (pp. 69–86) in J. Burton (ed.), *Keynes's General Theory: Fifty Years On*, Hobart Paper no. 24 (London: I.E.A.).

DOUGLAS, C. H. (1936) *The New and the Old Economics* (Edinburgh: Scots Free Press).

DROGHEDA, EARL OF (1984) pp. 8–9 in *Tributes in Memory of Lord Robbins* (London: L.S.E.).

DUNWORTH, J. (1980) Review of Robbins (1980a) *Economic Journal* 90, pp. 962–3.

EDGEWORTH, F. Y. (1925) 'The Revised Doctrine of Marginal Social Product', *Economic Journal* 35, pp. 30–9.

FRASER, L. M. (1932) 'How Do We Want Economists to Behave?', *Economic Journal* 42, pp. 55–70.

FRASER, L. M. (1937) *Economic Thought and Language* (London: Macmillan).

FRIEDMAN, M. (1953) *Essays in Positive Economics* (Chicago: University of Chicago Press, 1956).

FRIEDMAN, M. (1968) 'The Role of Monetary Policy', *American Economic Review* 58, pp. 1–17.

GLENDAY, R. (1939) 'The Export Problem: Another View', *Lloyds Bank Review* N.S. 10, no. 114, August 1939, pp. 250–62.

GREGORY, T. E. (1921) *Tariffs: A Study in Method* (London: Griffin).

GRIBBIN, J. D. (1977a) 'The Postwar Revival of Competition as Industrial Policy' (mimeo).

GRIBBIN, J. D. (1977b) 'The Development of United Kingdom Competition Policies from the War Until 1948' (mimeo).

GRIBBIN, J. D. (1985) 'The Wartime Contribution of G. C. Allen to the Development of UK Competition Policy' (mimeo).

GRIMMOND, J. (1985) 'Nasty, bullish but effective', *Daily Telegraph*, 4 March.

GUILLEBAUD, C. W. (1970) Review of Robbins (1970b) *Economic Journal* 80, p. 677.

HABERLER, G. v. (1936) *The Theory of International Trade* (1933) trans. A. Stonier and F. Benham (London: Hodge).

HABERLER, G. v. (1937) *Prosperity and Depression* (Geneva: League of Nations).

HARRIS, J. (1977) *William Beveridge* (Oxford: Clarendon).

HARROD, R. F. (1932) Letter to the *Economist*, 4 June 1932, pp. 1242–3.

HARROD, R. F. (1938) 'Scope and Method of Economics', *Economic Journal* 48, pp. 383–412.

HARROD, R. F. (1951) *The Life of John Maynard Keynes* (London: Macmillan).

HAYEK, F. A. v. (1931a) 'Reflections on the Pure Theory of Money of Mr. J. M. Keynes', *Economica* 11, pp. 270–95.

HAYEK, F. A. v. (1931b) 'A Rejoinder to Mr. Keynes', *Economica* 11, pp. 398–403.

HAYEK, F. A. v. (1931c) *Prices and Production*, 2nd edition (London: Routledge & Kegan Paul, 1935).

HAYEK, F. A. v. (1932) 'Money and Capital: A Reply', *Economic Journal* 52, pp. 237–49.

HAYEK, F. A. v. (ed.) (1935) *Collectivist Economic Planning* (London: Routledge & Kegan Paul).

HAYEK, F. A. v. (1940) 'Socialist Calculation: the Competitive "solution"', *Economica* N.S. 7, pp. 125–49.

HAYEK, F. A. v. (1978) *A Tiger by the Tail* (London: I.E.A.).

HEFLEBOWER, R. B. (1948) Review of Robbins (1947c) *American Economic Review* 38, pp. 445–6.

HENDERSON, H. D. (1935a) Review of Robbins (1934d) *Economic Journal* 45, pp. 117–23.

HENDERSON, H. D. (1935b) 'The Case Against Returning to Gold', *Lloyds Bank Review* N.S. 6, pp. 338–51.

HENDERSON, H. D. (1937) 'The Trade Cycle and the Budget Outlook', *Lloyds Bank Review* N.S. 8, no. 88, pp. 290–8.

HICKS, J. R. (1935) 'A Suggestion for Simplifying the Theory of Money', *Economica* 1935, reprinted in *Money, Interest and Wages. Collected Essays on Economic Theory*, vol. II (Oxford: Blackwell, 1982).

HICKS, J. R. (1963) 'Commentary' (pp. 305–15) in *The Theory of Wages*, 2nd edition (London: Macmillan).

HICKS, J. R. (1967) *Critical Essays in Monetary Theory* (Oxford: Oxford University Press).

HICKS, J. R. (1973) 'Recollections and Documents', *Economica* N.S. 40, pp. 2–11.

HICKS, J. R. (1979) 'The Formation of an Economist', reprinted in *Classics and Moderns. Collected Essays on Economic Theory*, vol. III (Oxford: Blackwell, 1983).

HICKS, J. R. (1982) 'LSE and the Robbins Circle' (pp. 3–10) in *Money, Interest and Wages. Collected Essays on Economic Theory*, vol. II (Oxford: Blackwell).

HICKS, J. R. (1983) 'A Discipline not a Science' (pp. 366–75) in *Classics and Moderns. Collected Essays on Economic Theory*, vol. III (Oxford: Blackwell).

HOBSON, O. R. (1938) 'The Budget', *Lloyds Bank Review* N.S. 9, no. 101, pp. 342–51.

HOWSON, S. and WINCH, D. (1977) *The Economic Advisory Council, 1930–1939* (Cambridge: Cambridge University Press).

HUTCHISON, T. W. (1938) *The Significance and Basic Postulates of Economic Theory* (reprinted New York: A. M. Kelley, 1965).

HUTCHISON, T. W. (1964) *Positive Economics and Policy Objectives* (London: George Allen & Unwin).

HUTCHISON, T. W. (1968) *Economics and Economic Policy in Britain 1946–1966* (London: George Allen & Unwin).

HUTCHISON, T. W. (1978) *On Revolutions and Progress in Economic Knowledge* (Cambridge: Cambridge University Press).

HUTCHISON, T. W. (1979) 'Robbins, Lionel', *International Encyclopaedia of the Social Sciences*, ed. D. L. Sills, vol. 18, *Biographical Supplement*, pp. 660–3 (New York: Free Press).

HUTCHISON, T. W. (1981) *The Politics and Philosophy of Economics* (Oxford: Blackwell).

JAMES, G. M. (1933) Review of Robbins (1932a) *American Economic Review*, 23, pp. 698–9.

JAMES, P. (1979) *Population Malthus* (London: Routledge & Kegan Paul).

JEVONS, W. S. (1871) *The Theory of Political Economy*, ed. R. D. C. Black (Harmondsworth: Penguin, 1970).

JOHNSON, H. G. (1972) Review of Robbins (1971a) *Journal of Political Economy* 80, pp. 835–6.

JOHNSON, E. S. and JOHNSON, H. G. (1978) *The Shadow of Keynes* (Oxford: Blackwell).

KALDOR, N. (1939) 'Welfare Propositions in Economics and Inter-Personal Comparisons of Utility', *Economic Journal* 49, pp. 549–52.

KALDOR, N. (1955) *An Expenditure Tax* (London: George Allen & Unwin).

KAUFMANN, F. (1933) 'On the Subject-Matter and Method of Economic Science', *Economica* 13, pp. 381–401.

KEYNES, J. M. (1924) 'A Comment on Professor Cannan's article', *Economic Journal* 34, pp. 65–8.

KEYNES, J. M. (1930) *A Treatise on Money*, 2 vols (reprinted London: Macmillan for the Royal Economic Society, 1971).

KEYNES, J. M. (1931) 'The Pure Theory of Money. A Reply to Dr. Hayek', *Economica* 11, pp. 387–97.

KEYNES, J. M. (1935) 'The Future of the Foreign Exchanges', *Lloyds Bank Review* N.S. 6, pp. 527–35.

KEYNES, J. M. (1936) *The General Theory of Employment, Interest and Money* (reprinted London: Macmillan for the Royal Economic Society, 1973).

KEYNES, J. M. (1978) *Collected Writings*, ed. D. Moggridge, vol. xxii (London: Macmillan for the Royal Economic Society).

KIRZNER, I. M. (1973) *Competition and Entrepreneurship* (Chicago: University of Chicago Press. 2nd Impression 1974).

KIRZNER, I. M. (1976) *The Economic Point of View*, 2nd edition (Kansas City: Sheed and Ward).

KNIGHT, F. H. (1921) *Risk, Uncertainty and Profit* (reprinted London: L.S.E., 1933).

KNIGHT, F. H. (1924a) 'The Limitations of Scientific Method in Economics', reprinted in *The Ethics of Competition and other Essays* (London: George Allen & Unwin, 1935) pp. 105–47.

KNIGHT, F. H. (1924) 'Some Fallacies in the Interpretation of Social Cost', *Quarterly Journal of Economics* 38, pp. 582–606.

KNIGHT, F. H. (1928) 'A Suggestion for Simplifying The Statement of the General Theory of Price', *Journal of Political Economy* 36, pp. 353–70.

KNIGHT, F. H. (1934a) 'The Nature of Economic Science in Some Recent Discussions', *American Economic Review* 24, pp. 225–38.

KNIGHT, F. H. (1934b) ' "The Common Sense of Political Economy" (Wicksteed Reprinted)', *Journal of Political Economy* 42, pp. 660–73.

KNIGHT, F. H. (1938) Review of Robbins (1937b) *Journal of Political Economy* 46, pp. 259–61.

KOOT, G. M. (1982) 'An alternative to Marshall: economic history and applied economics at the early LSE', *Atlantic Economic Journal* 10, pp. 3–17.

LACHMAN, L. M. (1976) 'From Mises to Shackle: An Essay on Austrian Economics and the Kaleidic Society', *Journal of Economic Literature* 14, pp. 54–62.

LAKATOS, I. and MUSGRAVE, A. (1970) *Criticism and the Growth of Knowledge* (London: Cambridge University Press, reprinted 1974).

LAVINGTON, F. (1921) *The English Capital Market* (London: Methuen).

LAYARD, R., KING, J. and MOSER, C. (1969) *The Impact of Robbins* (Harmondsworth: Penguin).

LEAMER, E. (1983) 'Let's Take the Con out of Econometrics', *American Economic Review* 73, pp. 31–44.

LEVY, A. (1984) 'Lord Robbins', *Annual Obituary* (London: St James Press) pp. 273–6.

LIPSEY, R. G. (1963) *An Introduction to Positive Economics* (London: Weidenfeld & Nicolson).

LITTLE, I. M. D. (1974) 'The right shape for a Budget', *The Times*, 6 February (15e).

MACFIE, A. L. (1953) Review of Robbins (1952) *Economic Journal* 63, pp. 651–60.

MACGREGOR, D. H. (1939) Review of Robbins (1939a) *Economic Journal* 49, pp. 491–3.

MACHLUP, F. (1979) 'Hayek, Friedrich A. Von', *International Encyclopaedia of the Social Sciences*, ed. D. Sills, vol. 18, pp. 274–82 (New York: Free Press).

MARSHALL, A. (1890) *Principles of Economics*, 9th (Variorum) edition (ed.) C. W. Guillebaud, 2 vols (London: Macmillan, 1961).

MARSHALL, A. (1892) *Elements of Economics of Industry*, 3rd edition (London: Macmillan, 1899).

MARSHALL, R. and PERLMAN, R. (1972) Comment on Robbins (1930c) *An Anthology of Labor Economics* (New York: Wiley) pp. 192–3.

MEADE, J. E. (1984) in *Tributes in Memory of Lord Robbins* (London: L.S.E.) pp. 5–7.

MENGER, C. (1871a) *Grundsätze der Volkwirtschaftslehre* (Wien: Bergmüller, 1871, reprinted London: L.S.E., 1934).

MENGER, C. (1871b) *Grundsätze der Volkwirtschaftslehre*, trans. J. Dingwall and B. Hoselitz as *Principles of Economics* (Glencoe: Free Press, 1950).

MENGER, C. (1883) *Untersuchungen über die Methode der Socialwissenschaften und der Politischen Oekonomie insbesondere*, trans. F. J. Nock as *Problems of Economics and Sociology* (Urbana: University of Illinois Press, 1963).

MILL, J. S. (1825, 1844) 'The Quarterly Review on Political Economy' and *Essays on Some Unsettled Questions of Political Economy*, reprinted in *Essays on Economics and Society* (ed.) J. M. Robson (Toronto: University of Toronto Press, 1967).

MISES, L. v. (1929) *Kritik des Interventionismus* (Jena: Fischer).

MISES, L. v. (1932) *Die Geimeinwirschaft*, 2nd edition (Jena: Fischer).

MISES, L. v. (1933) 'Sociologie und Geschichte' (pp. 64–121) in *Grundprobleme der Nationalökonomie* (Jena: Fischer).

MISES, L. v. (1934) *The Theory of Money and Credit*, 2nd edition (1924) trans. H. E. Batson (London: Jonathan Cape).

MISES, L. v. (1936) *Socialism*, trans. J. Kahane (London: Jonathan Cape).

MISES, L. v. (1949) *Human Action*, 3rd edition (Chicago: H. Regnery, 1966).

MISES, L. v. (1960) 'Sociology and History' (pp. 68–129) in *Epistemological Problems of Economics*, trans. G. Reisman (Princeton: Van Nostrand).

MISHKIN, F. (1986) *Money, Banking and Financial Markets* (Boston: Little, Brown).

MITCHELL, W. C. (1935) Review of Robbins (1934d) *Quarterly Journal of Economics* 49, pp. 503–7.

MOGGRIDGE, D. E. (1976) *Keynes* (London: Fontana).

MORROW, C. H. (1937) Review of Robbins (1937b) *American Economic Review* 27, pp. 813–14.

MOSER, C. (1984) in *Tributes in Memory of Lord Robbins* (London: L.S.E.) pp. 12–15.

MUGGERIDGE, M. (1966) *Tread Softly for You Tread on my Jokes* (London: Collins, repr. 1969).

MUGGERIDGE, M. (1973) *Chronicles of Wasted Time 2. The Infernal Grove* (London: Collins).

NORMAN, M. (1986) 'The rebels who lost', *Daily Telegraph*, 8 May.

NURKSE, R. (1955) Review of Robbins (1954) *American Economic Review* 45, pp. 437–8.

O'BRIEN, D. P. (1975) *The Classical Economists* (Oxford: Clarendon).

O'BRIEN, D. P. (1976) 'Customs unions: trade creation and trade diversion in historical perspective', *History of Political Economy* 8, pp. 540–63.

O'BRIEN, D. P. (1981) 'A. Marshall, 1842–1924' (pp. 36–61) in D. P. O'Brien and J. R. Presley (eds), *Pioneers of Modern Economics in Britain* (London: Macmillan).

O'BRIEN, D. P. (1983) 'Research Programmes in Competitive Structure', *Journal of Economic Studies* 10, pp. 29–51.

O'BRIEN, D. P. (1984) 'The Evolution of the Theory of the Firm' (pp. 25–62) in F. H. Stephen (ed.), *Firms, Organisation and Labour* (London: Macmillan).

PARSONS, T. (1934) 'Some Reflections on "The Nature and Significance of Economics" ', *Quarterly Journal of Economics* 48, pp. 511–45.

PEACOCK, A. (1982) 'LSE and postwar economic policy', *Atlantic Economic Journal* 10, pp. 35–40.

PECK, H. W. (1936) Review of Robbins (1935a) *American Economic Review* 26, pp. 495–6.

PEMBERTON, J. (1979) Review of Robbins (1979a) *Economic Journal* 89, pp. 950–3.

PESTON, M. (1981) 'Lionel Robbins: Methodology, Policy and Modern

Theory' (pp. 183–98) in J. R. Shackleton and G. Locksley (eds), *Twelve Contemporary Economists* (London: Macmillan).

PESTON, M. (1984) 'The free market paternalist', *Times Educational Supplement*, 25 May, p. 4.

PIGOU, A. C. (1924) *The Economics of Welfare*, 2nd edition (London: Macmillan).

PIGOU, A. C. (1925) *Memorials of Alfred Marshall* (London: Macmillan).

PIMLOTT, B. (1985) *Hugh Dalton* (London: Jonathan Cape).

PIROU, G. (1936) Review of Robbins (1934d) *Revue d'Économie Politique* 50, pp. 1222–3.

POPPER, K. R. (1934) *The Logic of Scientific Discovery*, trans. Popper *et al.* (London: Hutchison, 1959).

PREST, R. (1972) Review of Robbins (1971a) *Journal of Economic Literature* 10, p. 1202.

RAUNER, R. M. (1956) *Samuel Bailey and Classical Economics*, Ph.D. Thesis, University of London.

RIST, C. (1935a) 'Stabilisation', *Lloyds Bank Monthly Review* 6, pp. 391–403.

RIST, C. (1935b) Review of Robbins (1934d) *Revue d'Économie Politique* 49, pp. 233–4.

ROBERTSON, D. H. (1926) *Banking Policy and the Price Level*, 3rd, revised, impression (London: P. S. King, 1932).

ROBERTSON, D. H. (1935) Review of Robbins (1934d) *Economica* N.S. 2, pp. 103–6.

ROBERTSON, D. H. (1937) 'The Trade Cycle – An Academic View', *Lloyds Bank Review* N.S. 8, no. 91, pp. 502–11.

ROBERTSON, D. H. (1954) 'Utility and all What?', *Economic Journal* 64, pp. 665–78.

ROBERTSON, D. H. (1955) Review of Robbins (1954) *Economic Journal* 65, pp. 107–9.

ROBERTSON, D. H. (1959) 'A Squeak from Aunt Sally', *Banker* 109, pp. 718–22.

ROTHBARD, M. C. (1968) 'Von Mises, Ludwig', *International Encyclopaedia of the Social Sciences*, ed. D. Sills, vol. 16, pp. 379–82 (New York: Collier Macmillan).

RYAN, F. L. (1935) Review of Robbins (1934d) *American Economic Review* 25, pp. 93–4.

SAMUELSON, P. A. (1972) 'Jacob Viner, 1892–1970', *Journal of Political Economy* 80, pp. 5–11.

SAYERS, R. S. (1957) *Central Banking after Bagehot* (Oxford: Clarendon).

SCHUMPETER, J. A. (1908) *Das Wesen und der Hauptinhalt der theoretischen Nationalokonomie* (Leipsig: Duncker & Humblot).

SCHUMPETER, J. A. (1954) *History of Economic Analysis* (London: George Allen & Unwin).

SCOON, R. (1943) 'Professor Robbins' Definition of Economics', *Journal of Political Economy* 51, pp. 310–21.

SECKLER, D. (1975) *Thorstein Veblen and the Institutionalists* (London: Macmillan).

SHONE, R. M. (1935) 'Exchange Stabilisation – An Industrial View', *Lloyds Bank Review* N.S. 6, pp. 346–51.

SKIDELSKY, R. (1983) *John Maynard Keynes*. vol. I, *Hopes Betrayed 1883–1920* (London: Macmillan).

SOUTER, R. W. (1933) ' "The Nature and Significance of Economic Science" in Recent Discussion', *Quarterly Journal of Economics* 47, pp. 377–413.

SPENGLER, J. J. (1959) Review of Robbins (1958e) *American Economic Review* 49, pp. 722–4.

SPIEGEL, H. W. (1953) Review of Robbins (1952) *American Economic Review* 43, pp. 634–6.

SRAFFA, P. (1926) 'The Laws of Returns under Competitive Conditions', *Economic Journal* 36, pp. 535–50.

SRAFFA, P. (1932a) 'Dr. Hayek on Money and Capital', *Economic Journal* 42, pp. 42–53.

SRAFFA, P. (1932b) 'A Rejoinder', *Economic Journal* 42, pp. 249–51.

STALEY, E. (1943) Review of Robbins (1939b) *Journal of Political Economy* 51, pp. 291–2.

STEWART, I. M. T. (1979) *Reasoning and Method in Economics* (London: McGraw Hall).

STRIGL, R. (1923) *Die ökonomischen Kategorien und die Organisation der Wirtschaft* (Jena: G. Fischer).

THWEATT, W. O. (1981) 'Lord Robbins on Robert Torrens', *The Economists Refuted'*, *History of Economics Society Bulletin* 3, pp. 45–8.

TIMES HIGHER EDUCATIONAL SUPPLEMENT (1984) 'Lionel Robbins 1898–1984', 18 May (36b–g).

TIMES, THE (1984) 'Lord Robbins. Contribution to economics and higher education', 17 May (4f).

TOM, A. (1935) Review of Robbins (1934d) *Ekonomista* 35, no. 2, pp. 107–10.

VINER, J. (1953) *The Customs Union Issue* (New York: Carnegie Endowment for Peace).

WEBER, M. (1947) *The Theory of Social and Economic Organisation* (Part I of *Wirtschaft und Gesellschaft*), trans. A. R. Henderson and T. Parsons (London: Hodge).

WEBER, M. (1949) *The Methodology of the Social Sciences*, trans. E. Shils and H. Finch (Glencoe: Free Press, 1949).

WICKSTEED, PHILIP H. (1910) *The Common Sense of Political Economy and Selected Papers and Reviews on Economic Theory* (ed.) L. C. Robbins, 2 vols (London: Routledge & Kegan Paul, 1933).

WIESER, F. v. (1889) *Natural Value*, trans. C. A. Malloch (London: Macmillan, 1893).

WIESER, F. v. (1914) *Social Economics*, trans. A. F. Hinrichs (London: George Allen & Unwin, 1927).

WILSON, T. (1965) Review of Robbins (1963a) *Economic Journal* 75, pp, 439–41.

WINCH, D. (1969) *Economics and Policy. A Historical Survey* (London: Fontana).

WISE, E. F. (1931a) 'An Alternative to Tariffs', *Political Quarterly* 2, pp. 186–203.

WISE, E. F. (1931b) 'A Reply to Professor Robbins', *Political Quarterly* 2, pp. 411–16.

WISEMAN, J. (1985) 'Lionel Robbins, the Austrian School, and the LSE Tradition', *Research in the History of Economic Thought and Methodology* 3, pp. 147–59.

YEAGER, L. B. (1976) *International Monetary Relations*, 2nd edition (New York: Harper & Row).

YOUNG, A. A. (1913) 'Pigou's Wealth and Welfare', *Quarterly Journal of Economics* 27, pp. 672–86.

YOUNG, A. A. (1925a) 'The Trend of Economics as seen by some American Economists', *Quarterly Journal of Economics* 39, reprinted in A. A. Young, *Economic Problems New and Old* (Boston: Houghton Mifflin, 1927) pp. 232–60.

YOUNG, A. A. (1925b) 'Economics and War', *American Economic Review* 16, reprinted in A. A. Young, *Economic Problems New and Old* (Boston: Houghton Mifflin, 1927) pp. 1–20.

YOUNG, A. A. (1928a) 'Increasing Returns and Economic Progress', *Economic Journal* 38, pp. 527–42.

YOUNG, A. A. (1928b) Review of Gregory, T. E. and Dalton, H. (eds) *London Essays in Economics*, *Economica* 8, pp. 113–17.

Name Index

Subject Index

243